THE
QUEEN
AND MRS
THATCHER

THE
QUEEN
AND MRS
THATCHER

An Inconvenient Relationship

DEAN PALMER

The
History
Press

For Mum and Dad

First published 2015

The History Press
The Mill, Brimscombe Port
Stroud, Gloucestershire, GL5 2QG
www.thehistorypress.co.uk

British Library Cataloguing in Publication Data.
A catalogue record for this book is available from the British Library.

ISBN 978 0 7509 6265 0

Typesetting and origination by The History Press
Printed and bound in Great Britain by TJ International

CONTENTS

ACKNOWLEDGEMENTS

I would like to thank the following people who helped with the research and preparation of this book:

Darley Anderson, Mark Beynon, Kate Dunn, Andrea Messent, Juanita Hall, Jessica Bale, Kerry Green, Mary Darby, Peter Carington (6th Baron Carrington), David Owen (Lord Owen of the City of Plymouth), Jeffrey Archer (Lord Archer of Weston-super-Mare), Edwina Currie, Sir Bernard Ingham, David Steel (Lord Steel of Aikwood), Tim Bell (Lord Bell of Belgravia), Ronald Allison CVO, Michael Dobbs, Denis Healey (Lord Healey of Riddlesden), Dr Daniel Conway, Geoffrey Howe (Lord Howe of Aberavon), Nigel Lawson (Lord Lawson of Blaby), Maggie Smart and Angie Nuttall.

I should also mention friends and family who have been supportive throughout this process: Mary-Jane Evans, Deborah Wearn, Kate Shepherd, Jackie Moore, John Baldry, Patricia Turnbull, Rachel Himbury, Angela Holden, Kim Palmer and Kay Palmer.

The following archives and libraries also proved invaluable, foremost being the documents stored in the online archive at the Margaret Thatcher Foundation. Other sources include the British Library, the London Library and the Chichester Library. This book has also benefited from the release of new documents, particularly from the National Archives in 2013.

Most factual writers pluck fragments, large and small, from their predecessors' work. In writing this book I also found the works of the following authors extremely useful, in particular, the many excellent biographers of Queen Elizabeth II and royal writers, including the late Ben Pimlott, Sarah Bradford, Sally Bedell Smith, Piers Brendon, A.N. Wilson and Andrew Marr, as well as the biographers of Margaret Thatcher, including Penny Junor, John Campbell, Jonathan Aitken, Robin Harris, Charles Moore and Claire Berlinski.

Of great use were the two books written by Carol Thatcher, *A Swim-on Part in the Goldfish Bowl* and *Below the Parapet*. There were several incredibly useful articles in *Vanity Fair*, in particular 'The Blooming of Margaret Thatcher' by Gail Sheehy

(June, 1989) and 'The Invincible Mrs Thatcher' by Charles Moore (December, 2011). Andrew Neil's autobiography, *Full Disclosure*, was excellent in illuminating the facts of Michael Shea's press leak which opened the shutters on the relationship between monarch and prime minister.

The research done by journalists Mark Hollingsworth and Paul Halloran into Mark Thatcher is also revealing, as was an article about Prince Andrew entitled 'The Trouble with Andrew', by Edward Klein in *Vanity Fair* (August, 2011), and the various investigations carried out by the *Mail on Sunday*.

Around the time of Mrs Thatcher's death and funeral in April 2013, I found many newspaper articles and press reports useful. In particular, the coverage by the *Daily Telegraph, Sunday Telegraph, Daily Mail, Mail on Sunday, Daily Mirror, Sun, The Times, Sunday Times* and *Independent*.

Also of use was the Channel 4 documentary on *The House of Windsor* (December, 2007) presented by Dr David Starkey, and the four part BBC documentary series *The Downing Street Years* (September, 1993), based on the prime minister's own memoirs.

FOREWORD

We have become a grandmother.
Margaret Thatcher

On 28 February 1989, Mrs Thatcher emerged from the doorway of 10 Downing Street at great speed. Sporting blonde hair as rigid as fibreglass, over-sized pearl earrings and a purple winter coat trimmed with black fur, she had the distinct air of Cruella de Vil. Tottering over to the waiting television cameras, she smiled and then said the immortal lines, 'We have become a grandmother.'

It seemed to the world as if the prime minister was losing touch with reality. The use of the so-called 'royal we' (the majestic plural) is normally restricted to the head of state alone. Even then, it is heard only once a year when the queen reads her speech from the throne at the beginning of the parliamentary session. Its use by a mere prime minister was pure hubris. Such conceit resulted in some linguistic jokes at her expense: 'Why is Margaret Thatcher like a pound coin? Because she is thick, brassy and thinks she's a sovereign.'

This is the story of two powerful women who met and disliked each other on sight. For over a decade, they politely waged a quiet war on both personal and political fronts. Elizabeth found the means to snub and undermine her prime minister through petty class put-downs and press leaks. Margaret attacked her monarch by sidelining her, upstaging her and allowing Murdoch to crucify the royal family (although he was aided considerably in this by their own sheer folly).

In writing this book, I've identified four stages in their complex relationship: their first encounters, when the queen was suspicious of a female politician and the new prime minister was awed by her sovereign; Thatcher's victory in the Falklands, marking the start of her hubris and her usurpation of the queen's role; the queen's genuine fear that her radical prime minister was dividing her country and threatening her beloved Commonwealth, and finally, the shock and sympathy felt by the queen for Margaret when she was thrown out of office by her own Cabinet colleagues.

1

THE IRON LADY AND
THE ENGLISH ROSE

The meetings between the queen and Mrs
Thatcher are dreaded by at least one of them.
Anthony Sampson

At Conservative Central Office in Smith Square on 4 May 1979, Margaret Thatcher waited impatiently with her husband, Denis, her daughter, Carol, and favoured son, Mark, for the royal summons to Buckingham Palace for an audience with the queen. The previous night, Mrs Thatcher had won an astonishing general election victory defeating the rival Labour Party by 339 seats to 269. While she was still in her twenties, she had been told by a fortune teller at a fête in Orpington that she would be 'great, great as Churchill'.[1] Now she was on the verge of formally being offered the job of prime minister by her sovereign, Elizabeth II.

The atmosphere in the room was like the first day of a new school term, buzzing with feelings of anticipation, excitement and nervousness. Staff posed for a photograph, wearing slogan tops that read, 'I thought on the rocks was a drink until I discovered the Labour Government'.[2] Champagne and a giant chocolate cake, hastily baked overnight in the shape of the door to 10 Downing Street, home of Britain's prime ministers, were served up. Piped in white icing across the top were the words 'Margaret Thatcher's Success Story'.[3]

Margaret would not become prime minister until the Labour incumbent, Jim Callaghan, had tendered his resignation to the monarch. Protocol dictated that Mrs Thatcher would then kiss the regal hand and officially be asked to form a government by the queen. Only at that point would she become Britain's first female premier. Elected by the people, the job of prime minister remained, in theory at least, in the gift of the queen.

Now, dressed in a royal blue power suit, cream patterned blouse and her hall-mark pearl earrings, Mrs Thatcher waited. And waited. Each time the office phone rang the entire family jumped in anticipation. Was it Buckingham Palace this time? Margaret's biggest fear was that she would bump into the defeated James Callaghan en route to the palace, which she felt would be embarrassing. What if the two cars crossed? What was the etiquette for greeting a defeated political rival?

'I wouldn't want him to think I'm rubbing it in,' she declared.

Denis sensibly reminded her, 'Buck House has been doing this for years. I imagine they know the form by now.'[4]

Finally, the phone rang again. Everyone appreciated this must be *the* official phone call from the palace. Caroline Stephens, Mrs Thatcher's diary secretary, went to answer it. Everyone else strained their ears, listening.

'Wrong number,' she said. Silence fell for five minutes until the phone rang again. Tensions were running high. 'This is it!' declared Caroline, and she went through to take the call. Again everyone struggled to hear. 'Yes,' she said. 'Oh, thank you, would you hold on,' she came back into the room. 'Mr Heath would like to offer you his congratulations,' she whispered.

Margaret sat for a full thirty seconds without moving, then she replied, 'Would you thank him very much.'

She snubbed him and didn't take the call. For almost four years he had been her boss in Cabinet. However, Ted Heath, the former Conservative prime minister, had been anything but supportive after Margaret had surprisingly challenged him as the leader of the Conservative Party after the 1974 election defeat, and won. For the rest of his career, he would sit behind her on the backbenches in the House of Commons, the enduring detractor, never quite recovering from the bombshell of being trounced by a mere woman.

Five more minutes passed, and the telephone rang yet again. At long last, holding out the telephone receiver, Caroline announced, 'Sir Philip Moore from the palace.'

The queen had issued her summons, and Mrs Thatcher leapt into action. 'Right. We're off,' she said, jumping to her feet. Her restrained and sensible husband, Denis, pointed out that, with a police escort and no traffic lights they would do endless circuits of the Victoria monument until their scheduled appointment time. Carol chipped in that they might look like kerb-crawlers, which wouldn't give quite the right impression. For years, Margaret and Denis's sense of timekeeping had never been in sync. Mr Thatcher always complained that his wife didn't just want to catch the train, she wanted to be on the platform to welcome it in. Not surprisingly, that day Margaret won the argument, as she had on many other occasions, and their driver virtually had to crawl along the Mall so as not to arrive early.[5] It would be the last time she sat in the back of the Leader of the Opposition's car. Once she left the palace, she stepped into Jim Callaghan's old vehicle, and he into hers.

While Buckingham Palace officials swept Mrs Thatcher in to see the queen, Denis was whisked off to a private drawing room where he was offered a cup of tea. Not to his taste, he declined it, opting for a gin and tonic instead.

In the queen's private audience room, no one else except the monarch and prime minister were present. Thatcher would have kneeled before her sovereign and been invited to form the next government. The British constitution is unwritten and, unlike the United States, there is no single document outlining its fundamental principles. Rules have arisen out of legislation, precedent and custom.

The kissing of hands is a sober ritual that takes place in the queen's audience room. It is full of meaning and symbolism. The prime minister takes the official oath, receives the seal of office and kisses hands in a symbol of fealty and loyalty, before being asked to form a government in the sovereign's name. Following a general election, the monarch always calls upon the leader of the majority party in the House of Commons to form the government. Not until that moment is the election of the people's choice for prime minister ratified by the sovereign. In many ways, this is just a formality; in reality, the democratic process is already in motion, and no modern monarchy would ever question the people's choice.

Margaret would then, under full glare of the world's press, take possession of the highest political office in the land, and with it the occupancy of 10 Downing Street, and Chequers, a country house in Buckinghamshire also allocated to the British premier. Already, her personal assistant, Cynthia Crawford, known to everyone as 'Crawfie', was on her way to Number 10, with her staff and boxes of files, typewriters and other office equipment. The handover of power started the moment the election results were counted.

When the necessary formalities were completed by the queen and Mrs Thatcher, the new premier and her consort, Denis, were driven to Downing Street accompanied by a police motorcycle escort. The palace guards saluted Thatcher on the way out as she was now prime minister, something they hadn't done on the way in.[6]

The people's choice finally had the job she had craved. Downing Street was crammed with reporters, photographers, cameras and microphones. Crowds of enthusiastic supports sang 'For She's a Jolly Good Fellow' as the official car made its way through, and Mrs Thatcher was deposited just outside the most famous door in the land. Flanked by uniformed police officers she recited the prayer of St Francis of Assisi:

Where there is discord, may we bring harmony.
Where there is error, may we bring trust.
Where there is doubt, may we bring faith.
Where there is despair, may we bring hope.

After adopting the royal 'we' on her first day in the job, albeit in disguise, Mrs Thatcher then turned and walked through the door of what was to be her new home for the next eleven and a half years.[7]

Her success was a global news story, a new female head of government. It had happened before, Indira Gandhi in India, Golda Meir in Israel and Sirimavo Bandaranaike in Sri Lanka. That Britain, a nation bound by tradition and custom, could elect a woman was inconceivable. Margaret Mead, the noted anthropologist, once said that a clever woman must have two attributes to fulfill her intent: more energy than normal mortals and the ability to outwit her culture.[8] Margaret Thatcher could not only survive on four hours sleep, but she also had the wherewithal to break down the barriers of an inferior social background and gender handicap.[9]

On that first night in Downing Street, she shared a Chinese takeaway with her team in the grand setting of the State Dining Room, and worked until late.[10] She started as she meant to go on.

It would, however, be wrong to think of the queen or any British monarch as merely a crowned and anointed ornamental icon. Margaret said herself, 'Anyone who imagines that they are a mere formality, or confined to social niceties, is quite wrong; they are quietly businesslike, and Her Majesty brings to bear a formidable grasp of current issues and breadth of experience.'[11]

Prime ministers come and go with elections, but the monarch endures as head of state. Although Elizabeth II lacks direct power, she is a block on any prime minister having total control. For as long as she reigns, no premier can be number one, they will always remain in second place.

The reality is that the queen has far more power than she dares to use. She has been successful with most prime ministers because she has never rocked the boat or posed a threat as an alternative power broker. The monarch's role in the British constitution is limited to '… the right to be consulted, the right to encourage, the right to warn'.

Throughout Margaret Thatcher's premiership, Elizabeth exercised these very particular rights every Tuesday at 6.30 p.m. No one knows what was said during the weekly visits Mrs Thatcher made to the audience room at Buckingham Palace, but they took place for over a decade. No one else was present; no notes were taken on either side and both parties have an unspoken agreement never to repeat what

was discussed, even to their spouses.[12] The queen had received her seven previous prime ministers in the same room, starting with Sir Winston Churchill when
she was only 25 years old; Anthony Eden, Harold Macmillan, Alec Douglas-Home,
Harold Wilson, Edward Heath and James Callaghan all followed. The room they
meet in is large, and painted duck egg blue with high ceilings. On the walls are two
paintings by Canaletto and two by Gainsborough. At the centre of the room are
two chairs made by François Hervé in 1826 and upholstered in yellow Dupioni
silk. The colour was burgundy, until Queen Mary changed it for something more
cheerful, if less serviceable.[13]

These meetings had equipped Elizabeth II with a depth of political knowledge
and experience unrivalled by any political leader in the world. Now it was Margaret
Thatcher's turn to receive the benefit of that wisdom. However, the brutal truth
was that the new prime minister wasn't interested in listening.

At first, Thatcher was nervous because she didn't know how to treat the queen.
Margaret was merely a daughter of middle England, she had never been exposed
to the hunting, shooting and fishing crowd that made up the queen's set of people.
She found the meetings with her social superior difficult and could be overtly
diffident. Her alderman father had raised his daughter up to be a strident royalist
and stickler for etiquette. She never forgot that she once wrote to the queen and
ended the letter, 'yours sincerely, Margaret Thatcher', and received a letter back
icily pointing out that when writing to the monarch, people did not finish 'yours
sincerely'; a more obsequious salute was required, 'I remain Madam, your humble
and obedient servant'.[14]

Underneath Thatcher's armour of self-belief and simple Grantham philosophies
lurked deep insecurities, many of which were class based. On the way to a dinner
party given by Lord and Lady Carrington, she anxiously asked her secretary, Caroline
Stephens, 'Do you think I should wear white gloves?' She often had questions about
sartorial matters and social etiquette before events being attended by members of
the royal family, and was helped by Lady Tilney, the wife of a Conservative MP.[15]
'The first thing you have got to bear in mind is that Mrs Thatcher is a very ordinary
woman,' said Caroline.[16]

Socially nervous, Margaret was always scrupulously punctual, usually arriving a
full fifteen to thirty minutes early, rather than the required five. Before the appointed
hour, she would read through her notes while waiting for the royal summons. After
a few weeks, a palace advisor suggested that Mrs Thatcher might like to save time
and leave Downing Street a little later. Thatcher always said she was worried about
traffic. An interesting reply, because the drive only takes five minutes and as premier
she automatically had the privilege of a police escort. The queen could perhaps

have been more gracious and seen Mrs Thatcher when she entered Buckingham Palace. However, for Her Majesty the appointed hour, is the appointed hour and guests must be punctual, to show respect for her position. It was a lesson she continued to dish out to Mrs Thatcher repeatedly.

Meanwhile, the palace grandees sneered at the depth of Mrs Thatcher's curtsy, 'No one could curtsy lower,' they all gossiped. At a dinner party with friends, Margaret once demonstrated how the audience went, and leapt to her feet to enact the curtsy she was expected to deliver three times, first on entering the room, then on shaking hands with the queen and finally on retreating. For all that effort Margaret wasn't offered so much as a cup of tea.[17]

Ron Allison, the queen's former press secretary, explains how the prime minister got it wrong:

> They would've briefed Mrs Thatcher to just do the slightest of curtsies. That's how we always briefed people. I did it myself many, many times before press receptions on tours overseas and so on. And you call her 'Ma'am', as in jam, not 'Marm', as in marmalade, but you can say 'Your Majesty' just once and then after that it's 'Ma'am'.[18]

Elizabeth couldn't enjoy the lively banter she had enjoyed with many of her previous prime ministers, and Thatcher did love to lecture, which didn't go down at all well with Her Majesty.[19] William Whitelaw, Thatcher's deputy leader, said of his boss, 'If you have a sense of humour, you are always suspect with her.'[20] Thatcher had no sense of humour, whereas the queen has a dry wit. Clearly, in her opinion the encounters seemed counterfeit and awkward. Throughout their weekly meetings, over the years, the two women maintained a rigid formality. The ice never broke. Margaret would have expected the queen to make the first move, and that never happened.[21]

Over time, the waiting irritated the rather tense and uncomfortable PM, who clearly felt she had better things to do.[22] The palace ended up at the bottom of her priority list, and a mutual condescension crept in. The palace thought Thatcher vulgar, and the prime minister felt royalty was irrelevant. Denis Healey remarked, 'I think she [Thatcher] might have been jealous of the queen's role. I think because she thought she got there through her own efforts, and the queen got there simply because her father was … beforehand.'[23]

In theory, the Tory victory meant the queen exchanged a prime minister who headed a Labour Government critical of aristocratic privilege and position, for one who accepted the royal institution along with the House of Lords and Church of

England as part of the natural order. However, that was not the full story. The queen had been extremely fond of Margaret Thatcher's predecessor, Jim Callaghan.[24] For all their left-wing rhetoric, both recent Labour prime ministers, Jim Callaghan and Harold Wilson, had a tendency to be indulgent where the queen and the royal family were concerned. Margaret, on the other hand, had an evangelical's need to reform, to change. She could never just sit back and watch. Her entire character was an anathema to Elizabeth Windsor, whose constitutional role required her in many ways to do just that.[25]

Thatcher first met the queen shortly after she became Leader of the Opposition in 1974. During one of their early meetings at a Buckingham Palace function, the future premier fainted and rather irritated the stoic queen in doing so. Another version of the story was spread by a leading church man among his fellow bishops. Apparently Mrs Thatcher often felt faint at royal occasions. 'She's keeled over again,' said the queen dismissively to fellow guests when the Leader of the Opposition left the room to recover.[26] Harold Wilson couldn't resist passing on court gossip that the queen wasn't keen on this up-and-coming female politician. 'She doesn't like her,' Wilson confided to Joe Haines.[27]

For the queen, Thatcher was a new breed of woman to whom she had never been exposed. A scientist and barrister, she was entirely self-made and the upper classes have always traditionally preferred people who know their station and are comfortable in it. Thatcher had reinvented herself. Discontented with her place in the world, she had strove to better it. Immaculately groomed, she seemed intent on disguising her modest origins behind floral hats, pearl necklaces and elocution lessons.[28]

Margaret had erased her Lincolnshire accent, and acquired in its place something that sounded so affected even her closest advisors subsequently made her change it.[29] She was often deemed insincere because of her 'actressy way of talking'.[30] Elizabeth was suspicious of a woman in power, and disliked people she regarded as phonies. All Thatcher's manufactured self-improvements must have seemed very parvenu to Her Majesty. Broadcaster Andrew Marr summed up the situation deftly when he said the queen has an 'implacable aversion to insincerity ... The queen cannot abide pretence.'[31]

When Queen Elizabeth II took the throne on 6 February 1952, Thatcher was a fledgling Conservative politician trying to get a foot on the parliamentary ladder. She used the coronation to write a sycophantic article in the *Sunday Graphic* entitled 'Wake Up Women!' Margaret gushed that if the accession of the new young queen '... can help remove the last shreds of prejudice against women aspiring to the highest places, then a new era for women will indeed be at hand ... Should a woman be equal to the task, I say let her have an equal chance.'[32]

When Thatcher met the queen face to face there was little female solidarity evident on either side. They began on a basis of mutual condescension, said the queen's biographer, Ben Pimlott. 'The palace seems to have regarded Thatcherite fervour as vulgar, while the Thatcherites regarded the palace as irrelevant and effete. It was part personal, part political.'

Privately, both the queen and Prince Philip gave the impression that the new prime minister was 'not their favourite woman'.[33] Thatcher's biographer, Hugo Young, summed it up neatly, 'These were two women who registered different vibrations'. Their mutual dislike became obvious to staff at both Buckingham Palace and Number 10, as well as to outsiders. *The Times* described their relationship semi-tactfully as 'more businesslike than warm'.[34] Only once did the frost melt into something approaching girl talk, when the queen ended an audience by advising Margaret on her wardrobe when she visited Saudi Arabia.[35]

Matters were made more difficult because their roles seemed at odds with one another. The queen's style is matter-of-fact and domestic, while it was Mrs Thatcher (who is taller) who bore herself like a queen. Sir Charles Powell, Thatcher's advisor, explains his ex-boss's demeanour, 'You've got to think in terms of "Margaret Thatcher Productions" … there was the hair, the dress, the lighting and everything. She could have a tremendous dramatic effect … It was all packaged. It was almost like a great diva, giving a performance.'[36] The queen, however, is different, her cousin, Margaret Rhodes, explains, 'She can uphold the identity of herself as queen and still be humble. Her inner modesty stops her getting spoiled.'[37]

The queen had also found the previous Conservative Prime Minister Ted Heath hard work, but in that respect she wasn't alone. Heath, like Thatcher, spent the duration of his life shaking off his modest origins as the son of a carpenter from Broadstairs, transferring himself first to the lofty atmosphere of Balliol College, Oxford, and then to the Albany Apartments in London's exclusive Mayfair. His military service during the Second World War seemed to earn him an honorary place amongst the Tory elite. Despite this, it was known that the queen found Edward Heath 'hard going' and 'tricky' and they were never comfortable with each other.[38]

Surprisingly, it has been with Britain's two Labour prime ministers, Harold Wilson and James Callaghan, that the queen formed a closer bond. At least on a superficial level. When Harold Wilson first arrived at the palace, expectations were low on both sides to begin with. Martin Charteris, then the queen's assistant private secretary, described the day as a 'bit of a culture shock'. The queen knew nothing about working-class industrial Britain, Labour politics or trade unions. Wilson arrived with his wife and children, as well as his controversial and sometimes caustic political secretary, Marcia Williams.[39]

While Wilson had his first audience with the queen, his family and Marcia where served sherry by Patrick Plunket, master of the household in the equerries' room. Marcia sarcastically observed:

> A number of anonymous palace individuals were there. To me they all looked exactly alike. As I recall, the conversation centred on horses. Perhaps it was because it was assumed that everybody was interested in horses though my knowledge of them was minimal and the Wilson family's less. It struck me at the time as an ironic beginning to the white hot technical revolution and the government that was to mastermind it.[40]

Despite being from such different planets, where background and interests were concerned, the queen and Wilson got on extremely well.[41] He fed her desire for political gossip, even if it was salacious. He even told her about French President Valéry Giscard d'Estaing's alleged penchant for trolling the streets of Paris for women. 'Nothing would shock her,' said Marcia Williams.[42] It was a time when many of his colleagues were potential political rivals for his own job, so when he was worried about Cabinet disloyalty and backbiting, he could always cry on Her Majesty's shoulder. However, this warm relationship upset some of the hardliners in his own party, including the spiky Barbara Castle and ardent republican Richard Crossman.

Wilson, unlike most of his Cabinet colleagues, believed in the value of the monarchy to Britain. He worked well with the queen because he wasn't phony or pretentious. She was intrigued by him. He was socially from a very different place, but he didn't worry about the nuances of upper-class etiquette and the court. If it didn't worry him, it didn't worry her. 'Who would have thought of a chap like me ending up in a place like this,' was his frank and honest response to his elevation to prime minister. Although he had risen to one of the highest offices in the realm, he wasn't a social climber. He knew his place in the world, and where he fitted in. He was a man comfortable in his own skin. Besides this, a boyhood trip to Australia had bred in him a strong passion for the Commonwealth,[43] something the two of them had in common.

Wilson never patronised or lectured the queen. He treated her like an intellectual equal, as if she were a fellow member of the Cabinet. His press secretary, Joe Haines, said, 'He thought the advice often quite wise.' The queen, meanwhile, was flattered to be taken into his confidence.[44] As the years progressed, Wilson's audiences grew in length. Once he remained for two hours and was invited to stay for drinks. Usually prime ministers only see her for twenty or thirty minutes, and it is not normal for them to be offered any refreshments.[45] 'I think the queen talked very freely to Wilson,' one of her former private secretaries said.[46] 'Harold was very fond of her and she reciprocated it,' said Barbara Castle, 'He made her feel at ease, kept her well-informed … He really enjoyed his visits to her.'[47]

Her friendship with Wilson paid dividends for the queen. Despite the enormous cutbacks of the 1970s, he gave her two increases to her Civil List payments, much to the horror of many of his political colleagues, both in Cabinet and outside it.

Royal finances were always a political hot potato for Labour, their core supporters objected, not just to financing the queen's official obligations, but also to subsidising the assorted relatives who shared these duties with her, and they demanded to know why the monarch was immune from tax. Prince Philip put his foot in it when he broadcast:

> We go into the red next year. Now inevitably, if nothing happens we shall either have to – I don't know, we may have to move into smaller premises, who knows? … We had a small yacht which we had to sell, and I shall probably have to give up polo fairly soon.[48]

Philip lit a political fuse with his arrogance just as royal finances had become an issue. The press had a field day with bombshell headlines. A group of dockers in a Bermondsey pub wrote sarcastically to Philip offering to take up a collection for him to buy a polo pony. However, despite his pompous manner, what the prince was saying about the financial figures was accurate. The effect on the Civil List of rapid inflation meant the royal family could no longer cover their costs.

In 1970, *The Times* reported that the queen was overspending her allowance, and a concerned Wilson raised the subject in a meeting of the 'inner Cabinet.' The Labour Party was divided on the issue. Old school men like Wilson and Callaghan supported the queen, while fiery north London middle-class socialists like Richard Crossland noted that she already paid no estate or death duties, making her 'by far the richest person in the country'.[49]

When Crossland left Parliament to become editor of the *New Statesman*, he led an attack on the monarchy and the Civil List. During a visit to Harvard University he delivered a lecture called 'Bagehot Revisited' in which he described the British obsession with the royal family as a 'universal addiction … which canalizes and purges the emotions of mass democracy exposed to mass media in an irreligious age'.[50] He attacked the queen's 'truly regal cheek' arguing that she was seeking to have her cake and eat it by asking that the Civil List should take into account inflation, while not accepting that the net growth of her private assets should be taxed. In *The Times* he wrote, 'Money is an eternal dispute about which one monarch lost his head.'[51]

Wilson's objective was to take the issue out of politics. In agreement with Opposition Leader Ted Heath, he set up a select committee on the Civil List to meet after the June 1970 elections. By then, much of the royal spending was already being transferred to various departments; the Ministry of Works, for instance, now carried the cost of the royal palaces and castles, thus obscuring the true cost of the queen and the royal family.

The general election on 18 June delivered a shock result. Wilson lost. His resignation had to be delayed because the queen was attending Royal Ascot and couldn't give up watching the horse racing. In the end, a generous financial settlement was nevertheless passed by the new Conservative Government and Harold Wilson threw his weight behind her pay rise, although most Labour MPs abstained and forty-seven voted against it. 'The working-class members [among which he included both Wilson and Callaghan] love the queen and she loves them,' the left wing diarist and MP Tony Benn wrote rather crossly.[52] *The Times* stated that Wilson had been '... protective to the queen and her interests'.[53]

The 1971 select committee kicked the question of royal funding, the queen's private fortune and her tax exempt status, into the public domain. The Civil List Act, passed on 24 February 1972, was a watershed moment; from now on the queen's finances would be continually watched and scrutinised, whereas previously they had been largely secret.

When Harold Wilson was re-elected in 1974, he again delivered for the queen by authorising yet another Civil List increase, which amounted to £1.4 million overall. This was a significant deal, done against the backdrop of bleak economic conditions for the rest of the country, and a rebellious eighty-nine Labour MPs (including a young Neil Kinnock) opposed it, while another fifty abstained.

Wilson announced the increase on 12 February 1975, the very same day Mrs Thatcher made her debut as Leader of the Opposition in the House of Commons. On this occasion, both party leaders agreed with each other and Barbara Castle notes sardonically the new Conservative Party leader's 'not very notable intervention' on the subject of royal finances.[54] Thatcher was just keeping her powder dry. In her eyes, the prime ministers of the 1970s – Wilson, Callaghan and her own party's Ted Heath – had all been failures who presided over Britain's decline. They had given into the unions, given into Buckingham Palace, given into everything.

Thatcher felt that Britain under their leadership had become shabby, decayed and was heading rapidly for geopolitical irrelevance.[55] Margaret was determined to stop the rot and return Britain's status to that of a great global power. The enemy wasn't simply socialism, it was the old guard 'Establishment' who lived in a past that was no longer relevant. In Margaret's eyes they had allowed socialism to run wild; their crime, to stand by and watch it happen.

Margaret Thatcher, by contrast, was anything but laissez-faire. Sir Charles Powell described the environment around her as 'boiling – a permanent state of everything sort of red hot. Like some kind of lava coming out of a volcano.'[56] Meanwhile, the queen and her household became regarded by hardline Thatcherites as plodding and pointless. Her Majesty's 'chief flunky' was the Lord Chamberlain who, at this time, was a Scottish baron called 'Chips' Maclean. He was an ex-royal Guards officer and a former chief scout who perpetuated the tweedy atmosphere[57] of the royal household with a breed of 'yobbo aristocrats floating around'.

Chips was a figure from the 1920s, who arrived at 10 a.m. and had a dry martini at noon.[58] Press Secretary Ronald Allison vividly described another palace character, Lord Charteris, who succeeded Maclean as Lord Chamberlain:

> He [Charteris] lived just across the road in St James' Palace and walked across
> … before he left the house every day his wife, or somebody, if she wasn't
> there, brushed him down, 'cause he was a great snuff user. Brushed all the
> snuff off it. By the time he arrived at the privy press door which was, you
> know, three minutes I suppose he was covered in snuff again, 'cause not only
> had he taken some, but he was outside and he blew out. So someone at the
> privy press door brushed him off.[59]

It was all a very different world to Grantham. The lifestyle of Royal Ascot week, the yearly Windsor house party, shooting parties, skiing, weekends at Sandringham, summers at Balmoral, horses, dogs and hobbies were an anathema to Thatcher's Methodist roots. As Edwina Currie pointed out, 'Mrs Thatcher wouldn't have understood the concept of leisure.'[60]

Cecil Parkinson was left with the impression that the prime minister felt holidays were unnecessary, in stark contrast to the queen's view. While hosting a lunch for the queen once, Her Majesty asked Cecil what the prime minister was doing. He replied, 'Ma'am the prime minister thinks only lazy people have holidays.'[61]

Edwina Currie points out that Margaret in public 'was always a strict royalist and never spoke against the queen. However, if anything came out of the palace that she didn't like she would purse her lips.'[62]

The royal household could often be a source of irritation. While Buckingham Palace got hot under the collar about the merging of regiments, cap badges and so on, staff at Number 10 were trying to deal with issues that mattered to ordinary people.[63] Not surprisingly, Mrs Thatcher came to regard royal visiting as a tedious waste of time. In her mind, the royal family and the old guard encircling them were part of the unproductive rich.

Thatcherism, by contrast, with its middle-class work ethic, would succeed where the old-school-tie Tories had failed. Margaret Thatcher now coined the term 'wet' which meant, among other things, having a paternalistic attitude to the working class, and believed that the well-off should help the poor. Thatcher, on the other hand, was 'dry' and viewed this paternalism as guilt money. The new Conservatives, noting Mrs Thatcher's increasing indifference to the queen, concluded that 'wetness' was rampant in Buckingham Palace.[64] The view gaining ground was that the monarchy – like the bishops, Church of England and the House of Lords – were part of the problem that Thatcherite Conservatism needed to solve. They just happened to be lower on the list of 'things to do' compared to nationalised industries, the socialist menace and trade unions.

Particularly irritating to the new prime minister was the enormous gulf between the two households, royal and prime ministerial. The British Government is remarkably stingy to its prime ministers. Although their apartment at Number 10 is large, with six bedrooms, it isn't grand, and the layout resembles an extended railway carriage. When Mrs Thatcher moved in it was run down and old-fashioned, full of standard Government-issue furniture, and had the rather sad air of rented accommodation. There wasn't even a guarantee of hot water because the plumbing was so out of date.

Unlike most other world leaders, British prime ministers do not enjoy a full domestic staff courtesy of the tax payer, and they're left entirely to their own devices upstairs in the flat converted out of the attic. Government regulations strictly state that the incumbent prime minister has to pay a service charge and make their own housekeeping arrangements. The Thatchers paid out of Denis's private account for all entertaining except state dinners.[65] Mrs Thatcher brought her cleaning lady, Joy, from her Flood Street home in Chelsea, and a second one called Edwina to help out. Since no cook or housekeeper could cope with the long and irregular hours, Margaret didn't hire one. Joy and Edwina saw to most household chores, and everything else Margaret did for herself.[66] Visitors to the upstairs flat would be surprised to find the new prime minister of one of the world's most powerful countries dashing around reheating leftovers brought back from Chequers, or a 'shove in the oven' lasagne.

At Buckingham Palace, life is lived on a grander scale: private gardens, a swimming pool, horses, artworks and priceless jewels. There is no need to swap furniture or eat ready-meals. The working day for the queen at the palace starts when her maid taps on the door, which bears a white card in a plain brass holder inscribed 'The Queen'. She then enters the royal bedroom carrying the 'morning tray' with solid silver pots of Earl Grey tea and hot water, cold milk and a few Marie biscuits (named after a relative, the Grand Duchess Marie of Russia, who married one of Queen Victoria's sons). The cup and saucer are bone china, and there is a linen napkin with the royal cipher E II R.

The queen sleeps in a large pale green bedroom, in a double bed with monogrammed sheets bearing the name, HM The Queen, embroidered in letters exactly 3½in high. The same monogram appears on the pillowcases, except the lettering here is only 1½in high. The measurements are the old fashioned imperial system, rather than the continental metric system. The maid draws her bath, the temperature of which is measured by a thermometer. While the queen is having her bath one of her three dressers lays out her first outfit of the day in the dressing room which has floor-to-ceiling mirrors and is where her hairdresser brushes and arranges her hair.

Her Majesty may have to change up to three times in one day. All her clothes are stored in giant wardrobes in rooms above her bedroom.[67] Breakfast is served in the private dining room at 8.30 a.m. The cutlery is heavy solid silver and the crockery is Sevres china, but the food served is light – scrambled eggs or just plain toast. The newspapers are placed on a side table. The queen's preference is for the *Daily Telegraph* and, over the years, this first glance at the press must have been a tense part of the day. By 9.30 a.m., the queen is seated at her desk in her sitting room–cum–study accompanied by her Corgis, newly returned from walking in the gardens with a footman.[68]

The royal family has a vast retinue of servants. Buckingham Palace alone has over 800 staff. Many of them have bizarre, antiquated titles – Lord Chamberlain, Master of the Horse, Mistress of the Robes, Lady of the Bedchamber, Women of the Bedchamber, Yeoman of the Glass and China Pantry, Yeoman of the Cellars, Page of the Chambers and so on, through to the various secretaries, footmen, chefs, press officers and equerries. An entire department is devoted to horse drawn carriages, and a team of forty-three still wear 'livery': red and black tailcoats for the front of house and black for the senior attendants within.

It is a bewildering network of hierarchies, with enormous potential for the uninitiated to walk into a minefield of social booby traps or snobbish rules about protocol. According to Stephen Barry, the former royal valet who broke ranks and wrote a book about life inside the royal family, 'The royals do absolutely nothing for themselves. Everyone who works in the palace has a function and the end result is cosseting the royals … We used to say that the first thing that Nanny teaches a royal is how to ring for service.'[69] There was an 'ornamental futility'[70] to the whole system, if strict Thatcherite doctrine were applied.

The relationship between the two women went further downhill during the traditional summer visit the premier is required to make to Balmoral, the queen's vast country estate in Scotland. Previous prime ministers, even the Labour ones such as Harold Wilson and James Callaghan, had enjoyed the lifestyle of the great house. Thatcher, however, regarded these annual visits as a tedious waste of time and effort. The queen's jubilee biographer, Ben Pimlott, wrote, 'She [Thatcher] was not at ease with it. It was symptomatic that, on the last day of the obligatory visit, she would arrange to leave at 6 a.m. She couldn't get away fast enough.'[71] Lady Mary Coleman, a niece of the queen mother, was a fellow house guest at Balmoral when the prime minister visited. She confided to the infamous and indiscreet diarist, Woodrow Wyatt, that the queen was horrid to Mrs Thatcher, putting her down all the time, knowing that she was unaccustomed to that kind of society.[72]

Both Mrs Thatcher and the queen disliked other women, and this makes them problematic feminist icons.

The queen's attitudes were shaped in a bygone age. She is naturally suspicious of women in power, despite her own job description and the obvious role models in her immediate family, such as the queen mother and her grandmother, Queen Mary. 'She regards female inferiority as the natural order of things,' says historian David Cannadine. Anointed by God, she views her position as one of duty, which requires self-sacrifice and is an exception to the general rule that men are better at government. 'She is a believing Christian,' explains Ron Allison, 'She took those coronation vows seriously, and has kept and will keep to them. So that you can absolutely say she will never abdicate.'[73]

Consequently, the queen has done nothing to promote women within the royal household and, as head of the Church of England, she has ignored the cause of female bishops. Part of the problem is that she simply prefers men in senior roles, and if the choices in her own household are anything to go by, they're usually educated at Eton.

Intriguingly, Thatcher was equally adverse to powerful women. In eleven and a half years as prime minister, she brought only one woman, Janet Young, into her Cabinet as Leader of the Lords, and Baroness Young did not last long. Lord Carrington explained, 'She was just perfectly beastly to her [laughs], and she was a very nice, sensible lady. No, she [Thatcher] didn't like women. Or she didn't value them as politicians ... she wasn't interested in women ... She was only interested in power and men.'[74] Many other women, like the highly talented Lynda Chalker, were left languishing in junior government posts. Patricia Hewitt, a minister in Tony Blair's Cabinet, told the BBC News website, 'Margaret Thatcher broke through the glass ceiling in politics. But it is a tragedy that, having become the UK's first woman prime minister, she did so much to undermine the position of women in society.'[75]

Thatcher wasn't popular with Tory wives either. At the 40th birthday party of Michael Portillo, then a rising Thatcherite star, the prime minister made a speech and said, 'We'd like to congratulate Michael and ... [uncomfortable pause as she failed to remember the name] his wife.'

The handshake Mrs Thatcher extended to women was described as a wrestling hold; she would grab her opponent and pull her as hard as she could out of the way to get on to the man next to her.[76] Margaret preferred to be the centre of male attention, and didn't like other women who impinged on her. Although she could be charming to the women who worked for her in more menial roles, such as waiting on her at table at Chequers, professional women were viewed as a threat.[77] Tim Bell commented that she disliked women because 'she wasn't particularly enamoured of the fact that women talked about fashion, babies and housework and home building and she was talking about nation building'.[78] 'She didn't deal in small talk,' said Jeffrey Archer. 'She dealt in what you wanted to discuss or what she wanted to discuss ... she didn't deal in hours of discussing irrelevance or irrelevances. She got straight to the point and got on with it. She wasn't someone who wasted a moment of time.'[79]

Having two such women at the pinnacle of British life was always going to be awkward. Neither of them found any solidarity or common ground with the other. Their contretemps seemed very personal, class driven and distinctly female. Once, both the queen and Margaret appeared in public wearing almost identical dresses. Mrs Thatcher phoned the palace to suggest that she and the queen co-ordinate their wardrobes in future to avoid potential embarrassment. The queen's staff issued a very royal put-down. 'Do not worry. The queen does not notice what other people are wearing.' Margaret was left furious and humiliated.[80]

The queen was never the victim of the brutal sexism that Mrs Thatcher endured. Unlike Elizabeth, Margaret's gender was seen as part of her extremism, and her strongest detractors used sexism as a weapon. Indeed, many of the jokes used to attack her were sexist, often recycled mother-in-law jokes:

What does PMT stand for? Prime Minister Thatcher.

Denis Thatcher went into a bookshop and asked the assistant. 'Do you have a book called *How to Control Your Wife?*'

'Our fiction department is upstairs, sir,' the assistant replied.

After all these years of marriage Denis Thatcher has finally discovered an attachment for his wife. It fits over her mouth.

Thatcher represented a new breed of Tory, who drew their strength from the sharp-elbowed middle-class professionals and the ambitious working classes who wanted to own their homes, rather than from the old landed gentry and nobility. The PM declared herself a purposeful workaholic,[81] an idea quite alien to most aristocratic and royal circles, where stamina is a commodity hard to find. Old money has never liked the work ethic of social climbers, it makes them look idle. Thatcherites embodied the beliefs of Charles Darwin's 'survival of the fittest'. This meant a rejection of the unearned privilege brought to the attention of the public by the juvenile high jinks of the younger royals during the 1980s, such as Prince Andrew's affair with soft porn actress, Koo Stark, Fergie and Diana impersonating police women and the absurd *It's a Royal Knockout* television extravaganza.

Thatcher's free market economics depended on individual virtue to generate a robust, independent middle class. She tolerated none of the slackers or hangers-on that the Windsor dynasty accumulated. She nurtured the legend that her youth was spent in the family business learning housewife economics and the principles of thrift that subsequently informed her world view.[82] She made the queen and her family look out of step with reality.

Thatcherism was important because it ended the era of deference in British society. During the 1980s, the British became more democratic and less willing to bow and touch their caps to their 'class betters'. Respect now had to be earned by hard graft, it was no longer a birthright. For Margaret Thatcher, the USA, as a republic, was a model to follow politically, socially and economically. 'Europe was created by history. America was created by philosophy,' she famously said. America represented a new meritocracy and pointed towards the future, whereas 'heritage' Britain, and even the royal court itself, inhibited Britain's potential greatness.

Elizabeth Windsor has always felt most comfortable, as we all do, being surrounded by people of her class and background. The political aristocrats like Sir Winston Churchill, Sir Alec Douglas-Home, Sir Anthony Eden and Sir Harold Macmillan fitted into her world neatly. Mrs Thatcher was a bit of a shock. Margaret viewed the traditional, consensus, 'one nation' Tories favoured by the queen as failures; they were guilty of accommodation, a dirty word in the Thatcherite lexicon.

Lord Carrington explains:

> At first, she [Thatcher] was sensible enough not to sack all the people whom she knew disagreed with her, but she had them all in her shadow cabinet.
>
> But she made it perfectly clear from the beginning who was in charge, and she never allowed any sort of dissent from there. But you see, in a way she

couldn't stop dominating [laughs]. I mean, she was absolutely right to do it to begin with, but it became a habit.[83]

One by one she fired the remaining old guard of Tory posh boys, such as Francis Pym, Norman St John-Stevas and James Prior. What rubbed salt in the wounds of their collective political assassination was the fact that it was carried out by a woman who was born over a Grantham grocer's shop.

As she rose through the ranks of the Tory Party, Thatcher made little attempt to adapt and fit into the highest echelons of the Conservatives, dominated as they were by the public schools and land-owning classes. She made no pretence at being anything other than provincial lower middle class, displaying an assuredness and a self-confidence that was to inspire a new generation of Tories, even as it infuriated her snobbish opponents within the party. Furthermore, she had the temerity to replace them with the likes of Norman Tebbit, the son of a pawnbroker's shop assistant, men of the same ilk and class as her father. Thatcher had always been more Citizen Robespierre than Cardinal Richelieu, but the old school gentlemen of the Tory Party noticed that fact too late in the day. 'She should inspire anyone who has come from nowhere and wishes to achieve. She was not establishment,' explained Jeffrey Archer. 'She was not wealthy; she was not "one of the boys". Everything was against her, and she defeated every one of them in the end.'[84]

The popular BBC television show of this era, *To the Manor Born*, perfectly illustrated this class struggle. In this comedy series, national treasure Penelope Keith played Audrey Forbes-Hamilton, the snobbish lady of the manor who was forced to sell her stately home, Grantleigh Manor, after being widowed. Audrey finds, to her horror, that it has been bought by nouveau riche millionaire, Richard DeVere, played by Peter Bowles, a businessman of Czech ancestry who made his fortune with a company named Cavendish Foods. 'He's trade,' the departing lady of the manor shudders. The series began broadcasting during the autumn of 1979, four months after Thatcher's election victory. It captured the antagonism between the two wings of the modern Conservative Party: 'the estate owners and the estate agents' as Labour politician Denis Healey once described them. Audrey represented the old feudal traditions now in sharp decline, while DeVere stood as the embodiment of the rise of the entrepreneur. He was regularly referred to detrimentally as a grocer, echoing the occupation of Thatcher's father. The series captured the imagination of millions of TV viewers and was a massive ratings success.[85]

2

DADDY'S GIRL, THE GROCER'S DAUGHTER

Never do things just because other people do them.
Alfred Roberts

Mrs Thatcher, like the queen, was a daddy's girl. Both women were shaped by intransigent men who disliked compromise. Their fathers were born in an era when class and social position were fixed at birth and remained unchangeable until you died. The two men found it impossible to escape their respective birthrights. Margaret's father, Alfred Roberts, was a shopkeeper and local politician who rose to become Mayor of Grantham. With Alfred, life was about pulling yourself up by your boot straps and making something of yourself. By contrast, the queen's father, George VI, was determined to resist change in whatever shape it might appear; for him, maintaining the status quo was the highest virtue. These paternal philosophies would stick like glue to their respective daughters. To understand both women, you must understand the fathers.

After St Francis of Assisi, the next man Margaret Thatcher paid tribute to outside 10 Downing Street on the day of her election was Alfred Roberts, 'I just owe almost everything to my own father'.[1] At such a moment, personal reflections on life, events, and the choices made are inevitable. Thatcher's father had died in 1970, just before Margaret entered Ted Heath's Cabinet. His Victorian values and his sober commercial outlook, rooted in his corner shop, formed the basis of what his daughter preached to Britain throughout the eighties. Thatcher's biographer, John Campbell, perceptively wrote, 'Alfred Roberts' grocery shop had become a British equivalent of Lincoln's log cabin.'[2]

Sir Bernard Ingham, one of Thatcher's closest advisors and stalwart press secretary, stated:

> Hers was a narrow upbringing in a strict Methodist household which she grew out of. But instead of going off the rails, she retained a strong Christian ethic, a high sense of moral duty … Her father taught her not to go with the herd if she thought the herd was wrong.[3]

When Margaret Thatcher became prime minister, bizarre rumours persistently circulated that, somehow, through some aristocratic ancestral affair, blue blood pumped through her veins.[4] One version of the story is that Beatrice Stephenson, Mrs Thatcher's mother, was the illegitimate daughter of Henry Cockayne-Cust, the nephew of Lord Brownlow, and Margaret's grandmother Phoebe, who had briefly worked as a housemaid at the Brownlow stately home, Belton House, near Grantham. Phoebe had been a farmer's daughter who, after leaving service, went on to work as a factory machinist. In 1876, she married a humble cloakroom attendant called Daniel Stephenson. They were extremely poor, and after their marriage, her grandmother went back to work in domestic service.[5]

Although there is no evidence for this, the fact that these rumours made the rounds illustrates the depth of Britain's obsession with breeding, family connections and class.[6] Clearly, there was a group within the political class which felt Thatcher's power, leadership and charisma couldn't have originated from over a grocer's shop. Former Social Democratic Party leader, David Owen, thinks this is a sign of the outright snobbery that existed at the time within the Tory Party, 'That's the whole problem with the hereditary lot, they do believe their own propaganda'.[7]

Whether or not there was a secret aristocrat in Margaret Roberts' lineage, she enjoyed a secure, if humble, upbringing presided over by a thoroughly self-taught, self-made man. Alfred was a man of diligence and considerable naked intelligence. Educated only until the age of 12 like many working-class men, his ambitions were thwarted by circumstance. Alfred Roberts didn't complain; he just got on with it, fighting hard to gain respectability and security for his family.[8] He never tolerated the words, 'I can't', or 'It's too difficult'.[9]

One Tory MP indiscreetly, but accurately, observed that Britain was being governed by the wraith of Alderman Roberts, a sort of ghost of recessions past. He had handed on to his daughter a set of beliefs, values and social attitudes that she was now employing to guide the affairs of Britain. He added that, since Alderman Roberts had told her that you cannot spend more than you take at the till, she chopped away at public spending for all the world as if it were an unnecessary new hat.[10]

Margaret's entry in *Who's Who* is revealing. She describes herself as the daughter of Alfred. No mention is made of her mother, Beatrice. 'Well, of course I just owe everything to my father,' she gushed to Robert Harris, who was interviewing her for the *Observer* in 1988.[11] She always made a point of honoring daddy foremost, and it seemed to fuel her sense of being special, 'daddy's precious little daughter'. There is little, if any, sense of indebtedness to her mother. 'I loved my mother dearly, but after I was 15 we had nothing more to say to each other ... it was not her fault. She was always weighed down by the home.'[12]

There is no doubt about the intensity of the relationship between the young Margaret and her father. At home, Alfred ruled the roost and his word was law. He was tall, almost 6ft 3in, with horn-rimmed glasses and a thick mop of hair, which in later years turned pure white. He improved his mind with books, reading anything he could lay his hands on, from biography to history and politics.[13] Research shows that fathers who are challenging and somewhat abrasive raise the most socially competent, independent and intrinsically motivated daughters. In fact, social confidence in girls appears to be inhibited rather than enhanced by unconditional approval and passive acceptance.[14]

Whatever the romantic parentage of Beatrice Roberts, Grantham inhabitants described her as being poker-faced and 'a right old battle axe'.[15] She lived her life very much under her husband's thumb. Beatrice was a quiet and plain looking woman. 'Her mother was homely in every way,' recalls schoolmate Margaret Wickstead.[16] Beatrice was a quiet and gave the impression of someone who didn't enjoy life. She was never demonstratively affectionate towards her children and, although she worked all the hours God sent, she was no match for her husband's intellect and ambition.[17]

In one of Margaret's more revealing interviews to broadcaster Dr Miriam Stoppard, the prime minister explained how when she complained to her mother about her friends having more material possessions, she was repeatedly told, 'Well we are not situated like that!' When asked if she accepted this injunction, Margaret replied, 'one kicked against it, of course, one kicked against it. They [her friends] had more things than we did. Of course, one kicked against it.' But the kicking seems to have been directed more at Beatrice than Alfred, even though he was just as frugal as his wife. Her subsequent choice of a generous and affluent husband was at some level an expression of her resentment at having been forced to live so economically.

In the interview, Margaret also recalled going out to buy new covers for the settee:

That was a great event; to have new covers for a settee was a great expenditure and a great event, so you went out to choose them, and you chose something that looked really rather lovely, something light with flowers on. My mother: 'That is not serviceable!' And how I longed for the time when I could buy things that were not serviceable![18]

Margaret's resentment towards her mother is palpable. Beatrice, in Margaret's eyes, was someone who allowed herself to be sidelined. A contemporary at Oxford recalled, '... I used to feel, just occasionally that she rather despised her mother and adored her father'.[19]

The dominant matriarchal figure in the house was her maternal grandmother, Phoebe Stephenson, who ruled their cramped home with an iron grip, just as Alderman Roberts ruled the shop downstairs.[20] She was, said Thatcher, 'very, very Victorian and very, very strict'.[21] Beatrice wasn't even mistress in her own home.

Most daughters who distance themselves from their mothers retain a strong instinctive bond with them, even if the relationship has been overcast by tetchiness and mutual incomprehension.[22] The total absence of this bond suggests Margaret felt deprived of motherly love. Her extreme competitiveness, aggression and obsessive conscientiousness implied a need to fight for attention during a childhood that was not as rosy as she later chose to paint it.[23] Her anger with her mother would play out in her relationships with other women, from her school headmistress to female parliamentary colleagues and political wives, even to the audience chamber at Buckingham Palace.

Margaret also had an older sister, Muriel, four years her senior. In later life, Muriel never gave interviews, but she did write a few lines about Grantham life and stressed that Beatrice was an avid reader, perhaps in an attempt to give her an intellectual life in repudiation of Margaret's colder judgement.[24]

Grantham itself is a little backwater railway town just 24 miles east of Nottingham. Its population of 30,000 was then almost exclusively employed in the factories, building railway coaches and rolling stock.[25] Alfred Roberts had taken out a bank mortgage to open his corner shop on North Parade, the town's main commercial street. After years of prudent, and some say tightfisted, management the business grew and prospered.[26] A second store followed later. Margaret learnt to appreciate the free market as a simple and understandable manifestation, at the very front line where customers paid with cash in hand.[27] From childhood, the unfettered market appeared to be a reliable mechanism by which people could be served and an honest living made.

Although the Roberts family lived well compared to many in the town, there were no extras. Hot water for washing was boiled in the small kitchen and decanted into porcelain pitchers and bowls for the bedrooms. Bathing took place in a galvanised tin tub. Under each bed was a porcelain potty to avoid a cold walk to the outside privy in the middle of the night. There was a yard, rather than a garden. It was all terribly basic, but by owning property Alfred was the first in the family to lift himself out of the working class.[28] That was something of which he could feel very proud.

Eventually, the family moved into a sizable semi-detached property in a row of Edwardian houses just across the road from the shop. Here, for the first time, they had a garden and the comforts of modern plumbing.

Everything the Roberts family achieved was the result of grinding hard work, methodical savings and careful budgeting. Owning property made Alfred the master of his destiny, and life for the family revolved around the needs of the business. As Margaret would write:

> For one thing you're always on duty. People knocked on the door at almost any hour of the night or weekend if they had run out of bacon, sugar, butter or eggs. Everyone knew that we lived by serving the customer, it was pointless to complain, so nobody did.[29]

The Roberts' corner shop was unlike today's modern convenience stores. It had sacks of flour and sugar, lentils, dried peas and pearl barley which used to arrive in bulk, along with barrels of jam and treacle, chests of tea, bags of coffee beans, tins of dried fruit and giant slabs of butter. Everything had to be meticulously weighed, measured and decanted into smaller containers or brown paper bags. It was a job Muriel and Margaret helped out with.[30] If they made mistakes customers would be short changed, or profits eroded. The Roberts sisters learnt to be methodical and diligent.

Either Alfred or Beatrice would always be on duty during opening hours. This meant the family would never take a day off together, apart from bank holidays or Sundays. When the shop was closed, they might travel to Nottingham for afternoon tea and a visit to the cinema or, at Christmas time, a visit to the pantomime. Such days were a treat looked forward to for weeks. Summer holidays by the seaside at Skegness were equally prized, but, to keep the shop open, both parents took their break at different times. Margaret and Muriel went with their mother during the school holidays, Alfred took his holiday later to coincide with bowls week.

What little time was left over from the family business was taken up by the Methodist Church. 'I was born into a family which was practical, serious and intensely religious.'[31] Methodism, which was a popular denomination in Grantham, had a profound effect on her. Its religious regime was exhausting. Thatcher remembered, 'We had no alcohol in the house until (my father) became mayor at the end of the war, and then only sherry and cherry brandy.'[32] No newspapers or entertainment were permitted in the house on Sundays. There was no question of the girls being allowed to mix with friends or even play an innocuous game like snakes and ladders. Their grandmother Phoebe wouldn't even let them knit or sew. Sundays were reserved for God, religious thought and discussion:

> The values instilled in church were faithfully reflected in my home …
> The family went to Sunday morning service at 11 o'clock, but before that
> I would have gone to Sunday school. There was Sunday school again in the
> afternoon; later, from about the age of 12, I played the piano for the smaller
> children to sing the hymns. Then my parents would usually go out again to
> Sunday evening service.[33]

The Roberts family also practised Christianity through good deeds. Beatrice Roberts baked bread twice a week, and it was young Margaret's job to deliver surplus loaves and cakes to less fortunate neighbours.[34] 'There was always something from those Thursday or Sunday bakes which was sent out to elderly folk living alone or who were sick.'[35]

The church became Margaret's main source of amusement, there she learned how to play the piano and, briefly, the pipe organ. There she sang and listened to choral music. It was hardly a free and fun environment, but it was one that shaped her character. If the young Margaret objected, Alfred simply preached, 'never do things just because other people do them'. It became his favourite expression, and one Margaret adopted as if it were gospel.

Alfred Roberts sought to make something of himself beyond the realm of his little business by taking an active role in both his local Methodist church and by serving on the local council.[36] Lay preaching was one of the few ways working-class men could acquire ease and fluency in public speaking. Part of his Sunday would be spent visiting neighbouring villages travelling by pony and trap and, in later years, the church provided him with a taxi when he became one of the most popular preachers in the area.[37] This oratorical tradition was passed down to his daughter, who started her public speaking career reading passages from the Bible in her local church pulpit.[38] That preaching style never left her.

For Alfred Roberts, like Margaret later, there was just a small step between faith and politics. He was eager to do the right thing and, inspired by Christianity, he took a lively interest in both local concerns and the bigger issues of the day. There has been some debate whether her father was a natural Tory, then the party of privilege, land and wealth. His views were arguably more progressive. Even Thatcher conceded that, 'his politics would perhaps be best described as "old fashioned liberal"'.[39] Individual responsibility was his watchword, and sound finance his passion. Although he remained independent throughout his municipal career, without fail, he voted with the Conservatives in council on every single issue.[40]

At the time, both Conservative Prime Minister Stanley Baldwin and his successor, Neville Chamberlain, were great appeasers of Adolf Hitler, desperately trying to avoid a repetition of the slaughter of the First World War. Alfred Roberts was passionately interested in what went on elsewhere, particularly in ideological terms. Huddling around their kitchen radio, the Roberts family shaped their opinions differently and favoured swift rearmament:

> We had a deep distrust of the dictators ... Unlike many conservative-minded people, my father was fierce in rejecting the argument, put forward by some supporters of Franco, that fascist regimes had to be backed as the only way to defeat communists. He believed that a free society was the better alternative to both.[41]

This view would only have been reinforced in 1938 when Muriel's 17-year-old Jewish pen friend, Edith Muhlbauer, fled from Vienna to escape the Nazis and came to stay with the Roberts. Edith brought with her tales of life under the Third Reich, which Margaret listened to with horror and fascination. She became far more conscious than her school contemporaries of what the war was all about. However, the Roberts family didn't have the money or the time to take Edith in permanently. So Margaret, then 12, and Muriel, 17, set about raising funds and persuading the local Rotary club to help. Edith stayed with more than a dozen Rotary families for the next two years, until she could join relatives in South America.

While staying with the Roberts family, Edith slept in Margaret's room, and she left an impression. 'She was 17, tall, beautiful, evidently from a well-to-do family,' Margaret later wrote in her memoir. Most importantly, however, 'she told us what it was like to live as a Jew under an anti-Semitic regime. One thing Edith reported particularly stuck in my mind: The Jews, she said, were being made to scrub the streets. For Margaret, who believed in meaningful work, this was as much a waste as it was an outrage. Had the Roberts family not intervened, Edith recalled years later, 'I would have stayed in Vienna, and they would have killed me'. Margaret Roberts never forgot the lesson. 'Never hesitate to do whatever you can, for you may save a life,' she told audiences in 1995, after Edith had been located, alive and well, in Brazil.[42]

Everything changed with the outbreak of the Second World War. There were considerable disruptions to life; shortages, rationing, blackouts and air raids. For a relatively small town, Grantham felt the pressure of the war more than most. The mainline road and rail routes, along with its factories, made it a prime target for air raids. At one stage, it even had one the highest ratios of bombs to fall, per head of the population, in Britain.[43] Edith Muhlbauer wasn't the only new arrival. Hundreds of British and American airman arrived in Lincolnshire, and life in Grantham was turned upside down. Alfred threw himself into the war effort on the Home Front, gaining the distinction of being Food Officer for the town, as well as chairman of the Council Finance Committee, chairman of the National Savings Committee and, by 1943, he had served one term as mayor. In this later role, he was torn between upholding the tenets of his faith and keeping spirits up during the war. Eventually, he reluctantly allowed the town to relax the strict rules forbidding entertainment on the Sabbath and, for the first time, cinemas opened on Sundays. For Margaret, it was her only window onto a wider world. She wrote in her memoirs:

It was … the coming of cinema to Grantham that really brightened up my life. [My parents] were content that I should go to 'good' films, a classification which fortunately included Fred Astaire and Ginger Rogers musicals and the films of Alexandra Korda. On my visits to the cinema I roamed to the most fabulous realms of the imagination. It gave me the determination to roam in reality one day.[44]

Alfred was equally ambitious for his daughter, and her education reflected that. Although it included music and culture, he stressed achievement and vocational educational goals. Not surprisingly, his daughter studied to be first a scientist then a lawyer. Not for her the interpretive subjects such as classics, philosophy or history.[45] Margaret was sent to Huntingtower Road School, despite the longer commute, as it was better than other local schools both academically and socially. At 9, the hard-working little girl had been congratulated by a teacher for her luck in winning a poetry reading contest, 'I wasn't lucky,' she replied, 'I deserved it.'[46]

Margaret shone as one of brightest pupils in her year and, under her father's guidance, the learning never stopped. She was encouraged to read instructive books and to discuss them; she was taken to lectures and concerts, and preached to by her father on a wide range of topics, including finance. Margaret was encouraged to save her pocket money and buy savings stamps. She was never free to indulge in childish frivolity. There was no garden behind the shop to play in, and no bicycle to ride. This wasn't due to lack of money, but her father's extreme carefulness; not one penny was spent unless it was necessary.

In 1936, Margaret gained a place at the Kesteven & Grantham Girls' School where her sister was already a pupil. Manners, discipline and correct English were expected from every Kesteven girl, particularly the scholarship girls, who were all keenly aware of the opportunities that the school offered.[47] Margaret's desire to be recognised also expressed itself in a fascination with acting and she joined the dramatic society, acting in many of the school productions. She loved the glamour, but mostly a sense of being centre stage and the focus of attention.[48] She had a strong drive to be singled out and recognised as special, demonstrating an enormous streak of self-confidence. When visiting speakers invited questions at the end of their presentations 'it would always be Margaret Roberts that got to her feet … asking clear, well-formulated questions, while her friends just looked at each other and raised their eyes to heaven'.[49]

Margaret never made close friends at school, her time was always taken up with a combination of church, shop work and homework. As a consequence, she never quite fitted in with her peers and, because her father always expected her to be serious, she may have given the impression that she couldn't be bothered with giggly, silly girls.[50] Several of her classmates remembered her being ridiculed as 'priggish', 'bookish' and 'ambitious'.[51] Some classmates felt she was such a damper on the fun that they would walk a different route to school so as not to meet up with her on the way.[52] Many found her impeccable behaviour tedious.[53]

However, Margaret Roberts didn't value her peers' opinions much. Smart girl that she was, she quickly realised that education was the best way to escape the grim provincial world of Grantham. She had the zeal and higher purpose to apply for a place at Oxford University a year early because, at 17, she wanted to 'get on'.

Margaret had always come top in her exams through sheer effort and industry. The intellectual qualities most frequently attributed to her were 'logic and diligence'.[54] However, her ill-tempered Scottish headmistress, Dorothy Gillies, thought her star pupil was too young to leave home. 'You're thwarting my ambition,' Margaret reportedly said.[55] There was also another obstacle: Margaret hadn't studied Latin, an essential prerequisite to a place at such an august university. Not to be derailed, she conscripted her father's support and sweet-talked him into paying for private Latin coaching from a teacher at the local boys' school.

All that was to be done now was to apply. Alfred wrote the cheque out to accompany the examination fee, and Margaret took it to Miss Gillies as a fait accompli.[56] A local vicar, Canon Goodrich, whose daughter, Margaret, had recently gone up to Lady Margaret Hall College at Oxford, was also recruited to give extra coaching. The two

Margarets became friends. The Goodrichs' modest but comfortable middle-class home, littered with books, pictures and finer furniture, became a glimpse into a better, more elegant and comfortable way of life which she desired for herself.[57]

Not only did Margaret complete her High School Certificate a year early, she also successfully crammed a five year Latin course into a few months. It was with some satisfaction that she went up to Oxford to sit the entrance examination, hopeful for a scholarship to read chemistry at Somerville College.[58] Chemistry proved a shrewd choice. Far fewer girls applied for science degrees and, had Margaret switched to law or a more popular subject like English, the competition would have been far greater. However, the news from Oxford was initially disappointing. Margaret was turned down, but her name was put on the waiting list. This gave her two options, go to another university, like London or nearby Nottingham, or apply next year when she was 18.

Margaret chose the latter option and went back to school, where she was made joint head girl with classmate Madeline Edwards. She had shared this distinction for only two weeks when a telegram arrived from Oxford. Would Miss Roberts care to take up a place forfeited by someone else? In a fortnight, Margaret Roberts, always one to seize the main chance, disappeared from Grantham for good.[59]

Pulling up roots must have been painful at only 17. Arriving at Oxford, she appeared to be an unpolished girl whose homemade clothes and clunky shoes set her apart from the usual posh *Country Life* types.[60] Somerville was an all-women's college, its alumni included Indira Gandhi, Edith Summerskill and Shirley Williams. In those days the girls fell into three distinct social groups, exemplified by where a person sat at table in the hall. The foreign students took the top three tables, nearest the principal's chair. At the bottom three tables sat the wealthy and impeccably aristocratic girls from polished schools like Cheltenham Ladies' College and Roedean. In between sat the solid daughters of the middle classes and the scholarship girls, with brains and robust work ethics. It was this middle group with whom Margaret fitted in most, but again she came across as awkward and gauche; making herself an instant outsider and social misfit.[61]

'I was the first Roberts to go to Oxbridge,' she declared, aware that she was a meritocratic pioneer. However, she also witnessed at firsthand the huge advantages enjoyed by richer undergraduates with good connections. Their confidence and wealth were intimidating.[62] There is a note of animus and jealousy in her observation[63] that, 'I might have had a more glittering Oxford career, but I had little money to spare'.[64] Many patronised the earnest Methodist girl with small-town manners and a lingering Grantham accent. 'I began by keeping myself to myself, for I felt shy and ill at ease in this new environment.'[65] She was also mercilessly teased because of her naive and outspoken ambition to better herself. Her biggest faux pas was telling everyone that she had taken elocution lessons. She spoke like Eliza Doolittle in George Bernard Shaw's play *Pygmalion*, with a clear grip of the basic idea of what was needed, yet without the finesse to carry it off.[66]

Quickly and cruelly, Margaret became the subject of ridicule, just as she had at school. She never appeared to realise that she was making a fool of herself until it was too late, and once teased would blush crimson. She spoke incessantly about 'daddy'. Daddy, the Mayor of Grantham, rather than daddy, the grocer. What daddy thought of this and that, what daddy said she should do and how she should behave; and the books daddy said she should read.[67]

Meanwhile, Margaret also failed to integrate herself in the chemistry lab, where the students were tight knit as a result of the long hours of work carrying out laboratory practice. Margaret remained aloof, while the others joined in and had fun. As a result, she ended up spending her four years at university making few real friends, and inadvertently generated a feeling shared by many of her contemporaries that she was only prepared to offer friendship to those people who might be of some use to her.[68] Margaret, moreover, was never very close to any of her female contemporaries. The three for whom she had the most time were two fellow Methodists, Mary Osbourne and Jean Southerst, and Canon Goodrich's daughter, Margaret. She clearly preferred the company of men.

Margaret's social isolation was further exacerbated by the left-wing politics of Somerville College under its distinguished principal, Dame Janet Vaughan. Margaret arrived at Oxford an unshakable Conservative, and Dame Janet remembers no one quite as intransigent, as she never questioned her own political convictions once in all her undergraduate years.[69]

Barred from the Oxford Union, which only admitted men, she joined the next best thing, the Oxford University Conservative Association, which became both a refuge and inspiration.[70] Former members included ex-prime ministers such as Gladstone, Asquith, Salisbury, Macmillan and Heath. Margaret could easily hold her own in any political argument and found herself in a private club designed to forge social and political connections, as well as an unofficial marriage bureau with its social evenings revolving around dancing and dining. Margaret Roberts was too straightforward, naive and prickly to use this opportunity to find a rich husband.[71] Perhaps also, although attractive, she was too unpolished and unsophisticated to be viewed as good marriage material by the Oxford male population, but this didn't stop her trying.

For an ambitious girl, there were many potential suitors. As one contemporary, Pauline Cowan, said of her, 'We all knew that Margaret had set her cap at a young man with money and title.'[72] The grandest by far was Johnny Dalkeith, heir to the dukedom of Buccleuch. He was favoured by the queen mother as a potential beau for Princess Elizabeth. Margaret had a crush on him after he raised money from the other well-heeled students to buy the future prime minister a bicycle, because she was doing so much work on behalf of the student body and needed transport to get around. Mrs Thatcher would later describe him as a 'rather marvellous person'.[73] It is intriguing to speculate that Elizabeth and Margaret were once potentially interested in the same man.

Another male friend within the union was Edward Boyle, an old Etonian and baronet. She was taken to meet his mother in her apartment in Portman Square and was overwhelmed with its scale and treasures inside. 'To me it was a different world. I had never been in a flat like it.'[74]

However, it was Lord Craigmyle, a young history undergraduate at Corpus Christi College, with whom Margaret fell seriously in love for the very first time. This young aristocrat had a large shipping fortune and a title inherited from his father. He was also heir to his grandfather's grander title, the Earl of Inchcape. The unsophisticated Margaret made no secret of her feelings, and was quite gushing about him, although she laid herself open to further ridicule from female contemporaries who, by this time, were growing quite disillusioned by her blatant social climbing.[75] Unfortunately for Margaret, this shy young man was very close to his mother. When he took Margaret home to meet her at the family's London home, Lady Craigmyle found Miss Roberts provincial and therefore a highly unsuitable future countess. Her comment was, 'In trade and in science! We know nobody who is in either.'[76] Margaret thus failed to catch herself a title; yet again, another woman had blocked her progress.

Oxford made Margaret painfully aware that her background did not match up, and she never seemed to have much fun at the university. Not only was she trying to climb the matrimonial ladder, but also a political one as she socialised with the future Tory Party elite. Although she was enormously impressed by the wit of young war hero Quintin Hogg (a future Lord Chancellor) and the aristocratic charms of Anthony Eden and Alec Douglas-Home (both future prime ministers), the admiration wasn't returned. These sophisticated Tory grandees, who shared the same backgrounds and upbringing as the Buckingham Palace coterie, found her inherently vulgar, a viewpoint explicitly expressed by Prime Minister Harold Macmillan. Most spoke of her as 'that common woman'. To them, she was someone who served the carriage trade, someone whom they would be happy to patronise provided she was standing on the other side of the shop counter, ideally with an apron on. Although the Second World War had supposedly swept aside the old aristocratic Conservatives, Tory Cabinets which operated from 1951 contained no fewer than eleven hereditary peers. The old Establishment was holding on to power and privilege tightly.

Margaret Thatcher returned home from Oxford with a chip on her shoulder. After the urban world of university the social deficiencies of her own family were obvious. Oxford 'made her father seem a rather ordinary man,' guessed Margaret Goodrich.[77] But she wasn't crushed by the snobbish dimensions of Oxford. Her father had installed into her great confidence, which subsequently developed into narcissistic grandiosity and an incapacity to tolerate self-doubt.[78]

Politically she went far, meeting an array of up-and-coming young political stars alongside whom she would eventually work in Parliament, and becoming president of the university's Conservative Association. Academically, she gained a second, not a first-class degree. Her critics have made much of this, although the fact she later qualified as a barrister in just two years, while raising twins and securing a parliamentary seat suggests a great deal of intellectual stamina. She also won the Kirkcaldy Essay Prize in her third year, and no accolade from Somerville should be sniffed at.

Margaret saw and used Oxford, including the people she cultivated there, as a stepping stone to the House of Commons, and for very little else. She wasn't some dreary bluestocking, and the young men surrounding her had barely seen a woman before in their lives. She stood out from the crowd and captured their attention. 'Some of us were making it before women's lib was even thought of!' she infamously snapped.[79]

The obvious next step into politics for Margaret was via the law. However, further study required money which she didn't have. After graduation, Margaret needed to find work to make use of her chemistry degree and landed a research position at BX Plastics, situated in a drab factory outside Colchester, earning £350 per year (about £15,000 in today's money). She rationalised her position thus, 'Very few people greatly enjoy the early stages of a new job and in this I was no exception.'[80] Margaret was one of the first women ever to be employed in such a capacity. She found it agonising, and was quite incapable of communicating with the men on the factory floor. Her rather grand style earned her the nicknamed 'Duchess' or 'Aunty Margaret' which stuck to her throughout her three years working at the firm. Yet she was steering a precise course, quite indifferent to opinion around her. All her spare time was spent with members of the local Conservative Association where she made friends, or rather, useful contacts.

Marriage provided the big escape for Margaret, just as it did for Elizabeth. Matrimony transformed them both. Elizabeth became a grown woman at last, and Margaret married up and metamorphosed into a rich middle-class Tory wife.

When Margaret Roberts accepted Denis Thatcher's proposal, the story of a lower middle-class girl struggling against the odds ended.[81] Although her later career might have been possible without Denis's emotional and financial support, it would have been far harder. Marriage to Denis changed everything for her; their wedding was arguably one of the best decisions she ever made politically. It was also clearly a love match, as they were devoted to each other. 'I think Denis was very, very important,' said former Cabinet minister, Cecil Parkinson. 'I think he, you know, gave her a feeling of financial stability that the family if you like was well financed, and Margaret always liked to be sure that finances were in good order.'[82] 'Denis paid for all those things like child care and holidays that made life easier,' said Edwina Currie.[83]

As a couple, the Thatchers seemed to complement each other perfectly, where the queen and her husband tolerated each other's differences. The marriage between Denis and Margaret would also remain free from the scandals that engulf many in the public eye. Solid and middle class, the Thatchers left sexual indiscretions to the aristocracy.

The queen, by contrast, would be confronted by rumours of her husband's mistresses and various alleged adulteries (whatever the truth behind the rumours, at least the alleged affairs appeared to have taken place discreetly).

Margaret and Denis each admired the other's self-sufficiency and were supportive to each other. Both wanted their own careers and accepted the other's ambition. 'He [Denis] had a robust sort of good sense; he never pandered to her, he was immensely proud of her, but he always spoke his mind, and I think she just found that very refreshing,' said Cecil Parkinson.[84] Sir Bernard Ingham points out, 'She was an achiever, but whether she would have got as far without Denis Thatcher is entirely another matter. He brought financial security, emotional satisfaction … and the support that enabled her to go for it. She described him as her "rock".'[85]

Major Denis Thatcher was ten years older, a bit of a war hero who had been mentioned in dispatches and had served in France, Sicily and Italy;[86] not least of all, he was tall, athletic, good-looking and very taken with his bride-to-be. Denis was also managing director of the family paint and wallpaper company, Atlas Preservatives, in Kent, which made him comparatively rich, with a flat in Chelsea and a flash Jaguar motor car which he called his 'tart trap'. He took her to smart dinners at fashionable restaurants like The Ivy and L'Ecu De France.

Margaret did not say 'yes' at once to his marriage proposal. Denis was a divorcee and Margaret worried about becoming the second Mrs Thatcher. The first, Margot Kempson, a glamorous horse riding beauty from Hertfordshire,[87] was blonde, and a more sympathetic, more beautiful version of her successor, but the marriage suffered the separations of war. After two years, she left him for a second husband with a title, Sir Howard Hickman. Denis was shattered and refused to talk about it.[88]

Marriage to Denis was a smart move for Margaret. As mothers around the world have wisely reminded their daughters, it is just as easy to love a rich man as a poor one.[89] Denis understood the priorities of businessmen and informed his wife of them. Margaret was a great believer in commerce, she would never have fallen for a playboy. Denis's company, Atlas Preservatives, took him around the world and she admired that. She was a great advocate of enterprise and Atlas Preservatives was just the sort of British company the economy needed.

Their wedding was a quiet affair. The ceremony took place with fifty close friends and relatives in Wesley's Chapel in City Road. Margaret wore a blue velvet dress, a replica of an outfit worn by Georgiana, Duchess of Devonshire, in a painting by Sir Joshua Reynolds, complete with a little sapphire hat and ostrich feather. For their honeymoon, the newlyweds travelled to Portugal, Madeira and Paris, combining a little of the bridegroom's business with pleasure.[90]

As well as changing her name and class, Mrs Thatcher also switched religion from her Nonconformist Methodist roots to the more Establishment, Church of England.[91] Margaret was now the suburban Kent-based wife of a millionaire. After one year she became pregnant and gave birth to twins, Mark and Carol, in August 1953. They were looked after by a nanny during their early years, before continuing to elite schools, Harrow and St Paul's Girls. Only occasionally did her voice now betray a Lincolnshire lilt. Mostly, she sounded like a privileged and somewhat patronising stockbroker-belt southerner.[92]

Denis's money now meant she could afford to train as a barrister, and while still in the maternity ward of Queen Charlotte's Hospital in London she applied to the Council of Legal Education to study for the Bar. Women were then tolerated in the legal profession if they kept to subjects such as family law. That wasn't Margaret's style; after passing her exams she focused on building a taxation practice, which was then very much an elite male preserve. Qualifying as a lawyer was merely to prepare her to be a better parliamentarian.

Pursuing both a legal and political career took its toll on family life. It meant rationing her attention to her children in what Carol later called 'impenetrable tunnel vision'.[93] Margaret often forgot to wave to the twins when she left home, neglected Denis and refused to consort with his mother. The new young mother seemed to resent her domestic commitments, entitling the relevant chapter in her autobiography, 'House Bound'.[94]

In November 1954 she was shortlisted, but missed selection for, a by-election in Orpington. It was the same story again two years later in Beckenham, then Ashford and again in Maidstone. In her memoirs, Thatcher is clear about the sex discrimination she met:

> I would be shortlisted for the seat, would make what was generally acknowledged to be a good speech – and then the questions, most of them having the same purpose, would begin. 'With my family commitments, would I have time enough for the constituency? Did I really think that I could fulfill my duties as a mother with young children to look after and as an MP?'
>
> I detected a feeling that the House of Commons was not really the right place for a woman.

Margaret blamed women themselves as much as men. 'Perhaps some of the men at selection committees entertained this prejudice,' she wrote. 'But I found then, and later, that it was the women who came nearest to expressing it openly.'[95]

Eventually, success came with a safe seat in Finchley in north London, just after the Thatchers had rather frustratingly bought themselves a new house in Farnborough, south of London. To succeed, she still had to overcome considerable 'anti-women' prejudice in what had boiled down to a contest between racial and sexual discrimination. Her predecessor complained that, 'We've got to choose between a bloody Jew and a bloody woman'.[96] The bloody woman won.

Margaret threw herself into her constituency, giving speeches, attending social functions and bazaars, visiting old people's homes and schools and driving herself across London in her old blue Ford Anglia. Finchley may have been a safe seat, but Margaret fought the election with extreme passion, winning a majority of nearly 3,500 more than the previous incumbent. Her mission statement was, 'I will let the people know what Conservatism is about and I will lead the troops into battle.'[97]

At last, in 1959 Margaret Thatcher was a Member of Parliament. Aged only 34, she was the youngest woman in the House, and by 1961, she became parliamentary under-secretary for pensions and national insurance. Then, the Conservatives were in power under the old Etonian, Harold Macmillan. As Edwina Currie explains, Margaret was too clever to be ignored:

> The job they gave her in pensions was seen as the right sort of job for a bright woman. Pensions was very much seen as one of those female departments like education. They still exist in a sense, as you haven't seen a female Minister of Defence yet.[98]

Margaret made an impact, challenging colleagues and antagonising officials, usually correcting and occasionally tearing up letters they drafted for her. She crunched numbers and devoured raw data.[99] She hungered for work. She became known for her mastery of economic statistics as well as her good looks. 'I have the latest red hot figure,' she once stated in the House of Commons. It shows her lack of humour that she was baffled by the ensuing laughter.[100] Roguish members praised her vital statistics, others treated her with a galumphing chivalry which, in that all-male club, she quickly exploited.

Those whose only image of Margaret Thatcher is her *Spitting Image* puppet and the unflattering photos taken in middle age must remember that these show Margaret in her late 50s and 60s. When she first entered Parliament she was young, blond and clear-skinned. Her husband's money could pay for her immaculate grooming, expensive hair colouring and clothes. Because career women were a rare commodity in the 1950s, she stood out and very much enjoyed being the only woman in a room full of men. That was a character flaw which never left her. However, she used being a woman to her advantage and never allowed it to disable her.[101] Edwina Currie MP explained:

She flirted and twisted men around her finger … She wore a blue suit with a very white collar. Then she had this amazing gold hair, standing out like Joan of Arc. She stood out in the House of Commons amongst all the men, you could always easily spot her in the crowd.[102]

Tim Bell, one of the key figures behind Thatcher's success, explained:

She was perfectly capable of crying. She was perfectly capable of being coquettish, and she was perfectly capable of bringing her femininity to the way that she discussed things. But, only when it suited her to get her own way … they weren't deeply held views … they were just techniques. Politics is about relationships between people – and the relationships that the men in the Tory Party had with women tended to be their wives, mistresses and daughters. Suddenly they were confronted with a superior colleague, senior colleague. And, you know one or two of them found it quite difficult. I think it was Julian Amery who said, 'when you left home you left nanny and then suddenly you find she was running the office'.[103]

At this time she also returned to Kesteven as an honoured guest for an 'old girls' reunion. Miss Gillies, the headmistress who had counselled Margaret to wait a year before applying to Oxford and was, by that time, retired and rather elderly, misused a Latin phrase during a speech. Thatcher, who followed her to the podium, made a point of correcting her old headmistress's Latin to the horror of her appalled ex-schoolmates. It showed a streak of spitefulness that she never eliminated.[104]

In 1964, the Tories were ousted, and Margaret served in a number of shadow cabinet posts – being one of only a handful of women, she stood out. She worked very diligently and her hard work was noticed. Few who watched Thatcher in Westminster during the 1960s and early 1970s either identified her as the woman who would become the first female prime minister, or foresaw that she would espouse a philosophy that would radically reshape both her party and her country. While Thatcher was still a backbencher she frequently took on senior cabinet ministers and permanent secretaries, revealing a degree of political aggression that many disliked. Officials did not know how to handle such a forceful woman who did not play by bureaucratic rules.[105]

In 1964, Denis had some kind of breakdown after going through a particularly bad patch of business worries and working too hard. He spent several months away from home travelling in South Africa, where he saw old friends and relatives and took up photography. He found the long sea voyages to and from the Cape particularly relaxing. Margaret now became the stoic one, the fighter. Denis, later on, was always more likely to surrender. He became more emotionally and psychologically fragile than his wife. Finally, he decided to dispose of Atlas Preservatives, which was profitable but undercapitalised, and sold to Castrol Oil. It proved a profitable and shrewd move, as he joined Castrol's main board of directors and secured the financial stability of the Thatcher family.[106]

During the 1970 June elections, Ted Heath's Conservative Party promised the healing policies of trade union reform, lower taxes, public spending cuts and a free market for entrepreneurs. It was a winning combination, and the newly elected Heath named Margaret Thatcher Secretary of State for Education & Science.

However, Thatcher's aggressive posture did not decrease when she became a Cabinet minister. Although there is a distinct pecking order in Cabinet, with her role being in the lower echelons, ministers at this level are not normally expected to become involved in debate, except by express invitation or on the specific subject of their department. Margaret was either unaware of, or unimpressed by, such convention, speaking up about subjects that engaged her with an impressive display of facts and figures. 'That's enough from you Margaret,' Ted Heath barked.[107] In a very short time she was unpopular with her Cabinet colleagues,[108] with her determination to win arguments at whatever cost in bruised egos.[109]

When Mrs Thatcher finally found the publicity she craved, it almost destroyed her Cabinet career. After the election, Prime Minister Heath wrote to his cabinet with difficult news, 'We shall need determination and a willingness among spending ministers to accept reductions in programmes which, from a departmental stand point, they would be reluctant to make.'

In August 1970, as the new Secretary of State for Education, Thatcher responded to a Treasury demand by deciding to end free milk for primary school children to save £8 million. At the time, it was a stark choice between losing the milk and facing cuts to a new primary school building programme.[110] Throughout this period, Margaret fought attempts to cut the education budget overall, and although she failed, despite her wishes, to prevent local authorities closing grammar schools, she succeeded in saving the Open University, an egalitarian institution worthy of her father's ideals, which her Cabinet colleagues had wanted to scrap.

However, for public relations, the milk debacle was a gigantic personal catastrophe. The chant 'Thatcher, Thatcher, Milk Snatcher' rang out at almost every public meeting and made eye-catching tabloid headlines. Mothers throughout the country were astonished that a women would take free milk from children. Tory grandee, Lord Carrington, was a firsthand witness; she was, he said, 'unlucky to be called Thatcher because it rhymes with snatcher'.[111] In the House of Commons, MPs barracked her every time she rose to speak with screams of 'ditch the bitch'.

Oxford University would later refuse her an honorary degree because of her cuts to the education budget generally. 'Is Mrs Thatcher human?' asked the *Sun*, before declaring her, 'the most unpopular woman in Britain'. Margaret was hurt, she refused to talk to the press and then treated every question they asked as a trap.[112]

At this moment, it was to Ted Health alone that Mrs Thatcher owed her political survival. He invited her very publicly to Chequers and the press were briefed that the education secretary had the prime minister's full backing. The attack immediately ceased.[113] Lord Carrington said:

> Ted Heath actually did everything he possibly could to support her, he said to her, you know, 'this is not your policy; it's the government's policy, and we'll support you through thick and thin'. And he did. Um, whether or not that had any effect on his opposition to Margaret afterward – he may have felt that having, so to speak, supported her through thick and thin, when she challenged him, that was a poor reward, but that if it was, it was a very silly reaction.[114]

By 1974, it was obvious that Ted Heath's leadership of the country had failed. The Tory Party was disorientated and this provided Margaret's turning point. She looked around at 'her party' and feared it was sliding too far left. In her mind, only one person was capable of setting things right and that was Margaret Thatcher herself. It was the decision of a loner. No family discussions. No advisers. Early on in the leadership contest old school Conservatives wrote her off as a freak, and Heath regarded her challenge against him in the leadership contest a complete joke. When Margaret had gone to tell Heath that she was standing for leadership, he kept her standing while he sat at his desk and said, 'you'll lose'. The contempt was palpable.[115] Enoch Powell attempted to cut her down to size by stating that the party 'wouldn't put up with those hats and that accent'.[116]

However, she won to her cause three men who showed her the ropes of successful campaigning. The first was Airey Neave. Neave was a Tory Party legend who had escaped from the notorious Nazi prison, Colditz, during the Second World War. He had also trained women agents and he liked Mrs Thatcher's metal after his wife spotted her potential while sitting in the visitors' gallery.[117] Neave was not a particularly great parliamentarian. He operated best behind closed doors.[118] Airey's tactics, explained Edwina Currie, had been to go around back bench MPs telling them that Mrs Thatcher was a great talent, and she shouldn't have her career destroyed so early because of an embarrassingly poor vote, and that she deserved a decent show. Enough MPs believed him and voted for her. No one expected her to win.[119]

The second was Gordon Reece, a flamboyant television producer who reputedly lived on champagne and cigars.[120] He suggested that Margaret adopt a softer hairstyle and change her 'fussy' clothes. Crucially, he also advised her to speak more slowly and avoid hectoring people.[121] She also lost half a stone, which helped get rid of the double chin and slight tubbiness.[122]

The final mentor was Ronald Millar. For him, Thatcher was a twentieth-century Gloriana and he injected the spirit of Tilbury into her speeches and drilled into her the mantra, 'Cool, calm and elected',[123] and 'Remember dear, less is more!'[124] He worked on the pitch of her voice, drafting in experts, including Laurence Olivier, to make her sound less ladylike. Vocal training made her sound progressively deeper, more measured, less shrill and less like the queen did in 1953, the coronation year.[125] Millar would always hold a special place in her affections, she loved his camp showbiz qualities and he made her feel like a star.[126]

Together, these volunteers made history. On 11 February 1975, the grocer's daughter from Grantham was elected to lead a political party, made up almost entirely of the old guard Establishment that was both snobbish and chauvinist.[127] Observing from the Labour front bench, Barbara Castle wrote that Mrs Thatcher, 'the best man' the Tories had, looked radiant, 'She is in love, in love with power, success and with herself'.[128]

Her biggest strength was that she was different. She stood out as something new, exciting and optimistic. Margaret declared, 'It's been said that all that politicians are doing now is rearranging the deck chairs on the *Titanic*. Well, here is one who isn't.'[129] She was offering a fresh start.

The Conservative Party elected Margaret Thatcher their leader in a moment of crisis. There was no one else. Many in the actual shadow cabinet disliked her, finding her world view distressingly narrow and her personality both dominant and controlling. She displayed such command of even the minutest details of her government that even her friends felt that she looked too much like a child-ish know-it-all. They warned her against sounding 'too headmistressy'.[130] But Margaret was unapologetic, 'I have known some very good headmistresses who have launched their pupils on wonderful careers.' She went on to say, 'I am what I am. Yes, I do believe in certain things very strongly. Yes, my style is one of vigorous leadership. Yes, I do believe in trying to persuade people that the things I believe in are things they should follow.'[131] Take me or leave me, she was saying. There was no choice, and she knew it.[132] As she pointedly explained to her PR guru Tim Bell:

'If you've got a box of tricks that will get me elected please don't use them because if the people don't want me it won't work.' And that's what she understood. Want me doesn't mean like me or adore me. Want me means think that I can do the job better than anybody else.[133]

Bell saw that Margaret never courted popularity, she never thought that being pop-ular was what mattered for being elected.

All her potential rivals for the leadership of the Conservative Party during this period had made mistakes, she hadn't. Margaret beat off Ted Heath in the first ballot and he resigned the leadership. In the second ballot, she saw off William Whitelaw, Heath's preferred successor. A shadow cabinet colleague, Norman St John-Stevas, called it the 'assumption of the Blessed Margaret'. She gloated over the feeble showing of her chief rivals,[134] among them Edward du Cann. His shadowy dealings in the City excluded him, as he was about to be subject to a press investigation. As the chairman of the powerful 1922 Committee, he had led the back bench hostility towards Heath.

Then there was Sir Keith Joseph, who made an unfortunate speech on eugenics as a potential solution to immigration. Finally, William Whitelaw, who managed to anger the right-wing members of the party by being too close to the failed premier Ted Heath.

Thatcher was, in a sense, the last woman standing. According to historian Richard Vinen, had either Joseph or du Cann stood, Thatcher would almost certainly have withdrawn. He said, 'Thatcher had been almost no one's first choice for the leadership, probably not even her own.'[135]

Enoch Powell credited Thatcher's success to luck, saying that she was faced with 'supremely unattractive opponents at the time', and that, 'she didn't rise to power. She was opposite the spot on the roulette wheel at the right time, and she didn't flunk it.'[136] Old Etonian Whitelaw allegedly cried from shock when he didn't win, viewing the job as one he was entitled to. Ted Heath spent the rest of his career in a political huff, red-faced and sitting on the back benches.

In truth, she was very inexperienced by the standards of the time, having held none of the great offices of state, nor even shadowed them. She lacked a solid reputation.[137] Many just saw her as 'untried, unsympathetic and alarming'.[138] Tim Bell explains, 'I don't think we ever used words like sexism. We spoke in English.' He concedes, however, that there was caution inevitably, but 'it was just a perfectly natural caution people had about doing something for the first time'.[139]

Mrs Thatcher charmed all the back bench MPs who wanted a comforting maternal figure. She seemed to remind them of matron, or the school nurse from their respective boarding schools. No one should underestimate the fear that bank bench MPs suffer when they see their majority slipping away. In this despairing mood, Conservative MPs submitted to the lady and paved the way for the first woman prime minister in Europe.[140] Fearful, and in a state of panic, the old boys' club turned to the Grantham woman and the stoic provincialism that she represented.

'It is almost impossible to overestimate the difficulty she faced, in getting elected,' said Cecil Parkinson:

I mean, there was, I mean, the Labour prime minister summed up her dilemma, if you like, when, when he heard that she had won the leadership, he said, 'We have just won the next election.' He just didn't believe that the Conservative Party led by a woman was electable and he summed up the views of quite a few people in the Party. In fact, if you were to analyse her vote, I once said she led a peasants' revolt ... the make-up of her support was sort of the disaffected, the idealistic, the people who believed in ... the economic policies she believed in. But basically she was an outsider, and she rallied around her a group of people, who for various reasons preferred her to Ted Heath. But it was not a great, ringing enthusiastic endorsement of her, it was the fact that she represented the only viable alternative to Ted. And that is what attracted a lot of people; so she wasn't elected on a wave of popularity, you know, it was a slightly grudging election, that got her there, and I mean, I often think when she looked at her shadow cabinet, the first meeting she had after she was elected, there were only about four people around the table who had voted for her. So she took on a hell of a job leading a party that was questioning about what it had done and the shadow cabinet that in the main didn't agree with her. So you add all that up and she faced very substantial obstacles.[141]

The vote had polarised along right–left lines with, in addition, the region of origin, experience and education of the MP having their effects. Thatcher was stronger among MPs on the right, those from southern England and those who had not attended Oxbridge.[142] However, very few inside the shadow cabinet itself voted for her. Mrs Thatcher had a fight on her hands within her own Tory Government, from the old school club which dominated then, and still does, the British Establishment, government and monarchy. To them she was a shrill governess who had risen above her station.[143]

Thatcher may well have become party leader, but she was now surrounded by men like Sir Ian Gilmour and Christopher Soames, who struggled to conceal their disdain for someone they considered an arriviste. When Sir Edward du Cann invited Margaret and Denis to his smart London townhouse, he likened their manner to that of a couple coming to be interviewed for a job as 'housekeeper and handyman'.[144] Without doubt, Edwina Currie explains, 'she was the victim of snobbishness'.[145]

'Word came back from a lunch where a rather outspoken critic of hers, I think he would be probably classified as a grandee, said that the Conservative Party was a cavalry regiment led by a corporal in the Women's Royal Army Corps,' said Cecil Parkinson. 'The grandees felt very put out.'[146]

Lord Carrington feels it wasn't snobbishness, so much as surprise that such an unknown got the top job:

She [Mrs Thatcher] really took very little part in Ted Heath's Cabinet. I mean, when people say this is where she, sort of, made her mark, but she didn't make her mark at all – she hardly said anything.[147]

I don't think anybody was very hostile to her. I mean, she got people's backs up in various ways in the end – of course she did. But I don't think there was hostility – I think there was absolute astonishment that she'd been elected … She wasn't very club-able as a person, was she? No, she wasn't cosy. [Laughs]. But then, you … do you want your prime minister to be cosy?[148]

Tim Bell is more stoic:

> Everybody is the victim of snobbishness at some point or another in their lives. You have to cast your mind back to the era we're talking about which is the middle seventies and the Tory Party still had its ruling-class roots. Lord Salisbury was still an important person. The hierarchy of the Tory Party, the various area directors were all … either very successful businessmen or well-connected landowners. So, there was inevitably some snobbishness but nothing that was particularly aggressive.[149]

While the Tory Party had startled themselves with their new leader, the Labour Party clung to the hope that the long general election campaign would expose Thatcher's habit of making unguarded statements. The metropolitan elite deplored her vulgarity. Left-wing intellectual Jonathan Miller said he found Mrs Thatcher 'repulsive in every way' and excoriated her 'odious suburban gentility'.[150] Labour strategists were certain that Margaret Thatcher was the Tories' weak spot. Her advisors told her to save her energies until late in the campaign to keep her out of the firing line. Gordon Reece encouraged her to take her mind off the election by going to see a West End play or musical, so she took herself off to see *Evita*.

Eventually, under the guidance of Reece and Millar, Thatcher embraced a US-style campaign, much to the horror of some Tory Party snobs. Popular performers like Lulu and Ken Dodd provided the warm-up act, and she swept onto the political stage to the theme of 'Hello Dolly', although in Margaret's version it was re-lyricised to 'Hello Maggie'! It was something neither Ted Heath nor Harold MacMillan would have contemplated doing.[151]

Nothing served Margaret better for her public image than an insult from the Soviet Union, which turned into a backhanded compliment. The Soviet Army paper, *Red Star*, responded to her frequent anti-Communist speeches by dubbing her the 'Iron Lady'. Thatcher repeated the phrase whenever possible, and the jibe bolstered her efforts to distance herself from the shrill heckling housewife image that plagued her in the House of Commons. Callaghan's 'Sunny Jim' nickname, meanwhile, was fast becoming an unhelpful endearment during the winter of discontent.

Carol Thatcher points out that, for all her outward modesty, her mother was not surprised herself when the Conservative Party voted her as the leader:

> The outside world may have been surprised … but she had clearly seen herself in a central role. I was reminded of the famous scene in the Robert Redford film, *The Candidate*, where the victorious politician grabs an aide

in the loo and barks at him, 'OK, what do we do now?' My mother knew exactly what to do and embraced the leadership as if had been her destiny.[152]

When she visited the United States in 1976, everywhere she went she spoke with enormous confidence. 'The question is not whether we will win,' she told crowds in New York, 'but how large the majority will be.'[153] Election victory was within her grasp.

When power finally came on 4 May 1979, she had one man she could rely on completely, her husband Denis. Although much more relaxed about politics, he embodied her beliefs in practice. It was not an accident that Conservative politics bought them together.

Denis would transform himself into the perfect consort. When asked, 'Who wears the trousers in your marriage?' Denis replied happily, 'I do. I also wash them and iron them.' He was never subservient, and he was one of the few men whom she failed to domineer; in fact, she would meekly defer to him. Denis expected his wife to keep house, to entertain and to be a traditional 1950s housewife at one level.[154] Her speciality in the kitchen was Coronation chicken, cold chicken pieces curried in mayonnaise with chunks of apricot. The dish was invented for the queen's coronation banquet during the post-war austerity of 1953.[155]

'Better keep your mouth shut and be thought a fool rather than open it and remove all doubt,' Denis reportedly said another time.[156] He fully understood his role as consort and was socially useful to his wife, particularly at royal occasions. The queen mother was very fond of him, and he broke the ice at state dinners and Balmoral, exerting an easygoing charm with women and a chummy camaraderie with men. Denis knew that he had to be always present, but never there; he perfected the role of omnipresent discretion. He became her best friend, and they were much closer in Downing Street than they had been in the earlier part of their marriage.[157]

Denis also kept an eye on the most disloyal members of his wife's Cabinet and parliamentary party. He helped stiffen Margaret's resolve in 1981 when she had to stand up to what journalist Quentin Letts described as the 'sneering snoots' inside her first Cabinet. He was never browbeaten by the humbug of the old boys' club. He knew the type from his rugby days, and they failed to either menace or inspire him. Politicians he disliked he would describe as, 'as much use as a one legged man in an arse-kicking contest'. In doing so, he would lift his wife out of her darker mood.[158]

However, the media, through their inevitable requirement to report on something about the Thatcher marriage, set upon Denis. The satirical magazine *Private*

Eye introduced their 'Dear Bill' column, and painted Denis as an inebriated racist and henpecked dimwit. But he was in no way subservient to his wife, and neither was he the fool portrayed. The Thatchers played along with the joke, in one speech to the Scottish Tory conference Margaret claimed, 'Denis likes Scotland – particularly Glenfiddich, Glenmorangie and Laphroaig.'[159] She never saw him as this chumpish *Private Eye* lampoon. In her eyes, he was the staunch and steadfast older man who had given her the financial support and stability needed to juggle a political career and children.[160]

3

DADDY'S GIRL, THE KING'S DAUGHTER

The highest of distinctions is service to others.
King George VI

The queen, like Mrs Thatcher, was almost completely shaped by her father's philosophical inheritance. George VI was the reluctant king who only assumed the throne when his brother abdicated. His was a life spent resisting reform and viewing progress with deep suspicion. Thatcher's father couldn't have been more different, and this contrast made the two women fundamentally at odds in convictions and outlook. As prime minister, Mrs Thatcher wanted to embrace change and looked to America for inspiration. The queen closed her eyes to it until she was forced to respond.

Life for the queen and her prime minister was also viewed from two very different social vantage points, and the mutual bemusement of both women was largely derived from that old British chestnut – class. The Grantham woman, who transformed herself with a great deal of effort into a suburban lady in pearls, didn't see the world from the same place as a monarch with an ancient lineage dating back to William the Conqueror.

Elizabeth II would always view Margaret Thatcher as temporary. Politicians throughout her life had come and gone; and often it ended badly for them. By contrast, the monarchy stood for stability and continuity; two key factors that bred enormous confidence and security. Her Majesty had everything in life handed to her on a silver plate and the view from Windsor Castle was far more rarefied than the view from behind a grocery store counter. Thatcher, like her father, had to fight for everything, every day of her life. It was a habit she found impossible to break.

Margaret had to become somebody from scratch. Elizabeth had no experience or real understanding of that.

During the period when Mrs Thatcher was growing up in a tiny flat with an outside toilet, life for the queen-in-waiting had been very different. Princess Elizabeth's world only existed for most people, including Margaret Thatcher, in the 'Neverland' realm of Hollywood films and fiction. 'Lilibet', as she was known to her family, grew up in a carefree cocoon of privilege, wealth and isolation from the real world, surrounded by ponies, dogs, maids, footmen, nannies, governesses and tutors. When young high-born playmates visited they had to curtsy or bow and call her ma'am.[1]

The British royal family were a race apart, and their world hadn't changed much since Queen Victoria had occupied the throne. They lived in a succession of great houses, palaces and castles. Their collection of jewels and paintings was unrivalled. There was an army of servants, and the royal yacht alone had thirty. Every comfort and luxury was ministered to them by a select band of utterly loyal courtiers, drawn from the upper classes, who looked upon court service as a combination of hereditary duty and religious devotion. The monarch was at the apex of this world. It was what writer and broadcaster Andrew Marr has called 'a lost world of understatement' where people knew their place and protocol so well that these things were unspoken.[2]

During Elizabeth's childhood, class, station, title, degree and address still mattered very much. Inclusion in this society was by right of background alone. Originally, it had never been thought that Elizabeth would inherit the throne. Born Princess Elizabeth of York, she was only the daughter of the second son and 'spare heir', Bertie, the Duke of York. Then a twice divorced American called Wallis Simpson appeared on the scene, and everything changed. Edward VIII's decision to marry Mrs Simpson threw the royal family into turmoil and transformed Princess Elizabeth's prospects. In abdicating as king, her uncle, Edward VIII, made Elizabeth's father king, and Elizabeth the heir presumptive. This meant that, unless her father had a male heir, she would be the next monarch.

As the former King-Emperor went into exile with the new title of the Duke of Windsor, even his mother, Queen Mary, turned her back on him. It was a brutal demotion, from the sovereign of the British Empire which covered almost a quarter of the world, to a virtual nobody. The new Duke of Windsor later described his mother as having 'ice in her veins'.

For some years, Queen Mary had been drawing closer to her second son and working against her eldest who, in her eyes, was proving a big disappointment. Mary felt that Edward VIII was irresponsible and a 'gadfly'. He was having affairs with married women, gambling, travelling for fun, partying, clubbing with his racy circle of friends, suggesting sweeping reforms and living the sort of life she condemned as sinful.

The old queen had felt for some time before the abdication that her younger son Bertie, the Duke of York, and his wife, the former Lady Elizabeth Bowes-Lyon, could become the quintessential royal family. They would be a living example of the monarchy that embodied all the radiant domestic virtues she valued. Lady Elizabeth was the daughter of an earl and cousin of a duke, and therefore perfect royal marriage material, unlike the American divorcee Mrs Simpson. Queen Mary realised their enormous potential and sanctioned an attempt to glamorise the young couple and publicise them further with a documentary film. The programme depicted Bertie, slim, serious and neatly dressed, with his adoring wife, smiling sweetly. His daughters, Princess Elizabeth and Princess Margaret, were perfectly behaved and immaculately dressed in party frocks, playing together. The family was being promoted and exposed to the media.

Privileged royal-watchers from selected newspapers were invited to Buckingham Palace and Windsor Castle to see the two princesses at play or at their school lessons. Others came to watch the Yorks' own Christmas pantomime at Windsor, starring, of course, the two princesses.[3] Queen Mary was helping establish a substitute royal family, should the first son prove wanting.

Upon his accession as Edward VIII, the new king immediately swept in a series of reforms to Buckingham Palace. He slashed costs at Balmoral and Sandringham, suggested a more simple coronation ceremony, and he walked in the streets meeting his people, saying famously, 'something must be done' about the unemployed. All this was an attitude to refashion the royal institution rather than a serious agenda of modernisation. He was often contrary, mulish and willful. Edward found it difficult to concentrate, lacked application and was spoilt rotten by his cronies. Despite all these weaknesses, he was nevertheless a popular national figure. He also had the good fortune to inherit the blond good looks of his Danish grandmother, Queen Alexandra, and the intelligence of his grandfather, Edward VII. He was a good linguist, a natural charmer and popular with women.

Had the new king stopped to think, he would have realised that, in trying to change too much so quickly, Edward was building up enormous trouble for himself, not just in the royal household, but elsewhere in the Establishment, most notably with the Church of England, under the iron rule of Archbishop Cosmo Gordon Lang. Lang was a close friend of the York family and had even married Bertie and Elizabeth in Westminster Abbey. He also wanted to play a central role in the development of the so-called 'family monarchy'. Despite his own, probably non-practising, homosexuality,[4] the Archbishop led the opposition to the reform of the divorce laws under the guise of defending the institution of marriage. Queen Victoria had turned the British monarchy into a monarchy of duty. Archbishop Lang added a fresh responsibility, to have a flawless marriage. The Duke and Duchess of York fitted his brief perfectly. The new king didn't.

Much to Archbishop Lang's frustration, Edward VIII became a global star, much like Princess Diana in the 1980s. On spectacularly co-ordinated world tours of the British Empire, Edward VIII flaunted his sex appeal, glad-handed the people, defied protocol and embraced his celebrity status as a royal rebel. It was an unprecedented performance in a family noted for its dullness, and it didn't go down terribly well with the archbishop and his agenda for using the monarchy to put religion back into the centre of British life.

The Establishment cabal surrounding Buckingham Palace, with Lang at its core, were entrenched and sanctimoniously confident of their power; they wanted to be kingmakers. Before long they were telling all who would listen that Edward VIII was unfit to be king, and that the Duke and Duchess of York were better suited for the role.

The Establishment now decided on a campaign of denigration to bring down the pro-reform king.[5] Archbishop Lang's plot enjoyed the support of Lord Reith at the BBC, Geoffrey Dawson at *The Times* and various heads of government across the Commonwealth. By attempting to make Wallis Simpson queen, Edward simply played into their hands. It was no contest, and before the year was out, Edward VIII had abdicated and the more malleable Yorks were enthroned.

Together with their two daughters, they moved out of their private house near Green Park into Buckingham Palace. Their new palace home was a vast, grey and rather soulless building, more like a bank headquarters, with magnificent reception rooms and endless corridors. It was a big step up for Bertie and Elizabeth, for in royal circles sovereignty confers a sacred status on its holders. Bertie made the decision to be called King George VI, adopting his father's name as a symbol of stability and continuity. The new King-Emperor and Queen-Empress had no appetite for change, something that delighted most members of the royal household.[6]

'Does that mean you will have to be the next queen?' asked her sister, Princess Margaret Rose.

'Yes, someday,' Elizabeth replied.

'Poor you,' said her sister.[7]

The new titles and position were an enormous strain on Elizabeth's father. George VI was physically frail and plagued by anxiety over the public duties he would be expected to fulfill throughout the vast British Empire. All his life he had been compared unfavourably to his dazzling elder brother, who had charmed royal courtiers from the outset. One of them, Lord Esher, dismissed the unfortunate younger brother as 'backward but sweet'.[8] It was not a propitious verdict with which to start life. George VI was a slower and rather dimmer version of what people imagined a king should be. He was almost bottom of his school class, passing sixty-eighth out of sixty-nine pupils in his final school examination. He was knock-kneed and plagued with a bad stammer. But he did have the application, stamina and, at the age of 17, had become a convinced Christian. In short, the two brothers were the hare and the tortoise.[9]

However, this rather unimposing man who became king was the most important influence on the young Princess Elizabeth. It was her father who impressed her with his sense of duty and his conscientiousness. To understand her, you have to get to grips with him. He became her role model as monarch. Elizabeth noticed how methodical her father was in all official matters, even opening and reading his mail. He loved routine, for a king, the unchanging schedule was akin to a commitment. She saw him work gruelling hours at a job he never wanted. She saw him wrestle with his speech impediment and attend to all his duties with perseverance. Elizabeth would follow his ideals when she took the crown herself.[10]

Until their coronation, neither Bertie (now George VI) nor his wife (now Queen Elizabeth) had led particularly taxing lives. Apart from the occasional royal engagement they enjoyed the existence of idle aristocrats. As relatively minor members of the royal family, little had been expected of them. Art historian Kenneth Clark, a close friend and alleged lover of Queen Elizabeth, the Queen Mother, had been 'shocked to see how little she did with [the] day; she never rose before 11'.[11] Before the Second World War aristocratic life was effectively one long party that rotated around the annual London season and its balls, dances, dinners, luncheons, picnics, hunting, shooting and fishing functions. Although no one in the aristocracy worked, they were not footloose. They had a duty to maintain an active social life and, at the height of the season, that could mean attending three or four balls a night. Socialising was not only about pleasure, though it was focused around pleasant events, it was a way of confirming worth and status through connections. For an earl's daughter to marry a royal duke was the equivalent of an office promotion today. It was serious business, disguised as frivolity.

The Second World War changed everything for the ruling class, and George VI in particular. Sir Winston Churchill would state, the king 'lived through every minute of this struggle with a heart that never quavered and a spirit undaunted'.[12] From the moment when, six hours after the declaration of war on Germany on Sunday, 3 September 1939, the king donned uniform to broadcast to the empire, he became the focus of intense loyalty and identification on the part of millions globally.[13] He was now a war leader. However, George VI's relationship with his prime minister, Winston Churchill, was uneasy. Churchill had been one of the Duke of Windsor's most avid supporters, and neither George nor Elizabeth were keen for him to become prime minister. There was mutual suspicion on both sides. The king's official biographer went so far as to describe the new king as 'bitterly opposed' to Churchill's appointment.[14] And the new king wasn't above partisan politics.

Although he wasn't as pro-German as his brother, the Duke of Windsor, he was a major appeaser. When the previous prime minister, Neville Chamberlain, returned from his meeting with Hitler in 1938 promising peace in our time, he was paraded on the balcony of Buckingham Palace with the king and queen in front of huge waving crowds. It was an act of political partisanship worthy of Queen Victoria at her most unconstrained.[15] Once the war started, Churchill and the king were, to some degree, rivals for the role as a symbolic figurehead for the war effort. George was temperamentally unsuited for the task and viewed Churchill's status as a national icon with a degree of jealousy. Things came to a head when Churchill, with customary bravado, announced his plans to go to France after the first wave of troops in the D-day landings. Determined not to be outdone, the king scotched the scheme by threatening to accompany him. In the event, once the beaches in Normandy were secure, both the king and prime minister visited separately.

In the end, the war became as much of a public relations coup for George VI as victory in the Falklands was for Margaret Thatcher in 1982, projecting an image of royalty as a unifying symbol in a way that could never have been achieved in peacetime.[16]

While Churchill and her father were jockeying for status, Princess Elizabeth and her sister, Princess Margaret, spent most of the war at Windsor. They lived in the Brunswick Tower, a strongly built part of the castle, while their parents stayed at Buckingham Palace throughout the week. More than 300 high explosive bombs fell around Windsor Castle before the war ended. When the air-raid sirens sounded the girls were hurried down into the basement for refuge. They took with them little suitcases containing their favourite dolls, a book and their diaries. They slept in a two tier bunk which had been installed beneath the castle, where all the royal treasures, priceless paintings, furniture, tapestries and silver were also sheltered. The Crown jewels were wrapped in newspaper, tied with string and hidden in the vault ready to be taken to a ship in Liverpool. Along with the princesses, these valuables would sail for Canada should the need arise.

Elizabeth was 13 when the war started, and 19 when Japan finally surrendered. Having established the monarchy as the symbol of a united Britain, her father now had to ensure that it wasn't viewed as part of the old class structure (he never quite succeeded at this). The massive vote for Labour in the 1945 general election indicated a general desire to sweep away the old hierarchy.[17] The king knew they had to change. However, socialism and the house of Windsor proved not unhappy bedfellows and George VI got on particularly well with the unassuming Labour leader, Clement Attlee. They had much in common; both were quiet men with a strong sense of national duty.

Elizabeth, unlike her father, knew from an early age that she was destined to be queen. She was brought up to regard her future role with the seriousness of a zealot, embracing its religious significance, as it came with the role of Supreme Governor of the Church of England, as part of the job description. This burden seems to have made her an extraordinarily solemn and serious little girl, in contrast with her sister, Princess Margaret, who was frivolous and an enormous flirt. Margaret resembled, in many ways, her disgraced 'Uncle David', the Duke of Windsor. Both royal sisters lived in a narrow little world and bore the unmistakable stamp of the debutante. Their lifestyle revolved around the London season, country houses, horses, the racecourse, the grouse moor, canasta and the occasional royal tour. They socialised with a single social type, the landed class.[18]

George VI was intensely possessive about his daughters, treating Margaret as a spoilt plaything while Elizabeth was trained to have an elevated, almost Victorian, view of her role. Elizabeth reminded many members of the royal family, and the household, of Queen Victoria. Attending her confirmation in 1942, the Countess of Airlie observed her 'grave little face under a small white net veil' and felt 'the carriage of the head was unequalled, and there was about her that indescribable something that Queen Victoria had'. Lady Airlie concluded that this was the 'air of majesty'.[19]

Eleanor Roosevelt also commented on Elizabeth's 'serious nature'. She felt she was a child with a great deal of 'character and personality'.[20] Queen Mary noticed the likeness between Victoria and Elizabeth, and that the princess had adopted the regal habit of either staring hard at a person who said anything she disliked or ignoring them completely.[21]

Historian and country house expert, Jamie Lees-Milne, said Princess Elizabeth was 'imperious'. He described a scene where the little girl told a vicar that she disliked part of his sermon. Elizabeth once even alluded to her mother as a 'commoner', noting that she had been born merely Lady Elizabeth Bowes-Lyon and not a royal princess.[22] In her memoirs, her governess Marion Crawford related how Elizabeth, after her inspection of the Grenadier Guards, was very critical. An officer had to explain, via her governess, that this was not appropriate.[23] It made a lasting impression on the men, with half of them refusing in later years to contribute to her wedding gift.[24]

Elizabeth would never get to be queen *and* empress like Victoria and her own 'commoner' mother. In post-war Britain, George VI had to put on a brave face and accept radical social changes even if they included the virtual dissolution of the British Empire. Burma was the first to go, followed by Ireland, then India declared itself to be a democratic republic, but unlike Ireland it was prepared to acknowledge George VI as Head of the Commonwealth, but not as Emperor of India. The king quickly recognised that Britain was now a second-class power, but shrewdly saw a continuing role for the imperial monarchy as Head of the Commonwealth. He therefore embraced the idea of the New Commonwealth, which was to replace the old empire, as a free association of self-governing nations for which the Crown would provide the link.

He also saw the importance of switching British interests away from the Far East to Africa.[25] On 1 February 1947, the king, with his wife and two daughters, sailed from Portsmouth on his navy's newest battleship, HMS *Vanguard*, on what would be his last imperial tour to South Africa, where he was still officially recognised as king. The military correspondent of the *New York Times*, Hanson Baldwin, put it in terms of world strategy. He argued that Europe was now too vulnerable as a base in the age of the atom bomb and ballistic missile. South Africa, far from the threat posed by the superpowers, might be the answer for Britain, which could develop the country's mineral resources and restore itself to 'its historic position as the arbiter of world destinies'.

George VI's legacy to his daughter was the Commonwealth. Her father firmly believed that the monarchy still had a role to play outside the United Kingdom.[26] It was a belief that Elizabeth would cling to when she became queen. In a speech delivered during the royal tour of South Africa on 21 April 1947 to mark her coming of age, Elizabeth said, 'I declare before you all that my whole life ... shall be devoted to your service and the service of our great imperial Commonwealth to which we all belong.' Elizabeth's passion for Africa would eventually be the cause of major conflict with Margaret Thatcher, and push her towards a very public constitutional crisis.

Given that Elizabeth was in line for such a large and potentially troublesome inheritance, she never went to school. The future queen's education was left mostly to a few devoted governesses such as Marion Crawford, and even she complained that the princess's mother constantly interfered with her education, taking both her and her sister away from study for more frivolous diversions. While the scholarship girl, Margaret Roberts, had been studying hard to get into Oxford, the academic demands made on the princess were very modest, and there were few books in the classroom at Windsor Castle. Education was an alien concept to the Windsor family, compared to dogs and horses. Queen Elizabeth, the future queen mother, was determined to duplicate the happy childhood created for her by her mother, Cecilia, Countess of Strathmore, who didn't believe her children's enjoyment should be spoilt by too many lessons.

During her childhood, the queen mother inhabited a world where good manners and femininity were acceptable substitutes for actual knowledge. At Glamis Castle in Scotland and St Paul's Walden, a grand country house in Hertfordshire where she grew up, life had been idyllic, relaxed and given over to innocent pleasures. As a child, she was once even allowed to bring her Shetland pony into the house for a joke.

Things had almost changed when a governess, Fraulein Kübler, arrived at the Strathmores' London home to prepare the future queen mother for her basic school examinations. Horrified at the enormous gaps she found in Lady Elizabeth's education she studiously attempted fill them in, with little success. 'We worked at such a pace that Lady Elizabeth grew pale and thin.'

Lady Elizabeth immediately started to complain, 'I do hate my lessons, and [become] sicker every day of this beastly exam. I know less and less.' There is no surprise in how Lady Strathmore reacted.

'Her mother made us stop,' Fraulein Kübler wrote, 'and said with a smile, "Health is more important than examinations".'[27]

Predictably, the future queen mother never achieved a basic school certificate, but what Lady Strathmore managed to instill in her daughter was self-confidence. Exams, to women of her class and era, were just irrelevant. It was a policy she would carry forward with her daughter, despite the fact that she was potentially a queen-in-waiting.

In 1930, the royal family decided on the publication of a full-length biography of Elizabeth, then just 3 years old. *The Story of Princess Elizabeth* appeared with 'the sanction of her parents' and was written by Anne Ring, a former member of the royal household. The little book offered its readers such oozing drivel as:

From the moment of her birth not only has our little princess been wrapped about with the tender love of parents and devoted grandparents ... but she has been the admiring object of affection from thousands in the country and beyond the seas who have never seen her.

A description of her bedtime read:

When Princess Elizabeth's nurse descends to the morning room or the drawing room, and says in quiet tones, 'I think it is bedtime now, Elizabeth' there are no poutings or protests, just a few joyous skips and impromptu dance steps, a few last minute laughs at Mummy's delicious bedtime jokes, and then the Princess Elizabeth's hand slips into her nurse's hand, and the two go off gaily together across the deep chestnut pile of the hall carpet to the accommodating lift, which in two seconds has whisked them off to the familiar dear domain, which is theirs to hold and to share.

Not surprisingly, Wallis Simpson would later refer to Elizabeth as 'Shirley Temple', when such grovelling nonsense was being published about her as she was growing up.

This laxity was allowed because the queen's father, George VI, suffered a miserable childhood at the hands of nurses and tutors which left him a stammering wreck. He rarely saw his parents, and when he did it was an experience of anguish rather than pleasure. His mother, Queen Mary, was stiff and majestic. Bertie, as he was known in childhood, was only the second son: the 'spare heir'. Early difficulties were exacerbated by a nursery nurse who adored his older brother, but exhibited callous antipathy towards him. She didn't bother to feed him properly, and he developed serious digestive problems and a speech impediment which would stay with him for the rest of his life.[28] Queen Mary failed to notice all this until the harm had been done.

As time went by, things failed to improve. At 6, he was turned over to a tutor named Mr Hansell who attempted to correct the fact that he was left-handed, which was at that time viewed as being a sign of maladjustment, rebellion and moral failing. This only caused Bertie's stutter to get worse, and the schoolroom became a never-ending reminder of how inadequate he was. Even in his bedroom, he couldn't escape. He was knock-kneed, so doctors fitted him with splints that he had to wear most days and every night.[29]

In frustration, he would burst into violent temper explosions that became known as his 'gnashes'.[30] At 14, this unfortunate little boy was sent into the Royal Navy College for Cadets on the Isle of Wight, notwithstanding the fact he suffered from sea sickness and was almost pathologically shy. For most of his brief naval career, he was confined to the sick room with either acute depression or whooping cough.[31] Again the unfavourable comparisons to his brother always followed him. One contemporary wrote, 'Like comparing an ugly duckling to a cock pheasant'.[32] Although Bertie came to accept this as a fact of life, it hurt him deeply. Even the love of his wife and two daughters never fully eradicated his inferiority complex. He confessed to the prime minister's wife, Mrs Baldwin, how all his life he had been compared to his brilliant brother[33] and 'there had been times when as a boy he had felt envious that eighteen months should make so much difference'.[34]

With both Elizabeth's parents alienated at an early age by their education, it was left to her grandmother, Queen Mary, to take charge. Many historians go so far as to attribute the survival of the British monarchy during the first half of the twentieth century to Queen Mary. At this time, many European monarchies, such as the Romanovs in Russia, the Hapsburgs in Austria and the Hohenzollerns in Germany, were swept aside by war and revolution.

Although never a natural mother, she ruled the family with firmness and determination. When she was Princess of Wales, her father-in-law, Edward VII, ordered her to read all the official red boxes containing the government papers so that she would thoroughly understand the business of monarchy. It was a remarkable honour to involve a German woman so closely in government. Consequently, Queen Mary developed an uncanny understanding of the British people, and embodied the formidable ideals of middle-class womanhood. She persuaded the public that the royal family were 'just like us' and maintained the prestige and influence of the monarchy by example and public service. To demonstrate her dedication, she spent the First World War touring hospitals and tended the wounded soldiers herself. She made sure that her sons saw active duty at the front. Edward VIII was sent to the muddy waterlogged trenches, and George VI to a gun turret at the Battle of Jutland. For most of her life, she henpecked her children to toe the royal line of duty.

Queen Mary was horrified to find that both her granddaughters were learning so little. She discovered that the 11-year-old Princess Elizabeth and the 6-year-old Princess Margaret had only ninety minutes a day in the school room, from 9.30 a.m. to 11.00 a.m. The syllabus only covered the basic 'three Rs' of reading, writing and arithmetic. The lax schedule was followed by an hour's play and lunch, then another hour's rest, followed by singing, music, drawing and dancing. When weather permitted, the girls were taken outside for an hour's walk.[35]

There was a constant struggle between mother and grandmother. Queen Mary had a withering contempt for her daughter-in-law's anti-intellectualism, and she also despised her flamboyance. She made sure that Lilibet understood that real queens are modest and sincere rather than players to the public gallery.[36] Queen Mary decreed that Elizabeth would study history, with an emphasis on her family history; geography, with an emphasis on the British Empire; poetry for memory and religious studies so that she should understand her future role as Head of the Church.[37]

Sir Henry Martin, Vice Provost of Eton, was employed to instruct the princess on the British constitution.[38] Queen Mary also personally conducted both girls on cultural tours of London, taking them to the Tower of London, the Royal Mint, the Bank of England, Hampton Court Palace, Kew Gardens and Greenwich. These were rather fleeting visits and Princess Margaret later swore that their grandmother would never allow her and her sister to see more than three pictures at a time. When they pleaded for just one more, Queen Mary would just march on.[39]

Surprisingly, Queen Mary stopped there. There were no exams, no other pupils for Elizabeth to test herself against competitively and no science education. The two queens and the king were concerned that their daughters might become 'bluestockings' (studious young women). Princess Margaret remained angry as she grew up that she never had the sophisticated education her intelligence required, and always blamed her mother for this failing.[40] As a result, Princess Elizabeth succeeded to the throne, fifteen years later, virtually uneducated in all but the most rudimentary and basic disciplines. Neither university nor even finishing school was ever considered an option.[41]

To broaden her experience, she was sent to Girl Guides. However, rather than have her attend a normal pack, one was established in the gardens of Buckingham Palace on Wednesday afternoons. Its members were suitably vetted and included appropriately elevated girls of good breeding. In the winter, they met inside the palace, using its long corridors for signalling practice.[42] It was a rarefied bubble, and a wide gulf existed between the life lived by the royal family and their subjects.

The Second World War did bring two advantages. One was the arrival of Antoinette de Bellaigue, a vivacious Belgian viscountess who taught both princesses French and a little German. The second was that, finally, in 1945 Lilibet was allowed become a soldier of sorts and joined the Auxiliary Transport Service. For those last few months of the war, Elizabeth drove a 3 ton truck, changed spark plugs, adjusted brakes, greased axles and switched tyres. However, she still led a privileged, closeted existence and was never subjected to the rough life the other young women faced in the service.[43] While other girls slept in the army huts that constituted the barracks, she was driven back to Windsor Castle by 4 p.m. each day, and between lectures, she always ate in the officers' mess and not with the lower ranks. However, she did occasionally escape to have cups of tea with the other women.[44]

Nothing illustrates Elizabeth's cloistered life, cut off from the real world, better than her 16th birthday celebrations, when she was given a childlike tea party with jelly, ice cream and paper hats. A few people who attended, including her parents, sang 'Happy Birthday Lilibet' as though she were still a little girl.[45] Marriage would be as much an escape for Elizabeth as it had been for Margaret Thatcher.

Probably the future queen's biggest and only act of rebellion was over the choice of her husband. She met Prince Philip of Greece and Denmark at the outbreak of the war at the Royal Naval College at Dartmouth. At Christmas in 1943, Philip, who was on leave in England, was invited to attend the royal family's annual pantomime at Windsor Castle. Elizabeth played the lead role as Aladdin and Margaret played Roxana. During the show Elizabeth leapt from a laundry basket dressed as a young Chinese boy, tap-dancing, singing and cracking jokes. She tried to persuade the 22-year-old Philip to join in the 'fun' but he refused.[46] Then, he was interested in chasing more sophisticated women such as Georgina Wernher (now Lady Kennard), Deborah Mitford (later Duchess of Devonshire) and a Canadian called Osla Benning. He had played the field and taken them to places like Quaglino's and the 400 Club.[47]

Philip's romantic interest wasn't encouraged by either the king or queen. Elizabeth's mother had wanted her daughter to see many young men. She had even drawn up a so-called 'cricket list' or 'First XI' of suitable young English aristocratic men, including Sonny Blandford, the Duke of Marlborough, and Johnny Dalkeith, heir to the Duke of Buccleuch,[48] who had also caught Margaret Thatcher's attention at Oxford. Had the queen mother succeeded in her plan, Margaret and Elizabeth might have been in competition for the same man.

Behind the scenes, Philip was being encouraged by his highly ambitious uncle, Lord Louis Mountbatten, to pursue the greatest 'matrimonial catch' in the whole of European royalty. The queen mother was very suspicious of Lord Mountbatten,[49] she considered him 'pushy' and 'left-wing', something of a champagne socialist.[50] Philip had a mind of his own, was good-looking and independent, the pin-up boy for bevies of private school girls. Their fascination with Philip spread like influenza.[51] He totally lacked the courtly, understated manners of the English country gentleman, and palace courtiers found him 'rough and uneducated'.[52] Nor was Philip bound by the conventions that Princess Elizabeth slavishly observed. He was 'not all over her, and she found that very attractive'.[53]

Prince Philip's childhood could scarcely have been more different, at 8 years old his parents were exiled from Greece, where they had been part of a minor German-Danish royal family imported in 1863. Philip had no real home. His mother, Princess Alice, who spent eight years in German and Swiss mental sanatoria, suffered from 'paranoid schizophrenia'.[54] During the Second World War, Alice had been trapped in Athens where she helped rescue a Jewish family from the Gestapo. She eventually sold her jewels, became a nun and founded a convent, always struggling with her mental health. His philandering father, Prince Andrew, left her, to live with his mistress in Monte Carlo.

From the age of 8, until he was 15, Philip never saw his mother. Educated in Scotland at Gordonstoun, during the holidays he was parcelled around various family members. In England, he often stayed with the Mountbattens, or else he visited the various palaces and country houses of his family scattered across Europe –

his four sisters had each married German princes. At school, he was a natural leader, becoming head boy before he joined the Royal Navy, where he distinguished himself at the Battle of Matapan. He was mentioned in dispatches for bravery.

The queen mother, along with many in the royal household, thought of him as a bit of a gatecrasher, 'the Prince of Nothing, the Prince of Nowhere'. Margaret Rhodes, one of the queen mother's nieces, regarded Philip as 'a foreign interloper out for the goodies'. Princess Margaret said to friends that he simply was not good enough for her sister.[55] He had no money and his grandmother, the Dowager Marchioness of Milford Haven, paid all his bills at Gieves, where naval officers went for their uniforms. At Sandringham for Christmas, he wore heavily repaired hand-me-down clothes from his father and even had to borrow a bow tie.[56]

There was a fascinating standoff between the British Establishment's old guard and the young officer. He never showed them the respect an English boy would have done.[57] The Eldon, Stanley and Salisbury families, who were close friends of the king and queen, ganged up against him and made it plain that they hoped they were not going to let their daughter marry 'Charlie Kraut'.[58] One of the fiercest opponents of the match was the queen mother's brother, David Bowes-Lyon, who did his best to influence his sister against Philip.[59] The aristocracy surrounding the royal family did what they often did to any outsider, they closed ranks, something at which the British upper class has always been adept.

Finally, during a holiday at Balmoral in August 1946, Philip asked the 19-year-old Elizabeth to marry him, although her father was firmly against the match, she said. At first their engagement was kept a secret. George VI was anxious for his beloved Lilibet, and wary of his future son-in-law's man-about-town reputation.

Lord Mountbatten believed the king's devotion to his daughter had become too obsessive, even unhealthy.[60] His Majesty was miserable about the prospect of letting her go, and dreaded losing her; she was his constant companion in everything, work, shooting, walking and riding. He considered that Elizabeth was not only too young, but too unworldly, and was troubled that she had essentially fallen in love with the first young man who courted her.[61] Both the king and queen felt Philip was 'ill-tempered' and 'probably would not be faithful'.[62]

However, Louis Mountbatten wasn't going to be put off. Ever plotting to advance the royal romance in favour of his nephew, this intriguer telephoned his other nephew, King George II, who had just been returned to the Greek throne after a successful plebiscite, and suggested that the restored ruler leak the news of the engagement to the press. The story broke on 7 September 1946, in the *New York Times*. King George VI was furious with Philip, Louis Mountbatten and the Greek King; as he put it 'All those bloody Greeks'.[63]

The king fell back on a technique his daughter would later use as queen: delaying tactics. A royal tour was planned to South Africa, thus ensuring a long, forced separation from Philip. But Elizabeth was steadfast, and it became obvious to the king that he could no longer stand in the way of his daughter's wishes. However, he remained suspicious of Philip and refused him the title of 'Prince of the United Kingdom'. It would be a whole decade before he was given the full British royal title in 1957 by letters patent from his wife.

After the wedding at Westminster Abbey, the young couple honeymooned at Broadlands, the country estate of Mountbatten, or 'Uncle Dickie' as he became known. Mountbatten had plotted, planned and pushed for eight years to bring the couple together.[64] He had finally married his nephew into the British royal house.

For such a profoundly introverted girl, it was a breath of fresh air to be married to a man who didn't give a fig for the household at Buckingham Palace and their stuffy protocol. One diplomat, who was with them in Athens in 1950, talked to royal biographer Graham Turner and said:

> Both my wife and I felt that he [Philip] brought her out. She was very shy, rather withdrawn, a bit of a shrinking violet in fact, and he was young and vigorous and jollied her along ... she had a protective shell around her, and he brought her out of it.[65]

When George VI died in 1952, the queen mother, and Prime Minister Winston Churchill united against Philip. Both disliked his German roots and loathed his uncle, Lord Mountbatten, whom they felt had been an inadequate viceroy in India. The rest of the royal household took their lead. The new young queen, only in her mid-twenties, now had the world-famous prime minister as her adviser, and she was overwhelmed by him, allowing herself to be directed by him in everything. Her husband Philip was knocked sideways and struggled to find a role for himself.[66]

Within days of the king's funeral, a row also broke out over the royal family name. Would the new queen use her husband's name of Mountbatten, or her father's name of Windsor? When Queen Victoria had married Prince Albert, the family name changed from Hanover to Saxe-Coburg-Gotha, which remained the royal surname until George VI changed it to Windsor to avoid anti-German feelings after the First Word War. Queen Mary heard that Louis Mountbatten had boasted that since the accession of his niece-in-law, the 'house of Mountbatten reigned'. However, both the queen mother and Queen Mary, together with Churchill and the royal household, came down against any 'Mountbatten pretensions'.[67]

The queen, constitutionally obliged to take the advice of her prime minister, proclaimed the family name would remain Windsor.[68] Philip was furious, 'I am the only man in the country not allowed to give his name to his children. I'm nothing but a bloody amoeba.' It clearly remained a sore point for years and reduced Elizabeth to tears on occasion.[69] Even at the coronation, his role was undermined. Thanks to the scheming of Tommy Lascelles, the queen's private secretary, he wasn't allowed to walk with her down the aisle of Westminster Abbey. He was in the procession as her subject, not beside her, as her mother had been with King George at his coronation.[70]

Born with itchy feet, Philip at times hated his job as the Queen's consort and being tied on a royal leash. In the heart of London's infamous Soho he partied with the so-called Thursday Club, whose members included actors such as David Niven, Peter Ustinov, Jack Hedley, society photographer Baron Nahum and other members of the jet set, including Aristotle Onassis and Prince Bernhard of the Netherlands. Former Labour Foreign Secretary, David Owen, described Prince Philip as going 'pretty fairly wild'.[71]

By 1956 he had had a bellyful of 'pomping', as he referred to court protocol, and left on a four month trip on the royal yacht, *Britannia*, with its crew of 275, visiting Gambia, the Seychelles, Malaya, New Guinea, New Zealand, Antarctica, the Falklands, the Galapagos Islands, Australia and the West Coast of the United States, with his close friends, equerry Michael Parker and society photographer Baron Nahum. Presented to the public as a 'diplomatic mission' the entire trip was dogged by rumours of romantic trysts and a freewheeling lifestyle away from the palace. They sat on the deck sunbathing and drinking gin. The press slammed the trip as 'Philip's folly' and asked, 'who pays for it?'

When news of Michael Parker's imminent divorce was leaked to the press on the grounds of alleged adultery, the old guard at the palace forced his resignation. While the British press remained restrained, it was left to the American press to spread the bad news with headlines such as 'London Rumors of Rift in Royal Family Growing'.[72] Various articles linked Michael Parker's resignation to whispers that the queen's husband had more than a passing interest in an unmarried woman and met her regularly in the apartment of his close friend, Baron Nahum. The press concluded that the real reason for the four month cruise was that Philip was 'being got out of the country to cool down'. The queen put on a brave face.

George VI had left behind him a monarchy that was stable and surprisingly unaltered by the vast social changes that swept through Europe during the first half of the twentieth century. This was a not inconsiderable legacy to bequeath to a daughter determined to keep it all safe. However, he had an instinctive reliance on fossilised traditions, which he preserved while the rest of Britain declined.[73] Since his death, Elizabeth has followed the royal script written by him. Her philosophy and values of duty, service and self-restraint are what her father ordained. She tenaciously adhered to royal practices and protocol which, by 1980, seemed increasingly outmoded.[74] Surrounded by wealthy old Etonians and propertied ex-Guards officers she has shown a strong reluctance to step outside her class in any of her social relations.[75]

Although some reforms did happen, they were largely cosmetic and couldn't conceal the fact the queen had all the conventional prejudices of her class. With so much vested interest in the status quo, she was bound to resist real reform and modernisation.[76] Throughout the 1980s, Elizabeth II continued to turn her back on change, which came in the form of the Murdoch press, the cult of Princess Diana, and Thatcherism.

It was an attack launched by the Right Honourable Margaret Thatcher, who cast her personality so forcibly on the decade from 1979 to 1989 that, in many ways, proved the most destabilising. Thatcher once referred to herself as 'the rebel in charge of an Establishment government'.[77]

The queen and Mrs Thatcher were never going to agree. Elizabeth Alexandra Mary Windsor was the most famous woman in the world until Margaret Hilda Thatcher came along. Not since Elizabeth I and Mary, Queen of Scots had two 'queen regnants' lived in the British Isles, a regal state of affairs which ended very badly for one of them.

Mrs Thatcher would become far more than a mere politician. In newspaper cartoons she was depicted as the emblem of Britain itself: Britannia, a goddess, resplendent with trident and shield, wearing a centurion's helmet. For over a decade, during which the country had a more compelling icon to love or despise, Elizabeth II was overshadowed. The biggest threat to the monarchy came not from the Left, but from the Right,[78] from another woman who favoured pearls and a handbag, who curtsied very deeply, and who made 'Thatcherism' the defining word of the eighties.

4

DIPLOMATS AND SPIES

The Commonwealth … that's all she's got.
Denis Thatcher, on Her Majesty the Queen

Within days of Mrs Thatcher setting up home in Number 10, the public started to speculate about the phenomenon of a woman prime minister and her relationship with the queen. To begin with, relations were, in the words of Thatcher's biographer, John Campbell, 'punctiliously correct',[1] but insiders soon realised there was little love lost on either side. Margaret, having married a divorcee, was the second Mrs Thatcher, and even as late as the 1970s divorce remained an anathema to the palace. The queen harboured private suspicions of a woman in power and now took an active dislike to this new girl who clearly wanted to be head girl.

Mrs Thatcher's attitude to the queen was ambivalent. On the one hand she had an almost mystical reverence for the monarchy, 'Nobody would curtsy lower,' one courtier confided,[2] but on the other she gave in to school ma'am lecturing which didn't go down well, and she started to view Buckingham Palace as full of the 'unproductive' types.

Recently revealed memos written by Mrs Thatcher's aides show that, even during her first three years in power, the prime minister was constantly trying to avoid the audience with the queen. These documents hint at the early antagonism and tension between the two women, which they were both at pains to conceal. One, sent to Clive Whitmore, Mrs Thatcher's principal private secretary, and written by Caroline Stephens, Mrs Thatcher's diary secretary, reads, 'Tuesday, December 9 is not convenient as she has committed herself to entertaining a French high level mission (mostly bankers) for a drink'. When Mr Whitmore wrote to Sir Philip Moore, the queen's private secretary, he appears not to mention the French bankers and says only that the PM has a 'long-standing engagement'.[3] In one note Clive Whitmore cautions, 'I really think this will be pushing our luck with the palace', and Ms Stephens, equally concerned, writes, 'I don't want to spoil our relations with the palace'.[4]

Other memos reveal attempts by the prime minister to avoid attending the queen at Buckingham Palace, particularly when Parliament was in recess. Meetings between the two women were constantly rescheduled, and dates dropped. Finally, on 12 February 1981, an irritated Sir Philip Moore writes back stating that the audience time should now be 'regarded as firm', following yet another cancellation.[5]

Mrs Thatcher also declined to be a weekend guest at Windsor Castle for a 'dine and sleep' in 1979, the year she was elected, because her husband Denis had a board meeting the following morning.[6] She clearly wasn't over eager to socialise with the queen.

When the queen and prime minister were together in private, Thatcher was nervous and obsequious. She irritated Her Majesty with her combination of social anxiety, false humility and suburban pretensions. The queen wondered, 'Why does she always sit on the edge of her seat?'[7] and noted that she spoke with Royal Shakespeare Received Pronunciation from circa 1950.[8] Before long, she came to dread Mrs Thatcher's visits to the palace.[9]

Known for her mimicry, Elizabeth loved telling Margaret Thatcher jokes, her favourite being about the prime minister visiting an old people's home:

'Do you know who I am?' said the queen, imitating Thatcher's grandiose yet artificial accent as she shook the hands of an elderly resident.

'No,' replied the confused resident. 'But if you ask matron, she'll tell you.'[10]

However, jokes, for Margaret Thatcher, were no laughing matter. Irony was lost on the Iron Lady. On visiting a navy destroyer, she asked a sailor about the recoil of a naval gun on deck, 'Can this thing jerk you off?',[11] and on praising her deputy prime minister, William Whitelaw, she delivered her most notorious double entendre, 'Every prime minister should have a Willie.'[12]

There was one area in which the queen felt she was more expert than her lecturing, but less well-travelled, prime minister; and that was international affairs. Elizabeth II, by way of her position as Head of the Commonwealth, is sovereign of seventeen realms scattered across the globe. To Her Majesty, Mrs Thatcher was merely the eighth prime minister of the UK, and in 1979 when she took office, the queen had been in her job twenty-six years. Although Thatcher's ignorance of foreign affairs when she became prime minister was alarming, the queen's opinions were shaped by the former era of empire, when her royal cousins such as the Hohenzollerns and Romanovs sat upon the thrones of Europe and Britain ruled a large portion of the world.

To make matters more difficult, Mrs Thatcher had a loathing of the Foreign & Commonwealth Office. The Foreign Secretary at the time, Lord Carrington, acknowledged this:

> She [Thatcher] hated the Foreign Office ... she felt that anybody who tried to get along with foreigners was somehow disloyal and that they were the sort of people who would give in to foreigners ... She hated the idea of a consensus and, as a result, she never got on with the people in Europe, partly because I think she mistrusted people whose mother tongue wasn't English. Americans were alright; Australia was alright, Canadians were okay, but when you came down to French and Germans, well, that was a different matter altogether.[13]

Thatcher viewed all the inhabitants of the Foreign Office with great suspicion – public school boys with second-rate brains compared to those at the Treasury next door. 'Many in the department were Arabist scholars who spoke Arabic. Her constituency in Finchley was dominated by Jewish voters with whom she shared an affinity. The foreign office was very old-fashioned, if a woman got married in those days she had to leave her job,' Edwina Currie recognised.[14]

Mrs Thatcher's first adventure into international affairs was just before the 1979 election, when the Iranian Revolution forced the Shah of Iran into exile in Morocco. Thatcher sent word to the exiled emperor that she would allow Britain's old ally and friend to come to the United Kingdom should she win the election. The intermediary was a British television producer called Alan Hart, who had made several television documentaries in Iran. Thatcher told Hart, 'I would be ashamed to be British if we could not give the Shah refuge'. The Shah hoped to move into Stilemans, a large equestrian estate he owned in the stockbroker belt of Surrey.[15] Both the queen and Prince Philip, as well as the queen mother and Princess Anne, had all regularly visited their fellow royal when he sat upon his oil-rich throne. According to journalist, William Shawcross, the queen had been discreetly lobbying for the Shah, as she felt Britain should show him loyalty for the long years in which he had supported British interests in the Middle East. 'She believed that states must recognise personal as well as national obligations.'[16]

However, the post-election political climate was hardening against the Iranian imperial family, and the Foreign Office started making objections. They feared the Shah's life would be at risk from the thousands of Iranian students currently studying in the UK, thus adding a significantly large security bill to the logistical headaches. The tabloids ran stories of tank traps at Stilemans that made the neighbours nervous. There were also economic objections – if the Shah was granted a home in England, the new Iranian regime might block British trade, including oil. The loss of jobs to British workers could be enormous.[17]

Mrs Thatcher looked as if she was going sweep away any objections to the Shah retiring to the United Kingdom. However, what tipped the balance was the fear that the British Embassy in Tehran might be seized, and the ambassador and his staff held hostage, allowing the Iranians to demand that the Shah be traded for them. Lord Carrington, then Foreign Secretary, stated, 'The ambassador in Tehran sent me a telegram saying that if you offer asylum to the Shah, the 1,100 British citizens who are in Tehran will be shot.'[18]

Therefore, the 'Iron Lady' buckled under pressure, devastating the Shah, who felt betrayed. For the rest of his life spurned by those who had once fawned over him her searcher for a permanent home.

Back in London, during a dinner party with former government minister, Lord Shawcross (father of writer William Shawcross), the queen expressed her anger towards Margaret Thatcher for reneging on a promise to grant the Shah asylum. 'Once you give your word,' the queen said, 'that's it.' It was not a good start to the relationship, and a rare indiscretion by the queen.[19] Lord Carrington also felt sorry for the Shah. 'I always felt rather bad about it, because we'd been on very good terms with the Shah, and I was rather sorry for him, and he wasn't the evil man that people made out.'[20]

Another incident saw a clash of cultures between the old school Establishment and the new Thatcher model. This time it centred on the Surveyor of the Queen's Pictures, Sir Anthony Blunt, who had acted as a Russian spy while working at MI5 during the 1940s. Mrs Thatcher was fascinated by the work of the secret services and was a fan of Frederick Forsyth novels (she preferred the hardliners of MI6 to the 'wimps' of the Foreign Office). However, the new prime minister was shocked to learn that Blunt, who was at the heart of the British Establishment, had been a 'mole' for Russia.

In 1964, Blunt had been offered immunity from prosecution provided he co-operated in the inquiries of the security authorities. Buckingham Palace was also briefed on the immunity deal, which enabled Blunt to continue in royal service for the next fifteen years.[21] According to Peter Rawlinson, the government's solicitor general who arranged the immunity deal, the queen knew for years that he was a spy. He explained, 'it was essential to keep him in his position at Buckingham Palace looking after the queen's pictures. Otherwise, Russia would have realised that his cover had been blown.'[22] Palace officials knew Blunt's secret long before his public exposure. In 1948, former army officer Philip Hay attended Buckingham

Palace for a job interview. After passing Blunt in the corridor, Sir Alan Lascelles, the king's private secretary told Hay, 'That's our Russian spy'.[23]

Thatcher discovered the deal in 1979, when a book by Andrew Boyle, *The Climate of Treason*, hinted at who the mole was and led to questions in the House of Commons.[24] Instead of playing it safe, Margaret Thatcher overruled the director of MI5, Sir Michael Hanley,[25] and the cabinet secretary, Sir Robert Armstrong,[26] and went public on Blunt. Armstrong maintained that it would only 'shed light into corners best left publicly dark'. No corner was darker than Blunt's palace connections which helped him protest his innocence and even threaten writs, right up to the time of Mrs Thatcher's statement.[27] Former Labour Foreign Secretary David Owen said that Thatcher felt '... that the secrecy was being used to protect people, she is a radical, and she was confronted by the knowledge that Blunt had been pardoned in this sort of extraordinary way. So she did break it.'[28]

Thatcher's statement, which exposed Blunt, caused an international sensation.[29] As a story it had all the exciting elements needed to sell newspapers: class, spies, the Establishment, royalty, homosexuality and a villain who had betrayed his country. Satirical magazine *Private Eye* suggested that Blunt's royal connections had secured him immunity from prosecution.[30] The front page of the *Daily Mail* said it all, 'Traitor at the Queen's Right Hand'. In the *Daily Express*, columnist John Junor described him as a 'treacherous Communist poof'. The *Daily Telegraph* said Blunt had been a hopeless army officer and hinted at cowardice.[31] This, as Conservative MP Alan Clark confessed in his diary, was a lucky break for the government, as the story diverted attention from 'the really alarming manner in which our economy seems to be conducted'.[32]

Blunt, a crashing snob and homosexual, was the so-called 'fourth man' in the infamous Cambridge spy ring which included Guy Burgess, Donald Maclean and Kim Philby. After leaving MI5, he had become a distinguished art historian who was made director of the Courtauld Institute and advised the queen on the royal collection. He was also a third cousin of the queen mother (Blunt's mother was a second cousin to her father, the Earl of Strathmore). Blunt used to take tea with her and occasionally shared her box at the opera. She was rather fond of him.

Anthony Blunt had, on occasion, also performed the odd tricky 'diplomatic mission' on behalf of the 'family'. In the summer of 1963, only a few months before his confession, he had quietly acted on behalf of the Windsors to buy a series of drawings that Stephen Ward had made of Prince Philip.

Ward was a key witness in the infamous Profumo Scandal, named after John Profumo, the Secretary of State for War. Profumo had damaged Macmillan's Conservative Government by carrying on an affair with Christine Keeler, a London party girl, while she was also sleeping with Yevgeny Ivanov, a naval attaché at the Soviet Embassy in London. The ramifications for national security were grave. Stephen Ward, a fashionable osteopath and party arranger for the aristocracy, had introduced Keeler to Profumo. Ward had been charged with living off the profits of prostitution and committed suicide by overdosing on sleeping tablets on the last day of the trial. Any connection between such a notorious individual and Prince Philip, whom he met through the Thursday Club, was not desirable.

One of the many theories surrounding Anthony Blunt is that he obtained his immunity from prosecution by threatening to expose that the Duke of Windsor had been plotting with Hitler and the Nazi Party during the Second World War. In 1945, Blunt was sent by the Secret Intelligence Service to the Schloss Freidrichshof, the castle home of Prince Philippe of Hesse to recover potentially incriminating letters. Hesse, a cousin of the British royal family, was a great-grandson of Queen Victoria. The fact that the duke had been in favour of pursuing a pro-German appeasement policy with Hitler had long been an embarrassment to the royal family. Provided with official documentation and an army truck, Blunt set out for Germany with George VI's private librarian, Owen Morshead, to recover the letters. The official story was that Blunt was sent to recover private correspondence between Queen Victoria and her daughter Victoria, the Princess Royal, who became German Empress and Queen of Prussia.[33]

Arriving at the castle, Blunt and Morshead found it occupied by American forces and Prince Philippe in Allied custody for having served as a senior officer in Hitler's Third Reich. The American senior officer in charge was unimpressed by both Blunt's arrogance and his royal credentials, and refused to accept his demand to remove the papers. Determined to complete his mission, Blunt sought out the remaining Hesse family, recently evicted from the castle and now housed in a nearby village. Prince Philippe's mother, Princess Margaret of Prussia (a granddaughter of Queen Victoria) briefed Blunt on how to slip into the castle by means of a back staircase, which he did that night, providing him with a letter that instructed the loyal castle servants to help the two Englishmen. Blunt and Morshead removed two crates of documents from the castle's attics and drove off with them in a truck towards the safety of the British zone before the Americans discovered the theft. A week later, the documents were safely deposited in Windsor Castle, never to be seen again.[34]

In August 1947, a rumour surfaced that the Duke of Windsor had communicated with Prince Frederick William, the son of Kaiser Wilhelm II, who had also acted as an emissary for Hitler. Again, Blunt and Morshead were sent to the Continent, this time to Huis Doorn, the late Kaiser's residence in Holland, tasked with finding any more potentially embarrassing royal documents.[35]

Whatever Blunt's past services had been to the royal family, within minutes of Thatcher's statement to the House, Buckingham Palace announced that Blunt was being stripped of his knighthood.[36] It was as though the queen had just heard of the scandalous state of affairs for the first time.[37] Within days, Blunt's academic titles, honorary doctorates and fellowships all began to disappear[38] as he was cast out of the Establishment. The whole messy business illustrated MI5's ineptitude and the ability of the upper classes to protect one of their own.

Thatcher's statement to the House of Commons raised several questions: Had other traitors been offered immunity from prosecution in return for a confession? Why had immunity been offered to Blunt when other spies, who were not related to a member of the royal family and who did not hold positions at the palace, had been sent to prison? How much information did the queen know about the affair? The scandal, although something of a diversion from the daily work of politics, did raise issues about the relationship between Buckingham Palace, the government and the intelligence services.[39]

Mrs Thatcher believed that Blunt had 'by his own admission committed serious offences'.[40] Sir Bernard Ingham, her private secretary while she was at Number 10, had little doubt. 'I believe she did it because she didn't see why the system should cover things up,' he says. 'This was early in her prime ministership. I think she wanted to tell the civil service that the politicians decide policy, not the system. She wanted them to know who was boss.'[41] Alan Clark said that the whole affair was:

> ... disreputable; one of those episodes that indicated a kind of close society in the palace circle that regards itself immune for the norms of appropriate behaviour ... My view is that Anthony Blunt should have been executed because he had contributed by his actions to the deaths of our agents.[42]

Margaret Thatcher herself seemed personally affronted by Blunt's immunity. She had no time for liberal interpretations of his motives, which suggested he was fighting fascism. In her mind, a traitor was a traitor, and she found the whole episode thoroughly reprehensible and reeking of Establishment collusion.[43] Others felt Mrs Thatcher's decision to break the seal of confidentiality on Blunt's immunity deal was a home goal. The useful mechanism of offering a former spy immunity from prosecution in return for co-operation with the authorities would never again be trusted if they were going to be exposed later.[44] The head of MI6, Maurice Oldfield, had been against the move.[45]

Later that year, the newspapers disclosed the story of Blunt's mission to Germany, and it sparked imaginative speculations. Were the crates of documents merely the correspondence between Queen Victoria and her daughter, or final proof of the Duke of Windsor's Nazi sympathies? The royal family maintained their silence in public.

When the queen was asked about Blunt, she replied, 'I just can't remember whether they told me or not'. Perhaps she was dissembling, but she does have a known ability to put unpleasant facts out of her mind.[46] As for the queen mother, just after Blunt's exposure there was a lunch at Lady Perth's to which she had been invited. Gossip, of course, centred on the subject of Anthony Blunt and whether anyone dared ask her about it when she eventually arrived. As she swept into the room, Harold Acton had the audacity to ask the queen mother what she thought. 'Lovely day, isn't it?' she replied inscrutably, with her face fixed.[47] After Blunt's death she spoke to Sir Isaiah Berlin, the political theorist and historian. Berlin remembered that she spoken 'rather kindly' about him and that she was fond of gay men. She said, 'One can't blame them all. A lot of people made terrible mistakes, one shouldn't really go on persecuting them.'[48]

In 1987 Peter Wright, a retired British Intelligence officer with MI5, published a book called *Spycatcher*, that Thatcher banned in the UK. He revealed that he had interviewed Anthony Blunt, with colleague Arthur Martin, over a period of eight years with a wide remit to uncover his treachery. However, there was one subject Wright was not allowed to investigate. The palace emphatically insisted that any questioning of Blunt about his mission to Germany for George VI was out of bounds. Apparently Lord Adeane, the private secretary to the queen during the first twenty years of her reign, told MI5, 'From time to time ... you may find Blunt referring to an assignment he undertook on behalf of the palace, a visit to Germany at the end of the war. Please do not pursue this matter. Strictly speaking it is not relevant to considerations of national security.'[49] Wright would later comment:

> In the hundreds of hours I spent with him I never did learn the secret of his mission at the end of the war ... the palace is adept in the difficult art of trying to bury scandals over several centuries, while MI5 have only been in business since 1909 ...[50]

Mrs Thatcher's actions had unwittingly exposed the involvement of the old guard in a very British piece of hypocrisy which directly involved the queen. It was not a promising start so early on in their relationship, as it led to unwelcome criticism of Her Majesty.

International affairs again turned up the heat on the relationship between Elizabeth and Margaret. Three months after taking office, the newly minted prime minister found herself confronted with a surprisingly assertive queen, who apparently wasn't going to play by the constitutional rule of always 'acting on the advice of her prime ministers'.

The queen was deeply upset and annoyed by Mrs Thatcher's ill-concealed dislike of her beloved Commonwealth.[51] Elizabeth's parents had been the last self-styled Emperor and Empress of India, so it was hardly surprising that the queen should have grown up with a strong sense of her 'imperial responsibilities'. On her 21st birthday, as Princess Elizabeth, she had made a wireless broadcast not just to Great Britain, but to the entire empire. It was delivered not from London but Cape Town. In this speech she declared, 'That my whole life, be it long or short, shall be devoted to your service and to the service of our great Imperial Commonwealth to which we all belong'.[52] These were words that she sincerely meant, and she has gone on believing them, long after the political reality of the British Empire had vanished.

The Commonwealth is a world-straddling organisation as illogical as the British monarchy itself, and it embraces a curious mix of republics, despotisms and democracies. Historian Andrew Marr called it 'a strange half-empire' and successive prime ministers have all paid lip-service to this idea, largely for reasons of politeness. Mrs Thatcher, however, wasn't so tactful about this royal anomaly, and came to regard the Commonwealth as a pointless hangover from the days of empire, in which third world dictators would use the institution to hector properly elected leaders of democracies,[53] such as herself. In her mind, they were a bunch of greedy beggars looking for a handout. 'I think that she had very undeveloped views about almost all Commonwealth issues,' said David Owen. He pointed out that Margaret felt it was:

> Just talking shop, with no real morality, that ignores human rights when it's convenient to them. That it has an unrealistic view of South Africa, thinks we should effectively take economic sanctions but won't think through the consequence of economic sanctions for South Africa with already very high black unemployment and all this. And she has a rational case, no doubt about that.[54]

For the queen, the Commonwealth remains a viable institution capable of doing much good for its member nations. It was also a key part of her inheritance from her father. George VI saw the Commonwealth's potential to give the British monarchy enormous global prestige, something that the bicycling royal families of northern Europe didn't have, and Elizabeth was always her father's daughter. She saw her responsibilities as reaching far beyond Britain and merely British interests. Even at times when the British Government was at odds with individual member states, she was able to understand their viewpoint without taking sides and managed to convey that to them. It was this idea of the Commonwealth as a family that had the capacity to disagree without breaking up that was alien to Mrs Thatcher, who viewed it as a tiresome obstacle to realistic foreign policy.

The queen finds herself at the heart of this institution because the Victorian builders of empire wanted to knit together existing social hierarchies across the globe into one overarching system. The Victorians had learned from the American colonies, which had declared independence in 1776, of the danger in allowing countries to think about alternative ways of organising themselves.[55] These empire builders fostered a world of deference to one's superiors with local monarchies receiving their status from a central king-emperor or queen-empress based in London. In India, 500 maharajahs and other princes responded by accepting the recognition of the British Empire, building themselves vast new palaces and staging elaborate 'durbars' to show themselves off to their public. By the late nineteenth century, governing the vast empire through its local rulers was the only practical way forward, and where there was no local royalty, Britain invented one.

Winston Churchill claimed to be a kingmaker when he stated that Emir Abdullah of Jordan was, 'one of my creations'.[56] Royalty became the most exclusive club in the world. At the coronation of Edward VIII, King Lewanika of Barotseland, a tiny British protectorate in southern Africa, remarked rather grandly, 'When kings are seated, there is never a lack of things to discuss'. Although such institutions and arrangements may seem irrelevant in the modern world, that has never prevented Elizabeth II from trying the bolster them up. There was nothing Her Majesty enjoyed more than sailing around the former empire in the royal yacht.

The divergent attitudes towards the Commonwealth caused an early crack in the relationship between the queen and Margaret Thatcher that would soon develop into a full schism. The battle appeared to be shaping up between the two women, with Her Majesty even referring to her prime minister as 'that woman' in front of Commonwealth leaders whom she considered old friends.

One of the biggest events in the royal calendar is the Commonwealth Heads of Government Meeting (CHOGM), held every other year, which the new prime minister viewed as a complete waste of her time. One was due to be held in Lusaka, the capital of Zambia, just after Thatcher's election. The main issue for discussion at Lusaka was Rhodesia, where the white government led by Ian Smith had negotiated a power-sharing agreement with the moderate black party under a new prime minister, Bishop Abel Muzorewa. However, Black Nationalist guerilla leaders such as Robert Mugabe and Joshua Nkomo, who had been excluded from the electoral process, regarded Muzorewa as Ian Smith's stooge, and the international community, particular many of the African regimes, were hostile to his government.[57]

Mrs Thatcher had promised to bring Rhodesia to independence 'with wide international acceptance'. The plan was for the Commonwealth leaders meeting at Lusaka to endorse a peace conference between Ian Smith and the guerilla factions, and prepare for free elections. Mrs Thatcher, however, regarded the guerillas as terrorists[58] and, because Mugabe and Nkomo were operating out of bases in Zambia, the prime minister felt it would be inappropriate, even dangerous, for the queen to go to Lusaka.

In a radio interview, the prime minister called into doubt the visit of the queen to the Lusaka conference by claiming the right to advise the monarch about whether it was safe for her to attend.[59] Thatcher was speedily told to mind her own business, and reminded that the queen was free to take advice from all the appropriate Commonwealth leaders, of which Thatcher was only one.[60] Elizabeth II had been prevented from attending the Singapore meeting eight years earlier by Prime Minister Ted Heath, and she didn't intend to let such a thing happen again. The queen was now at her most determined, and on 2 July, Buckingham Palace announced that she would go to Lusaka. The prime minister was flying home from a trip to Tokyo and Australia. On her arrival in London, Mrs Thatcher said she had not yet seen the security arrangement for the Lusaka conference and, until she did, she was not sure whether she would advise Her Majesty to go. The queen had outmanoeuvred the prime minister, and the two conflicting statements highlighted the disagreement between the two women.

Mrs Thatcher would have liked to recognise the new Smith–Muzorewa regime fully. She did not want the Commonwealth heads of government, much less the queen, to go to Zambia in August, because any boost to the world stature of President Kenneth Kaunda of Zambia at the time would not have pleased the white, moderate, power-sharing Rhodesian Government whom Thatcher instinctively favoured.[61]

As David Owen explains:

She was treading into an area that the queen does consider her own, not totally her own, but cancelling her attendance at a Commonwealth Heads of Government Meeting is a joint decision between the queen and prime minister. It is not one made unilaterally by the prime minister through press briefings. And I'm convinced the counter-briefing in the press from the palace was authorised by the queen. Now whether or not it ever went into the audience with the queen, I don't know. I doubt it was necessary actually. I think the vibes had got through, and Margaret Thatcher, who was inexperienced but a quick learner knew she had gone too far on that. And it again showed her complete misunderstanding of the queen's relationship. The idea that the queen going to Lusaka with Kenneth Kaunda, who adored her, was going to be under threat and things like that was ridiculous.[62]

To make a delicate situation more tense, Kaunda, the host of the Commonwealth Conference, had a close relationship with the guerrilla leader Joshua Nkomo, whose headquarters-in-exile was Lusaka. Indeed, a state of war existed between the two countries and the city of Lusaka had been bombed recently by Rhodesian planes.[63] The British Government, by recognising the internal power-sharing settlement, had caused Kaunda considerable bitterness.[64] Thatcher had little political sympathy with Africa's struggle for liberation, and disliked the hypocrisy of African leaders who preached democracy while operating one-party states, reviling Britain one moment and then demanding an increase in international aid the next. She stated forcefully, 'Many of us do not feel quite the same allegiance to Archbishop Makarios or Doctor Nkrumah or to people like Jomo Kenyatta as we do to Mr Menzies of Australia'. Seldom has a point been more bluntly put.[65] She started referring to CHOGM (Commonwealth Heads of Government Meeting) as 'Compulsory Hand-Outs for Greedy Mendicants'.[66]

Her husband, Denis, went further, having been foolish enough to roar with laughter when an Australian journalist said that CHOGM stood for 'Coons Holidaying on Government Money'.[67] Journalists on the satirical magazine *Private Eye* were quick to see the comic opportunity that Denis Thatcher presented, and started running their 'Dear Bill …' letters, a fictional spoof correspondence between Denis Thatcher and his close friend, Bill Deeds. The column was such a popular success that it became a stage play called *Anyone for Denis?* The Thatchers, to prove they did, in fact, possess a sense of humour, went to see it and hailed it, probably through gritted teeth, as a marvellous farce. However, Denis only put his foot in it further by mistaking an actor who played a stage policeman for the real thing. He went on to compliment him and his fellow officers for sorting out 'Fuzzy wuzzies going on the rampage down in Brixton', referring to the notorious race riots that were taking place in the south London suburb, largely provoked by unemployment levels of 60 per cent among young blacks.[68]

After this incident, Denis was careful to stay out of the public eye, rather than become an embarrassment to his wife, unlike the queen's husband, Prince Philip, who was prone to notorious gaffes. These included telling British students during a state visit to China that they would become 'slitty-eyed' if they remained in the country too long, and reducing a teenage boy to tears by advising him to lose weight if he wanted to become an astronaut.

Newspapers in Africa branded Mrs Thatcher a racist. She even contemplated not going to the conference, and prepared for her arrival in Lusaka by donning dark glasses, fearful that acid would be thrown in her face. The *Zambia Daily Mail* compared Mrs Thatcher very unfavourably with the queen's 'extraordinary loving heart'. Indeed, Thatcher seemed bent on splitting the organisation apart while the queen worked hard to make herself the focus of unity.[69] Her Majesty, in contrast to her prime minister, was sympathetic to the black cause, both in Rhodesia and South Africa.[70] Indeed, many of the political leaders in the Commonwealth were old colleagues, and she had grown up with Kaunda and Nyerere. After her favourite refuge at Balmoral, it is said that the queen is always at her most relaxed when she is with the Commonwealth leaders.

Mrs Thatcher sympathised with the white population in Rhodesia and the power-sharing agreement with Bishop Muzorewa. But the Australian Prime Minister, Malcolm Fraser, tried to persuade Thatcher not to accept this settlement. After being warned by the British Foreign Secretary, Lord Carrington, that Margaret would never change her mind he found the queen more pragmatic, and the Commonwealth leaders saw that she was for a compromise. In an interview, Fraser compared the contrasting approaches of the queen and Mrs Thatcher:

> With Her Majesty ... there wouldn't have been any argument because she had a sense of these things, knew what it was all about from a very long involvement with an innate instinct for justice ... So [there were] two enormously different people with enormously different reactions, and you know one of the difficulties for Her Majesty must be the convention under which the monarch operates in Britain, at times living alongside a head of government with whom one disagrees.[71]

Constitutionally, the queen found herself in a potentially difficult position with split loyalties. Her title, Head of the Commonwealth, is a title held in the person of the monarch, not in the office of the monarchy. This subtle distinction is little known even in Britain.[72] As Head of the Commonwealth, the relationship to her prime minister is different from that pertaining to her role as queen of the United Kingdom. In Commonwealth affairs, Mrs Thatcher, as head of Britain's government, has arguably no more constitutional power over the monarch than does the President of Zambia or Prime Minister of Canada. Journalist Malcolm Rutherford, in the *Financial Times*, identified the potential source of trouble as the Commonwealth secretariat in London.[73] Because the queen receives advice on the Commonwealth directly from its Secretary General and not through the Foreign

& Commonwealth Office, the chances of a Britain vs. Commonwealth clash are, therefore, quite likely. It is a nightmare royal advisors fear.[74]

Enoch Powell always attacked the constitutional folly of having a monarch who was British, but not exclusively British, with the result that two distinct lines of authority from London could exist, devolving from both the government and the queen. Powell felt the queen was obstinate in refusing to accept reality, and thought that in any dispute she was honour bound to side with the British Government rather than her beloved Commonwealth, but his analysis failed to take into account her personal popularity and influence. Her royal tours, although infrequent, gave Commonwealth countries the perception that she was still their head of state, emphasising to citizens of the Commonwealth around the world the fact that the queen was someone who cared.[75]

The queen was determined to use her position to save the Lusaka Conference, and a former Secretary General of the Organisation, Chief Emeka Anyaoku, claimed it was only the direct intervention of Buckingham Palace that rescued it. Sir Sonny Ramphal, Secretary General of the Commonwealth secretariat in London, persuaded Joshua Nkomo to declare a ceasefire during the royal visit.[76]

On 27 July 1979, two days before Mrs Thatcher arrived, Elizabeth II landed in Lusaka, having spent the nine previous days touring the region, visiting Tanzania, Botswana, and Malawi, as well as Zambia. What she heard made her increasingly concerned that a number of African countries might leave the Commonwealth. She immediately urged President Kaunda to subdue the anti-British rhetoric in the local press. During the four day Commonwealth Conference, she followed the usual routine of hosting a banquet and reception for the nations' forty-two leaders. However, that evening she stayed until midnight 'quartering the room and talking to various heads of government,' said Chief Emeka Anyaoku of Nigeria. 'I am convinced that the intervention spurred the organisation, which was on the point of splitting up, on to compromise.' Her informal role, holding private talks with every leader in turn in her bungalow, was to convey sympathy for their position without explicitly stating her own. The leaders were impressed by her knowledge, and the temperature of the conference was reduced.

To her credit, Mrs Thatcher saw a way to emerge with some concessions, but without what in her mind would be surrender, a compromise that Lord Carrington and Malcolm Fraser had urged her to. The African leaders also yielded some ground, agreeing to consider a formula for white representation in Rhodesian's new government.[77] The conference even ended with the improbable sight of Margaret Thatcher dancing with Kenneth Kaunda. Mrs Thatcher was also far too polite to mention that, on returning to her accommodation, she found the ceiling had collapsed, and there was no running water.[78]

Thatcher signed the Lusaka Accord calling for a constitutional conference at Lancaster House in London in September, and she enthusiastically embraced the peace process which led to an agreement in December 1979, calling for a cease-fire and free elections. There was no recognition of Muzorewa as the interim authority. Observers thought the prime minister looked a little downcast at the end of the conference. The queen, in contrast, seemed elated.[79] At the time, it was a success of real substance for Margaret Thatcher and the Foreign Office that she so disliked. What was less recognised was the indispensable groundwork and the atmosphere of goodwill what had been achieved by the queen.[80]

Rhodesia declared independence in April 1980 as the Republic of Zimbabwe, the forty-third member of the Commonwealth, with Robert Mugabe as prime minister. Margaret Thatcher was upset that Zimbabwe ended up with Mugabe, but the political realities were on the side of the guerillas and she recognised that the Muzorewa Government could never have brought peace.[81] It quickly became apparent that Mugabe was a corrupt dictator. He crushed all political rivals and drove out the white farmers, destroying the agricultural economy while at the same time proving that Thatcher's fears about the regime were true.[82] As David Owen points out:

> She [Thatcher] lived with Mugabe during all her period in office basically knowing that he had committed huge crimes and became very disillusioned with the settlement, but didn't want to denounce it because it was a considerable triumph for her. But that fed through to her views on the Commonwealth and its refusal, to denounce ... this sort of thing.[83]

5

AMERICA, THE FALKLANDS
AND GRENADA

> Only two curtsies today.
> Her Majesty the Queen, on Mrs Thatcher

It was evident to all, including Her Majesty, that Margaret Thatcher would happily have abandoned the Commonwealth to pursue a special relationship with the United States, a country she greatly admired. In her opinion, the future lay not with the countries of the former British Empire, but across the Atlantic with the genial, right-wing and charming President Ronald Reagan, and Margaret set about making herself his closest political and ideological friend.

After his inauguration in January 1981, Margaret was accorded the honour of being his first foreign visitor, and the two of them bonded.[1] The American alliance was central to her thinking. She viewed the United States as the pivot in the coalition against Communism. The American anti-Soviet alliance cut across all other loyalties.[2]

Mrs Thatcher fed the United States' appetite for royalty by dispatching the queen and her family on a series of goodwill tours that were enthusiastically reciprocated. First lady, Nancy Reagan caught royal fever, and Thatcher fed this mania by inviting her to the wedding of Prince Charles and Lady Diana Spencer. Nancy arrived in London saying, 'I'm just crazy about Prince Charles', bringing with her twenty-six suitcases, eleven hat boxes, seventeen secret service men and a pair of borrowed earrings worth $880,000.[3] The queen arranged for her cousin, Jean Willis, to host her during her visit, and Mrs Reagan also took tea with the queen mother at the Royal Lodge in Windsor Great Park. At the wedding reception, Mrs Reagan sat with the queen and Princess Grace of Monaco for the buffet supper.[4]

The following year, the Reagans were invited to rub shoulders again with royalty by making a state visit to Britain. It was a diplomatic ruse on both sides. For the Americans, it was the crowning moment of Reagan's first European tour as president.

For Thatcher, it was a means of highlighting to the electorate the bond between herself and the US Presidency at a time when her ratings in the opinion polls were so low they were among the worst recorded for any sitting prime minister. Her imposition of strict monetarist economic policies, with accompanying redundancies and bankruptcies, lower taxation and low public spending, were making her extremely unpopular. She had come to power promising 'my job is to stop Britain going into the red', but the harshness of her policies led to riots breaking out in cities such as London, Liverpool, Leeds and Manchester, caused by unemployment, social deprivation and racial tension.

Jobless figures stood at 2.7 million, and police were battling against protestors throwing Molotov cocktails in the streets.[5] Denis Healey described her policy as 'sado-monetarism',[6] but Mrs Thatcher blamed criminals for the violence. After witnessing the destruction of property in Liverpool's Toxteth area, she reserved her sympathy for 'those poor shopkeepers'.[7] There were doubts about her political prospects in the US press and among many Reaganites. *Time* magazine had published an article about her entitled 'Embattled but Unbowed', reporting that her government was beset with difficulties.[8] Many people at home and abroad felt she wouldn't last.

Just before Ronald Reagan was about to set foot inside Windsor Castle, an international event blew up that would test their new friendship, take the focus off domestic failures and prove to be the Iron Lady's finest hour. On 2 April 1982, General Leopold Galtieri and his Argentinian military junta invaded the Falkland Islands.

Which side they should back was no easy call for the US to make. Jeanne Kirkpatrick, the American Ambassador to the United Nations, saw Galtieri as an important ally in countering the influence of Soviet and Cuban influence in South America. Galtieri had even been an early visitor to the White House, where he had met the president soon after Thatcher did. For the occasion, he had worn full military uniform with his chest emblazoned with medal ribbons.[9] This couldn't have made the timing of the presidential visit to Britain more awkward and potentially embarrassing for all sides. Mike Deaver, Reagan's deputy chief of staff, worried that it might look bad if the president was touring Britain during a bloodbath.[10] The British Ambassador to Washington, Sir Nicholas Henderson, even suggested to her that the Reagans call off their long-planned visit to Windsor Castle. Thatcher was indignant. 'It was the queen who had invited him,' Thatcher said. 'Did [Henderson] not realise how rude it would be to Her Majesty for the president not to come?'[11]

Uppermost in Thatcher's mind was the Suez Crisis in 1956, when Prime Minister Sir Anthony Eden used military force to liberate the British- and French-owned Suez Canal, which had been unilaterally nationalised by Gamal Abdel Nasser. President Eisenhower demanded that Britain and France end their efforts midway through the campaign or face the deliberate undermining of the value of Britain's currency by the US. Anglo-American relations had never fully recovered since then. Thatcher knew she had to keep the US Presidency on side and was prepared to use royal hospitality to help cement the bonds between American and Britain even further.

Ironically, Britain had almost handed over the Falkland Islands to Argentina, but procrastination and jingoism got in the way. Nicholas Ridley, a Thatcherite junior minister in the early 1980s, made no bones about the government's desire to shed, by hook or by crook, the burden of these bleak colonial relics.[12] He plainly shared Denis Thatcher's view, expressed after a post-war visit, that the Falklands were 'miles and miles of bugger all'.[13] There was a general acceptance that the islands were in decline, the economy was stagnant, morale low and that people were leaving.[14] Comedian Eddie Izzard quipped that we only needed them 'for strategic sheep purposes'.

Thatcher had passed the Nationality Act in 1981, which was designed to deny Hong Kong Chinese the right of abode in Britain, but it also excluded 800 Falkland Islanders, nearly half the population. In diplomatic terms, the Thatcher Government was sending out signals to the Argentinians that said 'come and take them'. There was even a confidential report containing the so-called Hong Kong solution, which suggested surrendering ownership of the islands to Argentina and having them simultaneously grant Britain a lease.[15]

Unlike Callaghan, who sent a naval force south in 1977, Thatcher did nothing to prove to them that she would defend the islands against attack.[16] The Labour prime minister had dispatched a Royal Navy mini-task force including the nuclear powered hunter-killer submarine, HMS *Dreadnought*, accompanied by two frigates and two support vessels. The Foreign Secretary credited this tiny flotilla with deterring a full-scale invasion. Papers released to the National Archives show that David Owen insisted the mission be conducted in intense secrecy. Not even the crews were told where they were going. While the Argentinian Government was privately warned by the British that there was a nuclear submarine in the area, the rest of the world was unaware. The papers show a high degree of nervousness within Whitehall over the operation; not least about its legality.[17] David Owen, then Foreign Secretary, explains:

We did put down a naval submarine with the rules of engagement to shoot torpedoes across them if they came in, in '77 which we feared they might during the negotiations. It all got rather down played because Jim Callaghan claimed that it was a deterrent. It wasn't a deterrent at all, he was wrong on that, he was just an old man who'd slightly forgotten, kidded himself and talked to MI6. But the fact is that I was in charge of that element, and it was [a] totally secret deployment because we thought we might have to do it again and again, difficult negotiations.[18]

However, no one expected Argentina to do anything quite so foolhardy, and when General Galtieri invaded, Thatcher was taken completely by surprise. This critical moment, more than anything else, saw the birth of her reputation for ruthless decisiveness. Shocked and angry, Mrs Thatcher launched a task force to retake the islands, 8,000 miles away in the South Atlantic, arguing that she was going to defend the islanders' choice to be British.

'Can we do it?' she asked Admiral Sir Henry Leach, the First Sea Lord.

'We can, Prime Minister,' said Leach. 'If we don't do it, if we pussyfoot … we'll be living in a different country whose word will count for little.'[19]

The prime minister was determined not to 'appease' the Argentine dictatorship, which had seized power in 1976 and presided over the disappearance of 30,000 of its citizens, a stance that resonated strongly with the British public disheartened by years of defeatism and retreats during the 1970s. Consciously modelling herself on Churchill, she insisted that the Argentine forces must be made to withdraw for the sake of British prestige and national honour. Galtieri had wrongly gambled that she wouldn't fight so hard, and had banked on retaking the islands to lend him a much-needed propaganda coup with which to shore up his flagging political karma at home.[20]

On the morning of Monday, 5 April, sixty hours after her first fighting words, the fleet sailed. 'She felt that dictators shouldn't just be allowed to use force to overrule the rule of law, and she felt that very passionately,' said Cecil Parkinson, a member of her War Cabinet. 'So from day one she was in deadly earnest that the armed forces would do their job.'[21] Lord Carrington felt it was, 'A courageous decision of hers, very courageous.'[22] Some among the military brass subsequently confessed that they were looking at the prime minister and thinking, 'How can we explain our activities to a woman?' However, Mrs Thatcher never delayed, or denied her commanders what they wanted,[23] although there was a pessimistic view at the Ministry of Defence, who believed that the British Navy wasn't prepared for a major battle in the South Atlantic.[24]

Alexander Haig, then Reagan's Secretary of State, was startled by the prime minister's determination and urged her to compromise. At the end of the first full day of meetings with Mrs Thatcher and her cabinet, the story goes that he walked into his suite at Claridge's, threw his jacket on a chair, and barked to an aide, 'Get me a drink. That's a hell of a tough lady.'[25]

A chill even developed between Thatcher and Reagan over the issue. Reagan sent a message to Thatcher urging her to accept the concessions the US were suggesting.[26] Haig persuaded Reagan to call Thatcher and encourage her to take her place at the negotiating table. 'Haig was bad,' states Lord Carrington. 'Weinberger, who was the Secretary for Defence, helped us a very great deal, but Haig was, you know, wishy-washy.'[27]

'Cap Weinberger was pushing every bloody available bit of stuff our way, he had huge importance in the Falklands War,' explains David Owen.[28]

Reagan found himself at the wrong end of a caustic phone conversation in which her words were 'more forceful than friendly'.[29]

'Just suppose Alaska was invaded,' Thatcher said, and continued:

I didn't lose some of my best ships and some of my finest lives to leave quietly under a ceasefire without the Argentinians withdrawing ... Ron I'm not handing over ... I'm not handing over the islands now ... This is a democracy and our island, and the very worst thing for democracy would be if we failed now.[30]

Reagan was left stammering out the odd word, trying to break Margaret's diatribe.[31] Margaret displayed the kind of candour which, in her words, could 'only be possible among the closest of friends. With everyone else, we're merely *nice!*'[32]

The queen supported the prime minister's action, not only in her role as monarch of the invaded country, but as Head of the Commonwealth. She was also in the position of being a mother. Her son, Prince Andrew, was a 22-year-old helicopter pilot in the Royal Navy, serving on the aircraft carrier HMS *Invincible*. There were those in government who felt that sending the prince to the Falklands was too great a risk, as he would become a natural target. The queen overruled that.

'Mrs Thatcher was very concerned about the queen's son,' said Cecil Parkinson. 'The queen made it quite clear that she did not expect her son to have any favours done, bearing in mind he was going to be a helicopter pilot which is a tricky job anyway, especially in the South Atlantic.'[33] Michael Mann, the queen's chaplain, stated she said, 'No. He's a serving officer. He must take his turn with the rest.'[34] Although Andrew was never involved in direct combat, he flew his Sea King helicopter in a number of diversionary actions, transported troops and conducted search and rescue operations which could have put him in danger. He was once even on the deck when Exocet missiles were fired at the ship.[35] When an Exocet missile hit the container vessel *Atlantic Conveyor*, there were excited rumours in Argentina that it was the prince's ship *Invincible* which had gone down.[36]

Like other army families, the queen and Prince Philip watched the progress of the war on the television. Unlike the other families, she also received bulletins from Downing Street. Six days after the first British landings on the islands the queen spoke publicly about the war. 'Before I begin I would like to say one thing, our thoughts today are with those who are in the South Atlantic and our prayers are for their success and safe return to their homes and loved ones.' After a moment's silence she added, 'Ordinary life must go on.' Alan Clark stated that:

> The queen's attitude during the Falklands War was something of a mystery to many of us. She was not nearly as forthright at the outset as one might have expected … She was also, by then, a little wary of the role that Mrs Thatcher was assuming, She was not gung-ho at all, whereas George VI would have been totally gung-ho, as so would George V; no question about that. As for Victoria, she'd have actually been at sea with the task force, stood off with *Britannia*.[37]

'The military,' explains David Owen:

> think they have a direct line to the queen, she encourages that and to some extent she has that feeling about diplomatic service and ambassadors … So she feels a very special responsibility to them during war, and I think on the Falklands, Philip and they must have told her, and she must have understood the extraordinary risks we were taking.[38]

The queen, like most of the Establishment, was haunted by the ghost of Suez and the burden of history. As her former press secretary, Ron Allison, explains, 'I think the queen would have the mixed feelings and reservations about going to war with its consequent loss of life.'[39]

Although the warrior queen and the real queen were not quite onside, the Falklands War served to remind the people of the traditional link between the royal family and the services. Her father, George VI, had fought at the Battle of Jutland during the First World War. Prince Philip had a hero's record earned in the Second World War at the Battle of Matapan, and now Prince Andrew was a serving officer. For all Mrs Thatcher's jingoism, the forces viewpoint was stated clearly by Brigadier Julian Thompson, the second-in-command of the British land forces, 'You don't mind dying for the queen and country, but you certainly don't want to die for politicians.'[40]

The only criticism the royal family faced at this moment was over *Britannia*, when it was announced that the royal yacht would not be used as a hospital ship, though this was meant to be her function during wartime. These rumblings grew louder when the *Canberra* was taken off a cruise and sent to the South Atlantic, as hundreds of people's holidays had to be postponed or cancelled. The official reason given was that *Britannia* used the wrong type of fuel and could not have been refuelled that far from home base. Many found that excuse not entirely convincing, although it was the truth.[41] As journalist Philip Hall stated, 'it is odd that such an oversight should have occurred when the Duke of Edinburgh was a frequent user of the ship and had spent twelve years in the navy.'[42]

On 7 June, in the middle of this conflict, the president and Nancy Reagan arrived at Windsor Castle to have a state dinner in the president's honour in the historical St George's Hall. The couple arrived by helicopter, and were assigned a seven-room suite in the Lancaster Tower, with two bedrooms, two dressing rooms, two bathrooms and a main sitting room with portraits of the queen's ancestors by Hans Holbein and with sweeping views of the Long Walk in the adjoining park. It was Mrs Thatcher's aim to buttress Reagan's ideological sympathy for her policies with a personal relationship between the Reagans and the Windsors.[43] It worked. For Reagan, the state visit to Britain was the pinnacle of a lifetime's achievement. For Nancy, a devotee of the British royal family, to stay overnight in the castle was an experience she would treasure.[44] Nancy had visited London the year before for the wedding of Prince Charles and Lady Diana Spencer, when she had arrived with a retinue of twenty-eight staff (including one astrologer) and irritated the queen by insisting on an invitation to a private family party. The queen had felt the reach of America's first lady was extending well beyond her rank, and at one point referred to her as 'that damned woman'.[45]

The queen and the president both had a passion for horses and went out riding.[46] For an hour, Elizabeth II and Reagan walked, trotted and cantered on their 8 mile ride. The president let it be known that he found the British Head of State 'charming', 'down-to-earth' and observed 'she was in charge of that animal!' The two heads of state chatted to each other like buddies, while Nancy Reagan followed behind with Prince Philip in a carriage. The British Ambassador, Nicholas Henderson, noted that the Reagan's key image-maker and deputy chief of staff, Michael Deaver, 'Invariably lit up at the prospect' of the ride. It was very successful and a photo opportunity not to be missed, although the queen was not much amused at having to parade up and down before 100 members of the invited press, irritated that she was being used for a political context. Reagan, in a perfectly fitted sports jacket, had gone for an old-time Hollywood look which he carried off with ease.[47]

In a speech to both houses of Parliament on 8 June, the president spoke of the alliance of the two countries against aggression, 'These young men fight for a cause, for the belief that armed aggression must not be allowed to succeed'. Later, at the state banquet the queen stood up to toast the president, 'Prince Philip and I are especially delighted that you have come to be our guests at Windsor Castle, since this has been the home of kings and queens of our country for over 900 years …' She spoke of drawing comfort 'from the understanding of our position shown by the American people'.[48] The president sat next to the queen, and Nancy was placed to the right of Prince Philip. The Thatchers were seated further down the table, with the royal dukes and duchesses.[49]

At that precise moment on 8 June 1982, news began to trickle in that British forces preparing for a final assault on Port Stanley had suffered a disastrous set-back. A daylight attempt to land troops had come under attack from Argentine planes. Two ships, *Sir Galahad* and *Sir Tristram*, were bombed. Fifty-one soldiers on board were dead and many more injured. The Argentines believed they had killed 900 British soldiers that day, enough to halt the British advance, a fact that could not be immediately denied in the House of Commons by John Nott, the Defence Secretary, for fear it would disabuse the government in Buenos Aires of the fatal news.[50]

Six days later, on 14 June, British forces retook Port Stanley and Thatcher immediately drove down to the House of Commons to announce victory. The queen also had a personal reason to be grateful: Prince Andrew, who telephoned her six days later, after the war ended, was alive and unharmed.[51]

The Falklands had been an enormous gamble, 255 British servicemen killed, 649 Argentines and three Falkland Islanders dead, not to mention the incongruity of spending billions fighting for a group of remote islands Britain didn't want. Winning the Falklands War was Thatcher's finest hour. It confirmed her courage and enhanced her stature, transforming her from mere party politician into a national leader. The war boosted Britain's credibility and prestige at a time when such a boost was badly needed. The nation rediscovered itself, and this created a bond between the people and their leader not seen since the Second World War.[52] Mrs Thatcher proved that she could unite the country behind her in times of crisis. Her personal popularity rating soared to 59 per cent.[53]

Immediately after the victory, Thatcher and the royal family enjoyed their warmest period. At a lunch Cecil Parkinson was hosting after being made Chancellor of the Duchy of Lancaster, he spoke to the queen:

The queen very kindly asked me what I was doing for a holiday and I told her; and she asked me what the prime minister was doing, and I made a rather flippant remark that 'Ma'am the prime minister thinks only lazy people have holidays'. And the queen said, 'Well that is wrong you know, after the Falklands she has had a very turbulent time, she must have a holiday and a proper holiday.' And at the end of the day she was about to leave and she called me over and said, 'They tell me you have influence with the prime minister … if you will tell her she should have a proper holiday so will I.' And I said 'Ma'am, it's, you know, rather easier for you than for me.' But nevertheless, I did tell her, but it struck me that the queen was genuinely concerned. And so I think she probably did think that Mrs Thatcher on occasions worked too hard … I think it was quite a revealing little incident.[54]

'The queen's view of Margaret Thatcher,' David Owen states:

I believe changed a great deal after the Falklands. I think the whole of the royal family's view of her changed. At long last they had a prime minister who made them feel proud to be the royal family and her proud to be queen … Margaret Thatcher gained a huge plus from the Falklands. You know, like a mother she watched that thing very, very closely. The queen had lived through the humiliation of Suez and now it could be argued that shame had been put to rest.[55]

There was a downside. 'The Falklands Factor' validated Margaret Thatcher as mother of the nation.[56] The queen no longer seemed solely to occupy that role anymore. There were two queens in the hive. In victory, Thatcher made the mistake of allowing herself, and not the queen, to take the salute at the Mansion House during the force's victory parade through the City of London. Eyebrows were now raised at Buckingham Palace[57] – no member of the royal family had been invited. In the 1945 parade celebrating the victory in the Second World War, Churchill and Attlee were positioned at a discreet distance from the saluting stage.[58]

'I mean, Churchill never held a parade,' said David Owen:

He never held a parade, they [politicians] were invited onto the thing, but the people who took the salute were the king and the queen. Churchill would never have countenanced that a prime minister should do that, and he understood the role, he had after all been in the military.[59]

Owen feels this is the moment Thatcher's ego took over:

My diagnosis of Margaret Thatcher is that she has naturally [a] hubristic tendency which most leading politicians have. The queen has got no hubris and is a fine example where she's not changed at all by it. Thatcher was changed by it, and it gripped her I think in particular for a period after the Falklands War.[60]

Indeed, as the crowds sang 'Rule Britannia', the victorious prime minister seemed transfigured. 'What a wonderful parade it has been,' she said, 'surpassing all our expectations.' Wearing a broad-brimmed white hat with navy ribbon, navy blue suit and white gloves, Margaret radiated vainglory. Writer Piers Brandon said, 'This pageant was her apotheosis. It sanctified a heroic egotism and aggravated a raucous intolerance of dissent.'[61]

'She wanted to be identified as the victor in the Falklands,' explained Edwina Currie.[62]

The queen may have reflected that the Falklands victory was very much Mrs Thatcher's, but other people felt it was odd not to see the queen, who is head of the armed forces, standing on the dais.[63] The sight of her taking the salute with her military leaders drove home a point not lost on either woman. As historian David Cannadine points out:

> It was Thatcher's war. She was responsible for the military direction of the war, so to the extent that the nation rallied, it rallied behind her rather than the queen. The queen was curiously low-key, an absentee.[64]

Mrs Thatcher allowed herself the pleasure of teasing those who doubted her. She hosted a dinner at Number 10 to thank about eighty of the officers who had carried out the Falklands campaign. She was the only woman present, and after dinner she stood up and said, 'Gentlemen. Shall we join the ladies?' The room convulsed with laughter.[65]

There was also positive news on the fiscal front. Just when 364 top economists sent a letter to *The Times* rejecting Thatcher's monetary policies and claiming they would deepen the depression to the point of provoking civil strife, the economy started to recover as inflation retreated and house prices recovered. The prime minister unabashedly claimed an economic miracle.[66]

Margaret now grew in self-confidence and a sense of her own rightness on every issue. The general election in 1983 was inevitable. Thatcher won an outright landslide with a 144 seat majority. On polling day, 9 June, her daughter Carol asked how, when other leaders had been exhausted by such campaigns, she managed to look 'younger and prettier'. 'It's the job I most want to do in the world,' was her mother's reply.[67]

Thatcher's election victory was almost a coronation. Until this point, her position in the Conservative Party had been an oddity. She was a woman, she came from outside the traditional ruling class, and she had held no great office of state before becoming prime minister. There had always been the risk that she would be deposed by her party the moment she became an election liability.[68] On the day Port Stanley fell, all this changed. This woman with no experience of defence or foreign policy was now a warrior queen. She was Boudicca leading the Iceni against the Romans, and Queen Elizabeth at Tilbury defeating the Spanish Armada. During the early stages of the war, Enoch Powell reminded Thatcher of her 'Iron Lady' soubriquet and added, 'In the next week or two this nation ... will learn of what metal she is made'. After victory in the Falklands, Powell said, 'The substance under test consisted of ferrous matter of the highest quality'.[69]

This new Gloriana developed her own court of flatterers[70] who came and went like Dudley, Essex and Raleigh in Tudor times.[71] 'Queen Margaret' even adopted the coldly regal expression when ministers displeased her – 'shall we withdraw our love?'[72] Those within her own Cabinet, who still believed consensus politics could work, had the love withdrawn. One by one, Ian Gilmour, Francis Pym, Jim Prior, Mark Carlisle, Norman St John-Stevas and Christopher Soames all found themselves in political exile.

Margaret would come to dominate the Cabinet to the point that her colleagues viewed her as the most overbearing leader they had ever known.[73] Lord Carrington argues, 'If you really want to change things, you have to be slightly blinkered ... if you're not blinkered, people will tell you you can't do it'.[74]

Robin Butler, her principal private secretary, felt her management style was because 'she lacked self-confidence. That was why she was so assertive. She had to pump herself up on adrenaline before any big occasion.'[75]

Another close colleague of Thatcher's, Jonathan Aitken, who dated her daughter Carol, felt she needed to master her brief right down to the smallest detail because of this. 'This over-preparation enabled her to browbeat her ministers.'[76]

There was also a new queenly, even imperial, style to the prime minister as her triumphs made her appear invincible. Insiders joked that the initials MTFS, which stood for Medium Term Financial Strategy, actual stood for 'Margaret Thatcher For Sovereign'.[77]

During the following January, when Thatcher visited the Falkland Islands, the event had the feel and tone of a royal progress. Conor Cruise O'Brien wrote in the *Observer* that she was developing a parallel monarchy, becoming 'a new style elective monarch, as distinct from the recessive ceremonial one'.[78] 'She got grander and grander,' recalls Whitehall advisor, Sir Clive Whitmore, 'and I thought this would have gone down badly with the queen.'[79]

Just as events were going so well for Margaret, her old friend President Reagan became an embarrassment, upsetting the queen, and putting a strain on the Buckingham Palace/Downing Street relationship. By invading the tiny Communist ruled island of Grenada, with a population of just 100,000, the president of the United States completely forgot that Elizabeth II was Queen of Grenada. Although the island had been ruled by Marxists since 1979, Grenada was part of the Commonwealth and retained Elizabeth II as head of state.[80] That the British Queen could be the sovereign to a bunch of communists was rather confusing to the Americans.

Reagan had been enjoying a golfing weekend in Georgia when the Cuban-backed Marxist Prime Minister of Grenada, Maurice Bishop, was overthrown and executed by a rival Marxist dictator, General Hudson Austin. The Governor-General of the island, Sir Paul Scoon, who acted as Her Majesty's representative, asked the US Government to send troops to restore order.[81] Legally speaking, Scoon was not obliged constitutionally to seek the queen's permission before exercising his residual powers. However, it was his duty to inform her of his intention to request intervention and his failure to do so could render the request constitutionally invalid.[82]

Scoon was not alone in feeling American intervention was needed. The leaders of Jamaica, Barbados, St Vincent's, St Lucia, Antigua and Dominica wanted US intervention without delay in case their positions were threatened by Grenadian inspired insurrections.[83] They were not alarmists. Prime Minister Dame Eugenia Charles of Dominica had survived an abortive coup launched from Grenada the previous year.

Reagan's sense of urgency was heightened by the fact that on the island were 1,000 American students who could be taken hostage, much like the sixty-six US Embassy staff kidnapped by an Islamic mob in Tehran in November 1979. When Reagan asked how long it would take to mobilise an invasion force to restore order to the island and protect the students and was told forty-eight hours, he simply gave the order: 'Do it!'[84] An invasion was quickly and efficiently mounted and the objective achieved.

Everyone, however, had overlooked the fact that one of Elizabeth's many titles was Queen of Grenada, and she was furious that she had neither been consulted nor informed by Scoon, or anybody else. It was as if she was irrelevant. Buckingham Palace let it be known (or did not effectively deny) that, as *The Times* put it, she disapproved of the 'notion that foreign powers may walk into member states' of the Commonwealth without warning.[85] The queen summoned Margaret Thatcher to explain why Her Majesty had been obliged to hear the news from the BBC and not from the prime minister herself.

Thatcher's view of the Marxist coup was that the new regime was a 'change of degree rather than in kind' and thought Reagan's concern 'exaggerated'. This opinion was shared by Reagan's defence secretary, Casper Weinberger, but he had been overruled by the president. Margaret had made her position clear to him, when he had floated the notion of an invasion to her just hours beforehand. 'This action will be seen as intervention by a western country in the internal affairs of a small independent nation,' she warned. 'I cannot conceal that I am deeply disturbed.'[86] The president wrote in his diary, 'She's upset and doesn't think we should do it. I couldn't tell her it had started.'

Reagan had made a conscious decision, knowing that Thatcher would disapprove, of not telling her in advance. 'We did not even inform the British beforehand, because I thought it would increase the possibility of a leak at our end and elevate the risk to our students,' he later explained.[87] That wasn't his only reason. He wanted to purge America of what he called the 'post-Vietnam syndrome' which meant that American military action internationally was always haunted by the ghost of the disastrous foreign war. He had also perhaps seen how Thatcher's victory in the South Atlantic had exorcised the ghost of the Suez Crisis. 'I understood what Vietnam had meant for the country, but I believed the United States couldn't remain spooked forever by this experience to the point where it refused to stand up and defend its legitimate national security interests.'[88]

On the morning of 25 October 1983, 1,900 Army Rangers and Marines stormed their targets. Nineteen Americans were killed and more than 100 injured as they met strong resistance for such a small island. The mission, however, was a success, the leaders of the coup were quickly rounded up, and the American students found safe and well. Thatcher was profoundly unhappy. 'I felt dismayed and let down by what had happened,' she recalled, 'at best, the British Government had been made to look impotent; at worst we looked deceitful.'[89] Thatcher pointed out to Reagan the effect his action was liable to have on British opinion at a time when her government was continuing with the deployment of cruise missiles. There were torrents of indignation in the British press about intervention in the affairs of a Commonwealth country.[90] Privately, the prime minister was 'apoplectic, the walls cracked,' said Edwina Currie, 'Reagan clearly didn't understand that British sovereignty was such an issue. To Margaret Thatcher it was everything.'[91]

Thatcher had to attend the House of Commons to explain how a member of the Commonwealth had been invaded by our closest ally, and then had to defend the invader in the face of widespread condemnation.[92] However, Reagan had pulled through for her during the Falklands War, and she would be a steadfast friend. 'We stand by the United States and will continue to do so in the larger alliances,' said the Prime Minister. 'The United States is the final guarantor of freedom in Europe.'[93]

Thatcher, as David Owen points out, knew post-Falklands that the president 'sacrificed quite a bit in South America to come on board'.[94] Thatcher knew she had to swallow the invasion, but as Lord Carrington pointed out, 'He ought to have known better, really. He ought to have said "do you mind?"'[95]

'Mrs Thatcher was outraged, and she let President Reagan know it, but they talked it through and they decided that the overall importance of the alliance was more important than the friction that this incident caused,' said Cecil Parkinson.[96]

The queen, however, was irritated with the prime minister for letting the Americans get away with it. A legend grew up around the incident. There was speculation that one of their regular Tuesday audiences was postponed because of the queen's displeasure, and when it took place, the queen showed her annoyance to the prime minister by not inviting her to sit down during the meeting. Afterwards, she reported Thatcher's reaction, 'Only two curtsies today'.[97]

'I think prime ministers have to take day to day decisions, which quite frankly the monarch is above,' said Cecil Parkinson. He continued:

The monarch can have a view, but it is a constitutional monarchy and the government of the day has to run the country ... you don't want in any way to get at cross purposes with the queen; but the government had to operate in the world where you do get your hands dirty from time to time, but would you want the queen to get hers? She is above all that.[98]

In fact, the queen's ignorance was beneficial, otherwise she would have been in the difficult position of either having to betray the secret of an independent country of which she was head of state, or else having to withhold important information from the British Government (which had also been kept in the dark). While the queen's possessiveness could be interpreted as an instance of her protective interest in Commonwealth countries, in Grenada the US troops were greeted as liberators and democracy was restored.[99]

On a BBC broadcast on 30 October, Thatcher offered her own principled view of her opposition to what the USA had done:

We use our force to defend our way of life. We do not use it to walk into independent sovereign countries ... If you're going to pronounce a new law that, wherever communism reigns against the will of the people, even though it's happened internally, there the USA shall enter, then we are going to have really terrible wars in the world.[100]

6

MURDOCH, MAGGIE AND HER MAJESTY

I always said a row with the queen would do Mrs Thatcher a lot of good.
You fought a civil war about this once.
Rupert Murdoch, to Woodrow Wyatt

As the British Establishment continued to turn up its nose at the grocer's daughter, Margaret Thatcher formed a powerful alliance with Rupert Murdoch, who loathed the British monarchy as deeply as any radical left-winger. Thatcher handed Rupert unprecedented control of the nation's media, and in return she got his newspaper editors' unwavering political support during three general elections. The republican press tycoon devised a commercially successful formula of royal gossip, anti-royal attacks, pro-Thatcherite articles and jingoism which he applied throughout his vast media empire. It undermined the queen, helped keep Thatcher in political office and made him very rich.

Throughout her 'reign' as prime minister, Thatcher's anxiety and determination to keep the Murdoch media empire on side was, in the words of her biographer, John Campbell, the 'grubbiest face of Thatcherism'.[1] Although Rupert shared the prime minister's sense of being an outsider, a dissident bent on smashing archaic vested interest and viscerally hostile to the liberal elite, theirs was largely a pragmatic alliance.

These two radicals were never fully in harmony. Murdoch disliked being shouted down by a mere woman. Mrs Thatcher, who never once mentioned him in her memoirs,[2] thought the *News of the World* 'such a filthy paper'.[3] Unlike subsequent prime ministers, including Tony Blair and David Cameron, she was careful not to be too beholden to him. Cecil Parkinson believed Thatcher was 'too much of a Methodist, if you like, to get indebted to people'.[4] 'Governments are rather pathetic if they allow the media to dictate their actions. Blair was often pathetic,' suggested Sir Bernard Ingham.[5]

Murdoch, nevertheless, enjoyed a powerful place in her inner circle, not as a courtier, but an influential independent ally rather like US President Ronald Reagan. Like Reagan, Murdoch had direct access to her whenever he sought it. He was the only newspaper proprietor asked to the Downing Street lunch to mark her tenth anniversary in 1989, and was several times invited to spend Christmas with the Thatcher family at Chequers. He was one of the privileged few given access to the back door of Number 10, which he kept using long after she had resigned. 'She and Rupert Murdoch believed in exactly the same things,' argues Tim Bell:

They both believed in work creation. They both believed in no taxation. They both believed in international free trade. They both believed in the person. They believed in the same things. If you saw Murdoch's first Thatcher lecture at the Centre for Policy Studies, he could have been her standing there speaking.[6]

Edwina Curries feels for Thatcher, 'Murdoch was all about free speech. His satellite television stations would have been broadcasting into the Eastern bloc. She saw him as a force for democracy.'[7]

Today, Murdoch is probably the most powerful anti-monarchist in the world. Everything about the British royal family annoys, repels and nauseates him. In his view, they're a symbol of an outdated class system which is unproductive, unearned and the 'apex of snobbery'.[8] Like the trade unions, they are the ultimate closed shop. Murdoch saw an opportunity to scrutinise the behaviour of the royal family and expose them if they misbehaved. To him this represented the double delight of chipping away at the monarch's standing and driving up his newspaper profits. The Murdoch empire came to rely on royal stories to the point of dependency. 'Diana mania' fuelled the great roaring bull market for newspapers in 1980s and 1990s Britain.[9] Stories of the Windsors sold copy, vast quantities of it, and the *Sun*'s profits jumped, throwing off $50 million a year in free cash flow. This meant the *Sun* could finance upward of $500 million in new acquisitions.[10]

When Murdoch bought the *News of the World* in 1968 he was only 37 years old, and was still referred to in his own country as the 'boy publisher'. To the British, Murdoch appeared to be an unsophisticated colonial, brash and without respect for the Establishment or royalty. He seemed completely without pretensions or social aspirations. Indeed, he carefully nurtured this image as an outsider who was willing to defend the hard-working common man and uphold democracy through the medium of his newspapers. When Murdoch appeared before Parliament at Westminster in July 2011, he stated incredulously that his father wasn't a wealthy man. This wasn't just him being disingenuous, it was a bizarre denial.

Murdoch was a posh boy who had been born into incredible privilege, had inherited wealth, influence and a first-class pedigree among the Australian elite. If he ever fought with governments, the battleground was more likely to be over regulation and fiscal controls than human rights or championing the under- dog. Young Rupert was sent to Geelong Grammar, an independent school whose alumni included Prince Charles, the King of Malaysia, and John Gorton, a former Australian prime minister. He later completed his education at Oxford University, where he could afford the best rooms, his own car and a generous allowance from his father, Sir Keith Murdoch.

Daddy had been head of the Melbourne Herald group of newspapers, and owned the *Adelaide News* (inherited by Rupert on his death) and the *Brisbane Courier Mail*. Murdoch's mother was Dame Elizabeth, who had been honoured by the queen for her charity work. The family lived in the wealthy suburb of Toorak and owned a country estate. Sir Keith wielded considerable political influence and was the ideal person to instruct his son on how to harness the power that could come from ownership of the press and to understand its interaction with politics. When Rupert was barely 30 years old, photographs of him appeared in the press standing beside US President John Kennedy. He was in every sense a member of an elite Australian aristocracy.

Although Rupert Murdoch enjoyed Oxford as a young man, he was critical of English values, and he displayed contempt for the English class system. He even had a bust of Lenin in his room at university.[11] Curiously, it did not prevent him from enjoying to the full a *Brideshead* lifestyle as an undergraduate. Few 21 year olds can blag a new Rolls-Royce for a weekend, or drive a new car around Europe, wreck it and then send it home to his father. Few are able to stay in the best hotels in Deauville, lose money at the gaming tables and then cable the 'not wealthy' family back home for more funds.[12]

While not an entirely self-made man, Rupert's Aussie roots meant he honestly favoured a more egalitarian spirit, and he refused to be held back by social convention or conservatism. Murdoch's first step on the path to political power in Britain was in buying the *News of the World* for a knockdown price from Sir William Carr. He would later describe this acquisition as the 'biggest steal since the Great Train Robbery'.[13] Carr represented everything Rupert hated about the decadent British upper class, he was a 'two bottles of scotch a day man', and said to be a brilliant mathematician before lunch. He would invite his staff to his palatial stately home in Sussex where they played croquet, and flunkies served champagne.[14] From their point of view, the Carrs were equally horrified by the arrival of the coarse colonial, and Rupert upset Lady Carr by lighting up a cigar before lunch. They took his money despite their misgivings and, although Rupert promised Sir William that he would remain as chairman, he later broke his word, claiming the British baronet had allowed the newspaper to decline into an even more parlous state than he had realised.[15]

At the *News of the World*, Murdoch lowered the tabloid's tone further with a formula of naughty vicars, knickers, sex and a sports section unrivalled by the competition. Rupert was reviled as a smut merchant and treated like a social pariah by London's elite, but the paper's circulation climbed to 6 million.[16]

Then he made the mistake of paying £21,000 to Christine Keeler for her memoirs of the Profumo Affair, six years after the event, thus reopening old wounds within the Establishment. Profumo had been rehabilitating himself following his resignation from the government by working for a charity helping drug addicts and ex-offenders in the East End of London, and Murdoch's conduct was viewed as ungentlemanly. The Australian outsider was invited to defend himself on David Frost's television chat show. In front of a studio audience, Frost ripped into him and accused him of attempting to destroy the newly reformed Profumo. Murdoch was badly shaken[17] and blamed the Establishment for whipping up the row. Frost ridiculed this as a conspiracy theory based on the anachronistic assumption that Britain was still governed by an old boy network scheming to resist change.[18]

However, the debacle only added to Murdoch's tarnished image as a coarse barrow boy, ignorant about the subtlety of British fair play. The satirical magazine *Private Eye* nicknamed him the 'dirty digger', an alias that he hated but it has now stuck for decades.[19]

Fleet Street in the 1960s and 1970s was a brutal place to work. Rupert clearly didn't know the rules, so he rewrote them. At first, the popular wisdom was that 'Rupert's Shit-Sheet' or 'The News of the Screws', as it was nicknamed, would last no longer than six months. When, a year later, Murdoch bought the *Sun*, the hacks on the street also felt that the Aussie had been sold a pup. However, at a more informed level, City analysts and newspaper boardrooms showed a patronising admiration for his success in the backwater that was Australia, and they felt his British papers suited his inherent vulgarity.

Murdoch now made the *Sun* snappy and sexy; choosing as its editor a talented Yorkshireman and former communist, Larry Lamb. Lamb drove to work in a company Mercedes sports car bearing the number plate SUN 1[20] and introduced topless models, the infamous 'Page Three Girls', into the mix. There was another sea change: from the moment Murdoch took power in Fleet Street he wanted the royals to be reported as any normal story would be, with no special favours. Tim Bell said:

> Rupert was a republican; he's a republican. He doesn't believe in the concept of monarchy. So, he considers that they can be talked about, in the same way that anybody else can be talked about. He doesn't think they have any privilege that should entitle them to do bad things and then not be commented on.[21]

Harry Arnold, one of the journalists who caused Buckingham Palace a large number of headaches, says he believes the queen's reign saw a revolution in attitudes. Asked what caused this, his reply echoes that of another colleague, Ann Leslie. They both answered in two words, 'Rupert Murdoch'.[22] Despite the fact that the National Union of Journalists censured Murdoch for debasing the standards of their profession, the *Sun* tripled its circulation to 3 million in four years, making it the most profitable unit in his growing empire.[23]

Once upon a time, in what must have seemed to the queen as the golden days, respectful court correspondents covered royal affairs virtually as dictated by the press office at Buckingham Palace.[24] Prurient interest in the royal family's private lives were off-limits, and the newspapers would be expected to obsequiously attend royal events and file servile copy that tiptoed around protocol.[25] Even when they knew a great deal about stories such as Edward VII's affair with Mrs Simpson, which led to the abdication crisis, they never broke ranks. It was a cosy little world that Murdoch blew apart.[26]

The queen and her family obviously do not want complete silence to reign. Otherwise, there might be no cheers for them when they ride out in their carriages and cut ribbons to open shopping centres. Invisibility can foster unpopularity, as the later years of the reign of Queen Victoria proved. The queen's old press secretary, Sir Richard Colville, always believed that no news was good news. His replacement, William Heseltine, believed that the queen must be seen to be believed.[27] In fact, the royals want it both ways, coverage of their public office, with the privacy that an ordinary person might expect. This is impossible, as the private lives of public figures are seen as a legitimate subject for press attention. The royal family don't accept this argument, and its members complain about intrusion with arguments such as 'the monarchy cannot answer back'.[28]

Over the years, the queen was repeatedly stung as she discovered that Murdoch's brand of cheque book journalism carried far more clout than the meagre wages she paid members of her household. His impertinent publications magnified the flaws in the royal family as they printed scurrilous stories and candid photos. Without the protective blanket of reverence, the royals and their advisors found themselves in a fluster. The queen attempted to lecture editors, obtained injunctions and went to court to stop servants selling secrets. The floodgates were opened as Murdoch declared it open season on the Windsors.[29]

One of the first victims of this new era was the queen's sister, Princess Margaret. In February 1976, a photographer snapped a picture of her with her toy boy, Roddy Llewellyn, on the island of Mustique. The *News of the World* published the photo and the princess's husband, Lord Snowdon, asked for a divorce. He then held a press conference in which he wished his wife well, asked for their children's understanding and professed his undying admiration for the royal family.[30]

The queen's second son, Prince Andrew, was soon identified as another potential target for stories by the red top hacks. The prince fulfilled his tabloid potential by earning himself the nickname, 'Randy Andy'. His girlfriend Koo Stark had even appeared in a British soft porn movie called *Emily* which showed her taking part in a lesbian shower scene. Andrew did himself no favours either, when pictures were published of him skinny-dipping in Canada under the byline, 'it's strip ahoy as naked Prince Andrew larks about in the river'.

Next came breakfast-in-bed details about Andrew's entertaining women in his private apartments at Buckingham Palace. 'The women were always young and fanciable,' a former palace kitchen aid told the *Sun*, 'and Andrew was always so sure of his chances, so cheeky, that he would order double bacon and eggs the night before.' In selling his story, the former kitchen helper violated the confidentiality agreement he had signed as a condition of employment. The queen was more incensed by his breach of contract than she was by his revelations, and she sued.

The *Sun* had paid the servant more than half a year's wages, so it wasn't that surprising that he had spilled the beans. His story made great reading, with much delicious tabloid detail that became a signature of the paper. Andrew's lover, Koo Stark, had romped through the palace kitchen in short skirts and skimpy T-shirts, wearing bright red dog tags that Andrew had given her after the Falklands War. The actress ordered the staff around and helped herself to the queen's favourite chocolates. The story ended with the promising teaser about the Princess of Wales: 'Tomorrow. When Barefoot Di Buttered My Toast.'[31]

The queen's lawyers obtained an injunction and the *Sun* responded with the headline, 'Queen Gags the *Sun*'.[32] She then sued for damages, deciding that a line must be drawn between legitimate public interest and salacious intrusion into their private lives. Her Majesty's press secretary issued the following terse statement:

The servant had breached an undertaking of confidence which all palace employees sign. In this declaration, they agree not to make any disclosures about their work at the palace. It is a legally binding document under civil law.[33]

Her Majesty was awarded damages which the *Sun* agreed to donate to the Newspaper Press Fund, plus payment of her legal costs. Koo Stark departed gracefully and maintained a discreet silence, but she could never shake off her identification with the queen's son.[34]

Her Majesty was further incensed after a photo appeared of her 6-year-old grandson, Peter Philips, twirling a dead pheasant by the neck during a bird shoot. She ordered reporters and photographers off the estate at Sandringham and barred them from Windsor. She tried, to no avail, to keep them away from all family events, including royal christenings.

Margaret Thatcher had also been an early victim of Murdoch's brutal brand of popularism, but she reacted very differently. As the new education secretary in 1970, the *Sun* had given her the infamous tag of 'Margaret Thatcher – Milk Snatcher'. It was an epithet that almost derailed her career, and Margaret had been in tears over the perceived cruelty of the *Sun*'s left-wing editor 'Red Larry', as he was known on the street. 'Why don't you chuck it in?' Denis sympathised when the family were together at Christmas. She responded with her now familiar steely glare and rasped, 'I'll see them in hell first. I will never be driven anywhere against my will.'[35]

The *Sun* had, at one point, even gone as far as to call her the most 'unpopular woman in the country'. In her autobiography, Thatcher wrote how she learned a valuable lesson from the experience. 'I had incurred the maximum of political odium for the minimum of political benefit.'[36] Five years later, she would manage to transform the *Sun*'s view of her. Its editorial staff would become 'her boys' and its editor her important political ally.[37]

The success of the *Sun*, particularly with its younger readership, made Murdoch a political power in Britain and Thatcher needed his support if she was ever going to become prime minister. As Conservative leader, Margaret knew she could rely on the support of papers such as the *Mail* and *Express* in the mass market. Both papers were already preaching to her existing supporters. The *Mail* did amazing work amongst the loyal Tories with its circulation of 1.5 million. However, during the 1970s the *Express* was more important, with a circulation of 3 million. Unfortunately, it had an aging readership and its circulation had fallen by half from 1970. When Thatcher won the leadership contest in 1975, she made every effort to woo both Rupert Murdoch and Larry Lamb.

The Thatcher-Murdoch alliance started to be forged when Thatcher sent key advisors like Geoffrey Howe and Nicholas Ridley round to Red Larry's office for 'chewing the fat' sessions in the evening. Margaret seemed, to Lamb, a more inspiring figure than either Ted Health or Harold Wilson and he saw real potential in her leadership. However, Murdoch was initially unenthusiastic about Margaret Thatcher, worrying that Larry Lamb's support for her would alienate the paper's working-class readership. He would telephone Lamb, asking with exasperation, 'Are you still pushing that bloody woman?'[38] However, when Murdoch began scenting her success he changed his anti-Thatcher position.[39]

Margaret, or 'Maggie', as the hacks liked to call her, also began to pay court with visits of her own. Sessions would begin with the new Leader of the Opposition being offered a glass of whisky, something she wasn't used to, which made her eyes water and her skin turn pink. She swallowed it to show she could be one of the boys. As the meetings warmed up, she would cross her legs demurely, flex her ankle and allow her shoe to dangle from the tip of her toe. She could play the girl card better than most, when needs must.

Lamb assumed a commanding but relaxed position, informally resting his back-side on the desk. When the hacks asked Mrs Thatcher questions, she would coyly turn to Larry and in a quiet voice ask, 'What do you think Larry?' Lamb would puff himself up with pride and lecture on the solutions to the country's problems. 'You know that's marvellous,' she would say. 'If I only had people like you who really know how to communicate. Absolutely marvellous.'

An important political partnership was thus forged between the ex-communist and the lady with the pearls. Mrs Thatcher's courtship was so effective that Lamb decided that she had become the 'tool' for causing a *Sun*-led political sea-change for the country. However, the switch to supporting the Tories was unpopular with many of the *Sun*'s journalists. Roger Carroll, the Labour-supporting political editor, left and was replaced by the ultra-Tory Walter Terry from the *Daily Express*. Murdoch further strengthened input by 'suggesting' Lamb should hire leader writer Ronnie Sparks to write, 'The *Sun* Says' column that always adopted an uncompromising Thatcherite line about everything.

Lamb became a regular visitor to the Thatcher family home in Flood Street, Chelsea, while the election strategy was being planned. Lamb was given freedom to lecture at great length about his own and his paper's merits in communicating with his readers. Thatcher was particularly grateful for headlines such as 'The Winter of Discontent' and 'Crisis, What Crisis?' Lamb also provided help in speech writing and, in return, Thatcher gave the *Sun* the inside track on the Tory campaign, carefully briefing the paper on the party's star performers.

Both Lamb and Murdoch realised the 1979 election wasn't about politics, but about personalities, in line with the growing influence of television. The Tory manifesto was tailored to the *Sun* readers' preoccupations with housing, the cost of living and immigration, including the sensational offer of selling off council houses at a discount to their tenants. On polling day, Lamb weighed in with his biggest single contribution, a 1,700 word leader, by far the longest political piece ever written in the *Sun*, or any other Fleet Street paper on election day:

> This is D-day, 'D' for decision. The first day of the rest of our lives. The *Sun* today wishes particularly to address itself to the traditional supporters of the Labour Party ... The *Sun* is not a Tory newspaper ... The *Sun* is, above all, a RADICAL newspaper. And we believe that this time the only radical proposals being put to you are being put by Maggie Thatcher and her Tory team ... The choice you have today is quite simply the choice between freedom and the shackles.

The leader went on to attack the Labour Party. 'The party has become the refuge of militants, Marxists, bullies and class war warriors it ... has all but destroyed the spirit of Britain ... That is the heaviest charge to lay against this government. That it has contrived to destroy Britain's belief in itself.'

Mrs Thatcher was cast in the role of national savior: 'With Jim (What Crisis?) Callaghan we look into the abyss. With Margaret Thatcher, there is a chance for us to look again to the skies ... The *Sun* says: Vote Tory. Stop the Rot. There may not be another chance.'

It worked. Margaret Thatcher won the election with 43.9 per cent of the vote against 36.9 per cent for Labour, giving her a comfortable majority of fifty-seven seats in the House of Commons. Courtship of the *Sun*'s working-class readership paid Thatcher large dividends. The 9 per cent swing among this demographic was almost double the national average of 5.1 per cent, and it delivered into the Conservative Party's hands a string of marginal seats in the midlands and north-west.[40]

The press and media went wild with excitement at the election of Britain's first female prime minister. The only major paper not to mention the election of Margaret Thatcher was *The Times*, still closed in the midst of an epic industrial dispute. The strike was symbolic of the crisis, and many speculated that it would never open again. The fact that two years later it was bought by Rupert Murdoch was symbolic of the 1980s triumph of meritocracy over Establishment.[41]

Mrs Thatcher was very, very grateful to the *Sun*. Larry Lamb was sent a letter thanking him for his help, and Margaret stated that she would strive to be worthy of his readers' support. The *Sun's* offices were decorated in blue bunting, rosettes, union jacks and portraits of the new prime minister to mark her regal attendance at the paper's victory celebrations.[42] Larry Lamb also found himself knighted, and after his investiture he insisted on being called 'Sir Larry', which only caused hilarity amongst the journalists on the paper.[43]

Sir Larry wasn't the only useful left-wing convert to Thatcherism. Another was former Labour MP, Woodrow Wyatt, who lost his seat in 1970 and became head of the Tote – the office that governs horse racing in the United Kingdom. Wyatt moved to the far-right of politics with such astonishing speed that he became *persona non grata* amongst his former Labour colleagues. Never shy of the spotlight, he became a flamboyant television personality best remembered for his floppy bow tie and preaching right-wing opinions.[44] Woodrow Wyatt became a paid lobbyist and go-between for Murdoch and Thatcher, part of a network that made up Britain's powerful political elite.[45]

Wyatt, an inveterate social climber who knew everyone who was anyone in the capital, met Murdoch just at the point that the Australian needed a guide to show him around the city. Wyatt was considered a snobbish eccentric, with several former wives, but he was astute enough to spot a man on the rise and offered the newcomer friendship. The Wyatts and the Murdochs holidayed and socialised together.[46] Rupert was schooled by Wyatt in the belief that the real cause of rot and decay in British life was the ungovernable trade unions and the real hope for Britain in the future was Margaret Thatcher.

Murdoch embraced Wyatt's credo wholeheartedly, and Wyatt became something of a go-between for Thatcher and Murdoch. Bernard Ingham, Thatcher's press secretary, spent a great deal of his time attempting to fend Wyatt off, and referred to him as 'a bloody menace. He thought he was running the country by ringing her up at eight in the morning. Poisonous little twerp, he was.' Similarly, inside Murdoch's News Corp, no one except Rupert had any time for him. However, Thatcher's victory in 1979 was a massive promotion for Wyatt inside the Murdoch business machine, and he found himself rewarded with columns both in *The Times* and the *News of the World*. Amidst the stories of randy vicars and spanked school girls, Wyatt's column, named without any trace of irony, 'The Voice of Reason', advocated the virtues of free market economics. It gave a forum for Wyatt to write political love letters eulogising Margaret Thatcher's leadership. They were also reportedly Margaret's first read of the day and, some say, her only news read of the day.[47]

Although Wyatt was annoying and had a sometimes comic persona he was a key influence on Murdoch's anti-union position, bringing moderate union leaders to meet him who were willing to supplant the more radical ones. It was through

Wyatt that Murdoch was introduced to Frank Chapple, head of the electrician's union, who agreed to undermine the printers union by allowing members of his union to be drafted in to keep the presses running.[48] (Chapple would be created a life peer in 1985.) Wyatt not only became the ultimate courtier to Murdoch's *Sun* king, but he was also vital in shaping his pro-Thatcher stance.

Murdoch's first deal in the 1980s was his acquisition of *The Times* and the *Sunday Times* in 1981 for £12 million.[49] Thatcher did all she could to help him snap it up.[50] The prospect of the 'Dirty Digger' taking over such an institution as *The Times* caused enormous disquiet, not just in Establishment circles[51] but throughout Fleet Street. People were horrified that the 'top people's paper', known around the world as the *Times of London*, would be sold to a brash Australian whose reputation had been sullied by his antics at the *News of the World* and the *Sun*. However, these two national institutions were being put up for sale by a disillusioned Lord Thomson, who had lost his battle with the print unions following a strike that had kept both papers out of circulation for a year.[52] Thomson, a Canadian, had inherited both his newspapers from his father who had made Thomson Newspapers Canada's most powerful media group, and his family the richest in Canada. He now moved the family business away from newspapers and towards new technology-based communications.[53]

While the *Sunday Times* made a profit (even in the depths of a recession it was turning away advertising), the daily edition lost millions every year. Eager to avoid the severance costs of more than £53 million associated with closing the paper, this was officially a distress sale. None of the potential buyers except Murdoch would agree not to close the daily *Times*, but despite this fact, bitter controversy broke out over Margaret Thatcher's failure to refer the purchase to the Monopolies & Mergers Commission.

Murdoch got what was seen as his political reward when the government put on a three-line whip in the Commons and decisively defeated the motion for referral. Thatcher was clearly bending the rules to allow Rupert Murdoch to purchase both papers, 'it illustrated her political dependence on his newspapers,' said Jonathan Aitken.[54]

'I think they should have applied the Mergers & Monopolies policy much more rigorously,' states Tim Bell.[55]

The loyal Bernard Ingham points out, 'I think before we say she gave Murdoch too much power, we have to ask what would have been the fate of *The Times* and *Sunday Times* without him.'[56]

Woodrow Wyatt had been instrumental in the abandonment of the inquiry. In his diary he wrote, 'At [Murdoch's] request and at my instigation [Margaret Thatcher] had stopped *The Times* acquisition being referred to the Monopolies Commission though the *Sunday Times* was not really losing money and the pair together were not.'[57] In 1987, Woodrow again urged Thatcher to prevent another inquiry by the commission, this time into Murdoch's purchase of the *Today* newspaper. And two years later, Wyatt spoke to Thatcher and helped Murdoch to avoid further inquiry into his media dominance. Murdock told Wyatt, 'I am very grateful to you.'

Wyatt continued to prove crucial after Murdoch moved into Sky TV, telling him, 'Margaret is very keen on preserving your position. She knows how much she depends on your support. Likewise, you depend on hers in this matter.'[58]

Although Murdoch gave assurances of editorial independence and elaborate safeguards were erected, in practice they turned out to be worthless.[59] The so-called independent directors were docile and acquiescent, although one of them, Lord Dacre, denounced Murdoch as a 'megalomaniac twister'.[60] Rupert Murdoch, the upstart Aussie, was now the world's most famous newspaper proprietor, and arguably the most important private citizen (or actually, non-citizen) in the United Kingdom.[61]

Like Thatcher, Murdoch often used the royal 'we' to disguise the absolutist nature of his authority.[62] At the offices of his latest acquisition Murdoch slashed staff, who were either abruptly sacked or made redundant. Murdoch called the place a 'graveyard'.[63] He was scornful of high-minded broadsheet newspapers and the self-important journalists who worked on them. He was especially vehement about any articles that failed wholeheartedly to support either Margaret Thatcher or Ronald Reagan. In the words of Hugo Young, the deputy editor, Murdoch 'didn't believe in neutrality'.

It was also time for a changing of the old guard at the *Sun*. Sir Larry Lamb, who had done himself no favours in Murdoch's eyes by accepting a knighthood, was replaced with Kelvin MacKenzie, who enthusiastically embraced the macho two-fingers-to-society, 'I don't give a fuck' mentality Rupert now wanted. Throughout his 'reign of terror' he abused 'darkies', 'poofters', students, royals, 'krauts', 'royal krauts', 'frogs', gypsies and celebrities. He transformed news into the greatest vaudeville show in town with memorable headlines such as 'Freddie Star Ate my Hamster'. He delighted in lewd and titillating stories, but made gargantuan mistakes in the process. He wrongly blamed drunken Liverpool fans for the fatal crush at Hillsborough football stadium and alleged that Elton John had sex with underage rent boys, a libel that cost the paper £1 million in damages. Murdoch called him 'my little Hitler' and encourage his worst excesses.[64]

MacKenzie conveniently arrived at his post when Princess Diana was injecting new glamour and drama into the otherwise stuffy house of Windsor.[65] The arrival of a fairy tale princess transformed the Windsors into an entire industry, neatly segueing into the national obsession with American soaps such as *Dallas* and *Dynasty*, driven by the fantasy of enormous wealth and glamour.[66] Royal stories became essential to the success of Murdoch's business empire, but the pressure it placed on the new Princess of Wales was enormous. Although Diana behaved flawlessly in public, she found herself exhausted by each performance. At home, she started to throw tantrums that fell outside Prince Charles's realm of experience. Not knowing how to handle his wife's fluctuating emotions, he called his mistress Camilla Parker Bowles for advice and played more polo. The more elusive Charles grew, the more upset Diana became. Frustrated by an absent husband and tabloid intrusion, Diana protested to the queen.[67]

Her Majesty summoned Fleet Street editors to the palace[68] and her press secretary, Michael Shea, told them to rein back stating that the princess felt 'totally beleaguered'.[69] Later the queen entered the room and told photographers it was unfair to hide in the bushes tracking the princess without her knowledge. The queen citied a picture published the day before of Diana with her arms around her husband's neck, smiling affectionately at him as they stood outside their private country home, Highgrove, in Gloucester. Most editors agreed to back off except Kelvin MacKenzie, who failed to attend. He sent a note informing the palace that he had a meeting with Murdoch, which he deemed more important.[70]

The truce between Buckingham Palace and the rest of the press pack lasted about six weeks. Then Diana threatened to kill herself. Shortly after the Christmas holiday at Sandringham, which the princess always hated, she warned Charles that if he left her alone again to go riding she would make an attempt on her life. As he stormed out, she threw herself down a flight of stairs. The queen mother, then 81, heard the uproar and found the pregnant princess in a heap sobbing. Except for a slight bruising around her abdomen, she was fine. However, hours later a footman sold the information about the princess's fall to Murdoch's *Sun*, proving nothing weighs as heavy as a royal secret worth money. The tabloid ran the story on the next day's front page, but did not say it was an apparent suicide attempt.[71]

The queen proposed that Diana and Charles should take a trip, feeling that they needed to get away together to sort things out.[72] After the New Year, a break was set up in the Caribbean in the hope that the princess would find some respite from the media attention.[73] As the Prince and Princess of Wales left for the island of Windermere in the Bahamas, they were only setting themselves up for yet another Murdoch front page. On the island, royal reporter Harry Arnold secured one of the biggest scoops of his career: photographs of the five months' pregnant princess wearing only a bikini. The pictures appeared on the *Sun*'s front page. The palace, caught on the hop, reacted with an angry statement that Charles and Diana were shocked at the tastelessness of the pictures. The next day, using the row as a pretext, MacKenzie ran the pictures again, this time describing the new rules according to the *Sun*. The paper was 'deeply sorry' if it had caused offence but, a '*Sun* Says' editorial proclaimed, the pictures had, 'brought back a breath of summer into the lives of millions of readers back in chilly Britain'. The *Sun* was exercising 'a legitimate interest in the royal family not merely as symbols, but as breathing people'.

The royal pursuit continued undiminished. Every Monday the *Sun* had a policy of running a royal story, as it was traditionally a slow day for news. Many journalists saw the royals living a lifestyle that had lasted for centuries virtually unaltered, and regarded them as fair game.[74] For the 'New Thatcherite Tories', Her Majesty reflected the unchanging, aristocratic mentality that Mrs Thatcher had made it her mission to attack. For many, the monarch embodied the glamour of a lost age and was the upholder, not of capitalism, but of tradition.[75]

Mockery and intrusive reporting sold newspapers because the public mood had grown coarser and less deferential. While the queen was lampooned for not paying taxes, it was her family that suffered. They were now downgraded to the status of mere 'celebrities' and they were sucked into the tabloids' favourite game of 'set them up, knock them down', a pastime which also chewed up and spat out footballers, rock stars and famous actors.[76] MacKenzie treated the royal family like dumb animals, creatures to be kept healthy so they could be shooting targets. The paper's photographers rudely called them 'the Germans' and described taking their pictures as 'whacking the Germans'.[77]

However, the attack on the royals didn't just come from Murdoch's downmarket tabloids. Beyond the red tops, there was also a north London intellectual debate raging, stoked by Murdoch's 'quality' newspapers. The *Times*, once the backbone of the Establishment, now did a volte-face. Together with Charter 88, a left-of-centre reform group, the paper organised a conference on the monarchy. The event took place at the Elizabeth II Centre in Westminster and gathered legal brains, journalists, theatrical and literary personalities from across the spectrum. It mostly consisted of outspoken republicans, with a few token defenders like Charles Moore of the *Daily Telegraph* debating such topics as cutting the Civil List and removing the queen's constitutional powers.

The left-wing playwright David Hare stated, 'Newspapers led by the Murdoch group have begun a project of putting the royal family in such a state of tension that their lives will become unlivable ... We shall mock them until they wish they had never been born.'[78] This, he recognised, gave no one any kudos, but it was, as he saw it, the only practical stratagem against a royal family which the nation was reluctant to tackle head on.

Murdoch made it possible for the first time to be anti-royal, but still pro-Britain, and the greatest shared Murdoch-Maggie triumph was the Falkland's War. MacKenzie's *Sun* quickly moved from whacking Germans to whacking Argentinians. The paper had been fortunate enough to have sent reporter David Graves to the islands before the invasion. He was there covering a humorous story based on Foreign Office statistics that the population was made up of three women to every man, the highest imbalance in the world. Think what that meant to the forty-two marines garrisoned there, sniggered the *Sun*.

MacKenzie never had a flicker of doubt as to where his loyalty lay – Maggie Thatcher. His mindless jingoism and patriotic fervor were typical of most tabloids during a war, but the *Sun* took it to a new level. 'The *Sun* Says Knickers to Argentina!' the paper informed readers on page three. 'Britain's secret weapon in the Falklands dispute was revealed last night ... it's undercover warfare.' According to the *Sun*, thousands of women were sporting 'specially made underwear embroidered across the front with the proud name of the ship on which a husband or boyfriend is serving'. This was followed by the equally comic, 'Stick It up Your Junta' and the infamous 'Gotcha!' when the *General Belgrano* was sunk by a British torpedo. For many people, it summed up the crass bloodlust of the popular press. For others, it identified that the public were getting fed up with the lack of action, and the brash headline encapsulated what many readers would have felt on hearing the news.

The paper cruelly lampooned Foreign Secretary Lord Carrington as a mouse against Churchill's bulldog, along with a splash of 'We'll Smash Em!' The '*Sun* Says' column castigated the Foreign Office as a 'safe haven for appeasers' while Murdoch's newly acquired *Times* followed the same line by denouncing Argentina's action as 'naked aggression' without equal since the days of Hitler. Carrington resigned.

While the BBC maintained its tradition of impartiality and the *Guardian* newspaper cast doubt on the official British versions of the sea battle with the *General Belgrano*, the *Sun* dutifully turned its big-gun leader writer Ronald Spark on these two 'enemies within'. Spark came up with the line 'Dare Call it Treason'. He continued, 'There are traitors in our midst. The prime minister did not speak of treason. The *Sun* does not hesitate to use the word ...' He specifically named the BBC's defence correspondent, Peter Snow, and the 'pygmy *Guardian*'.

On the eve of the Falklands War, the Conservatives' opinion rating had fallen to 25 per cent, a drop of twenty points in two years. After the Falklands, the 1979 election-winning figure of 45 per cent miraculously returned. The paper was now selling 4,224,000 copies a day and had increased its lead over the *Mirror* by 900,000. MacKenzie's extraordinary barnstorming style seemed to be working. Maggie had regained her popularity and the *Sun*'s deification of her knew no bounds. MacKenzie, along with Murdoch, felt an affinity with Margaret, as they were all outsiders amongst the Establishment. They would forgive her anything because of her firm convictions and unshakeable beliefs. Even when MacKenzie disagreed with her, he would always say, 'she's wrong, but she's strong'. As the Murdoch press saw it, Maggie had saved the country from the soggy 'wets' and the unproductive public school boys.

Murdoch had been repaid for supporting Thatcher in the 1979 election with ownership of *The Times* and the *Sunday Times*. Now his support for her during the Falklands conflict would pay dividends as he declared war on his workers, the print unions. In 1984, the Thatcher Government had passed the Trade Union Act which made strike ballots mandatory and outlawed secondary picketing, triggering a major shake-up of the newspaper industry.

Murdoch knew that to make his UK newspapers profitable he had to break the power of the print unions, and their restrictive practices known as 'old Spanish customs'. This phrase originated during the first Elizabethan period, when anti-Spanish feeling was strong as a result of an attempted invasion by the Spanish Armada in 1588, and was used to describe 'deceitful, perfidious and treacherous' practices. Originally designed to protect print jobs in the industry, these customs were now out of control, causing grotesque overmanning and wildcat strikes that amounted to little more than systematic fraud, extortion and sabotage.[79] One technique was to hold up production of the *Sunday Times* on Saturday nights by complaining of a bad smell in the foundry that could only be wafted away with £5 notes. Union 'chapels' run by quasi-independent shop stewards known as 'fathers' ensured that their members received, according to Rupert, 'the most pay for the least work of anyone else in Britain'.[80] Thatcher's union reforms now handed newspaper proprietors a chance to change the status quo if they dared to, and Murdoch did.

Both Murdoch and Wyatt were invited to an intimate lunch with Thatcher and her husband Denis at the prime minister's official country house, Chequers. On the way back to London, Murdoch gave Wyatt a tour of the new printing works in London's docklands, which looked as if they had come straight out of George Orwell's *1984*, a real life 'Ministry of Truth', guarded by CCTV camera, searchlights, electronic gates, 12ft fences and razor wire.

Murdoch struck a secret deal with the maverick electricians' union to enable journalists to type their copy directly from desktop computers, making the role of the print-worker entirely redundant. This was all done under the secret pretence of launching a new evening paper from Wapping. His next step was to provoke a strike; as Wyatt explained, he wanted the printers to go on strike so he could 'sack the lot'. Murdoch thus fired 5,500 employees without compensation, saving £40 million in redundancy payments.

He then moved his entire newspaper operations to Wapping,[81] which was immediately besieged in one of the longest, ugliest and most violent strikes in British history. Murdoch tried to pay the workers off, even offering them the Gray's Inn Road premises to start their own paper, but the offer was rejected. He relied on Margaret Thatcher's measures outlawing secondary picketing and making trade unions liable for damages. She supported him to the hilt, as he had done for her in the 1979 election and Falklands War.

Thatcher's support for Murdoch's new plant was key, and not only through the restrictive trade union laws that her government had introduced, but also the nightly presence of police at the gates of Wapping.[82] His delivery trucks were protected by British police, who met the picketers' violence with violence and sometimes got their aggression in first.[83] They became known as 'Murdoch's paperboys'.[84]

The streets around 'Fortress Wapping' became a nightly battleground. Margaret decided to treat the strike as a law-and-order issue which had to be won. This was, however, an intensely political confrontation and a vital test of the Thatcher revolution at a ground level.[85] According to Andrew Neil, editor of the *Sunday Times* during this period, Murdoch obtained Mrs Thatcher's personal assurance before the dispute began that enough police would be available to allow the papers to continue.[86] As with the National Union of Miners, she wanted victory, not compromise.[87] While the strikers loathed Murdoch and declared him bad news,[88] the prime minister trumpeted 'Rupert is marvellous'.[89]

The year 1986 went down in newspaper history as the year of the 'Wapping Revolution' and the printers' strike finally collapsed after a brutal fifty-four weeks. Other press barons embraced the new technology, moving to Docklands and consigning the bygone, inky world of Fleet Street to the dustbin of history. For ideological as well as commercial reasons, Murdoch's papers became even more stridently Thatcherite after the move to Wapping. When Labour MP Ken Livingstone said on television that his party's defeat in the 1987 general election had been caused by media lies and smears, Murdoch cried out delightedly, 'That's me!'[90]

Murdoch's early teenage flirtation with left-wing politics soon changed to espousing the hard right-wing views common among the super-rich: strong leadership, low taxation and light regulations, and against trade unions, the European Union and global warming science. His newspapers would sabotage defiant politicians and advance his own political and business agenda, especially if it led to getting favours in the heavily regulated TV industry.

In 1986 *The Times* editor, Charles Douglas-Home, was reported to have said, 'Rupert and Mrs Thatcher consult regularly on every important matter of policy especially as they relate to his economic and political interests.'[91] News Corporation, the company that controlled Murdoch's media interests, was deeply involved in the Institute of Economic Affairs, a think tank which played a vital role in laying the intellectual foundation on which Thatcherism was built, shaping the policies on free markets, deregulation and privatisation. Murdoch's *Sunday Times* and the institute co-published a series of pamphlets attacking the welfare state for producing an intractable 'underclass'. From 1988 to 2001 the founder and director of the institute, Lord Harris, was a director of the Times Newspapers Holdings Ltd, Murdoch's holding company for both *The Times* and the *Sunday Times*.[92]

In the 1987 election, Thatcher said of Murdoch privately, 'We depend on him to fight for us. The *Sun* is marvellous.'[93] That year, Murdoch travelled to London to personally oversee his newspapers for the month before the election. According to Wyatt, Thatcher 'was delighted that Rupert had promised to come over especially for the election to keep in touch with me and to have an input of advice'.[94] His advice was that the Tories should tell the public that they stood for low tax.

'Appeal to their greed,' Murdoch said.

'Rupert is marvellous,' repeated Margaret.[95]

The *Sunday Times* veteran and Thatcher biographer, Hugo Young, argued that Murdoch 'did not believe in neutrality. Indeed, rather like politicians themselves, he had difficulty in comprehending it. As far as he was concerned, journalistic detachment was a mask for anti-Thatcherism. If we were not for the government, we were quite plainly against it.'[96]

Thatcher turned a blind eye to his crucifixion of the royals. Of course, she knew all about it, but she ignored Murdoch's diet of sleaze, sex and royal bashing in exchange for his determined support. Thatcher biographer, John Campbell, claims she rationalised it as 'the price of freedom', without saying *whose* freedom. The public mood was ready for change and Murdoch fuelled it. Reform of the monarchy, in particular the Civil List, was placed firmly on the prime minister's 'to do' list, although not as high up as the unions or the nationalised industries.

In unpicking the relationship between Thatcher, Murdoch and the royal family, we witness how his empire came to exert such a poisonous influence on public life and how he used his vast power to bully, intimidate and cover up.[97]

Thatcher herself didn't always escape totally unscathed. While the *Sunday Times* under Andrew Neil supported the Conservatives at election time and during the worst moments of the miners' strike, it also revealed how the queen was distressed at Thatcher's social policies and exposed the business dealings of her son, Mark.

Other newspapers in the Murdoch empire supported the Thatcher Government unconditionally, but the *Sunday Times* was distinguished by being prepared to be critical of the Tory leader.[98] Murdoch had changed the economics of the press by breaking the print unions. His media empire, swollen by the enormous power Mrs Thatcher had given him, could now make the politicians dance to his tune.

By contrast, while Mrs Thatcher was embracing Murdoch's growing empire, her relationship with that other media tycoon of the 1980s, Robert Maxwell, was very different. Maxwell created for himself an image as one of Britain's richest men with a fortune of £1.1 billion. However, his debts were almost twice that, and he survived by moving money around his companies, 'borrowing' from the pension fund and dreaming up new schemes. Maxwell, an ex-Labour MP, was endlessly litigious and reeked of the sulphurous aroma of financial scandal. He was dubbed the 'bouncing Czech' by Prime Minister Harold Wilson, under whom he served during the 1960s. The full extent of Maxwell's fraudulent dealings was only revealed after he died in 1991, when his body was found in the sea near his luxury yacht, the *Lady Ghislaine*, off the Canaries.

Mrs Thatcher kept him at arm's length. At one stage, Maxwell tried to get Margaret Thatcher and her Conservative Government to back him in a barter deal with the Soviet Union worth up to $20 billion (£11.2 billion). Maxwell talked his way into meeting her at 10 Downing Street in 1990, the year before his death, to reveal details of the scheme. Maxwell's percentage as fixer could have given him enough money to stay afloat, and would have prevented his £450 million raid on the Mirror Group Newspapers pension fund ever becoming known. Thatcher sent him away. She developed the means of deflating Maxwell, by saying he looked ill whenever they met.

Charles Powell explained:

Margaret Thatcher rather reluctantly saw him, but she had a marvellous technique. He would come and sit down, and she would look at him and say, 'How are you?'

He would say, 'Very well.'

She would say, 'You don't really look too good.' He would feel anxious and start to sweat. 'Are you sure your wife is looking after you?' she would say.

By now he would be reaching for his handkerchief and dabbing his brow and wishing he had never come in.[99]

7

THE DEATH OF
CONSENSUS

Politics is a dirty game, but we politicians could
never teach those at the palace anything.
Margaret Thatcher

On 12 October 1984, just as the queen was leaving for a holiday inspecting race-horses in America, she was told that a powerful IRA bomb had exploded at the Grand Hotel in Brighton during the Conservative Party Conference. Margaret Thatcher, who had been the prime target of the attack, had escaped unhurt, although she had been minutes away from being killed. Five people died, and thirty-four were injured, including Cabinet colleague, Norman Tebbit, and chief whip, John Wakeham. Alan Clark put it in his famous diary, 'Mrs T had been saved by good fortune (von Stauffenberg's briefcase!) as she was in the bathroom, had she been in the bedroom she would be dead.'[1] The morning after the attack, Mrs Thatcher addressed the conference at 9.30 a.m., giving a defiant speech announcing, 'All attempts to destroy democracy by terrorism will fail',[2] and 'it was an attempt to cripple Her Majesty's democratically elected government'.[3]

Thatcher had taken a hard line in Northern Ireland against the 1981 hunger strikers, when ten IRA members being held in the infamous Maze prison for terrorism starved themselves to death, demanding the status of political prisoners. During this period, one of the strikers, Bobby Sands, had been elected to Parliament, prompting worldwide media interest, and his funeral was attended by 100,000 people. After her 1983 election triumph, her opposition to any political demands from IRA only heightened.

The Buckingham Palace press secretary, Michael Shea, censured the attack as a 'dreadful outrage' and the queen sent a message of 'sympathy and concern' to the prime minister.[4] She then got on a plane and went on holiday. The almost successful attempt to assassinate a sitting prime minister was not considered of sufficient importance for Her Majesty to delay her equine adventure in the legendary bluegrass horse country of Kentucky with her close friends the Porchesters. (There are gossips who persist in believing that Prince Andrew's natural father was Henry Porchester, 'Porchey', 7th Earl of Carnarvon, suggesting the conception took place when Philip was away on one of his long sea voyages on the *Britannia*.[5]) It was not until the royal flight landed in Wyoming that the queen called Mrs Thatcher, whose first words were, 'Are you having a lovely time?'[6] This story is often quoted to illustrate the stiffness of Margaret Thatcher and her inability to express any real feeling even in the face of death.[7]

The queen's close relative Lord Mountbatten had been murdered by an IRA bomb in 1979, and Mrs Thatcher had lost one of her earliest political supporters, Airey Neave, in a car-bomb attack a few months earlier. These two incidents were a reminder of the danger both the queen and prime minister faced daily.[8] Only twenty days after the Grand Hotel attack, Indira Gandhi, a friend to both women, was shot dead by her own Sikh bodyguards in New Delhi. Margaret made a point of attending her funeral, but it could so easily have been the other way around.

The Brighton bombing might have forged some bond between the sovereign and her prime minister, but it failed to. Both women adhered to the strict formalities of their two respective offices and were separated by class, outlook and experience. The queen remained in the United States looking at horses, and Mrs Thatcher got on with the conference. It was business as usual.

This dramatic escape from a terrorist bomb, along with victory in the Falklands and the election, combined to inflate Margaret's beliefs. For her, politics was a battle between good and evil which had cast her as a modern day Joan of Arc. Assassination, the curse of all world leaders and monarchs, had been aimed at her personally. She emerged from it resolute, and it confirmed on her a status enjoyed previously only by Winston Churchill.[9]

Mrs Thatcher's fiercest critics and enemies sat directly behind her on the back benches of her party.[10] Within the higher echelons of the Tories there was a feeling that someone with such an inferior pedigree as Thatcher ought not to be prime minister; she was, in their eyes, still only a grocer's daughter. Until Margaret's takeover of the Conservative Party, it had been controlled by old-school landed gentry types. The prevailing rationale was that these Establishment figures, groomed at Eton and Oxbridge, were compassionate, broadminded, intellectual chaps who embraced the principles of *noblesse oblige*.[11] To Margaret this was just humbug, she found them patronising and felt they wanted power to dictate to other people what they thought was good for them. The Thatcherite Tories called them the 'Wets', a public school term meaning soppy or weak.

Indulging in a bit of class revenge, she told Brian Walden in an interview, 'Success is not an attractive thing to many people ... and of course, some of them are snobs. They can never forgive me for coming from a very ordinary background.' Thatcher, unlike the old Tories, understood the passions that drove everyday folk for policies that led to them buying their own home or running their own businesses. Her intuition caught political fire. If the 'Wets' had dared to face Margaret down when they had been in the majority in Cabinet, history would have been different. But the 'Wets' were wet, and they lacked the stomach for a fight.[12]

The shake-up over the old boy network wasn't just taking place in Westminster, it was nationwide. Britain changed more during the 1980s than at any time since the queen's coronation. There was an expansion in private business and the service industries. Old state-owned industries were transformed into modern public companies as they were sold off. 'Privatisation' became a word that Thatcher had invented. Deregulation in the City, known as the 'Big Bang', revolutionised British banking traditions. Hard-working, ambitious, noisy, south London boys flocked to the city trading floors, waving fistfuls of cash and swigging champagne in overpriced bars after work.[13] Some traders were earning £100,000 a year by the time they were 23. Another word, 'Yuppie', standing for 'young urban professional', entered the vernacular. To the pure Thatcherite, the free market encouraged individual virtue. It produced people who were robust, independent and willing to take responsibility for their actions.[14]

David Owen feels that Margaret Thatcher never understood the non-strivers:

That incomprehension was a huge weakness. That's rare, you don't see that very often these days in prime ministers, most of them are pretty much on all fours with their fellow citizens, she wasn't and she couldn't understand the failing of the people who can't ... the non-achievers.[15]

This was in direct contradiction to the queen's personality, states Owen:

The queen is quite good at understanding ... she's gone around a lot and seen the disadvantaged, the weak and the inadequate, and she can empathise with them and she knows they exist in all societies. She isn't a do-gooder, but she's on all fours with it.[16]

In Peter Morgan's play, *The Audience*, the queen asks Mrs Thatcher to remember:

> Not everybody is as strong as you Prime Minister. Or prodigiously gifted. Or driven. I can't help thinking about the rest of us sometimes. Those that are just ... normal. That have to read things twice to understand. That need a prevailing wind to get thorough life. And rarely get it. [17]

The Thatcher revolution seemed unstoppable, and Margaret began to question anyone who did not embrace the principles of her credo, including the royal family. Were the Windsors 'true believers'? On close inspection, members of the royal family looked suspiciously liked a collective of Tory 'Wets'. They were worried paternalists who instinctively favoured the type of Conservative Party and society Thatcher now challenged. [18] They believed in compassion and caring, just so long it didn't mean giving up their palaces, cars, holidays and horses.

Prince Charles was seen as the 'wettest' royal of all. As the prince fretted over urban poverty and green issues he became a real irritation to Mrs Thatcher, giving speeches about how Britain was becoming a selfish consumer-orientated society in a state of spiritual decay. [19] In October 1985, Charles was quoted as saying that he feared inheriting a 'divided' Britain, when the *Manchester Evening News* ran the headline 'Prince Charles: My Fears for the Future'. The article stated that the prince was 'prepared to force his way through parliamentary red tape to ensure that his country is not split into factions of the haves and have-nots'. Charles was reported to be worried that 'when he becomes king there will be no-go areas in the inner cities, and that the minorities will be alienated from the rest of the country'. [20] The voicing of the Prince of Wales' opinions ignored the warning of the great constitutional expert Walter Bagehot about the danger of having on the throne 'an active and meddling fool'.

When the *Manchester Evening News* story broke, Margaret Thatcher was addressing the United Nations in New York. Incensed, she phoned Buckingham Palace demanding an explanation and was less than convinced by the royal courtiers, who insisted that Charles had intended no criticism of her government. The provenance of the royal remarks was murky. They had, however, been leaked by Rod Hackney, one of Charles's architectural advisors, following a private conversation on the royal train. Hackney, whose brand of 'community architecture' had seen him forge an alliance with the prince, now found himself rebuked and banished from the prince's inner circle. Tory Party hard man, Norman Tebbit, said on television, 'I suppose the Prince of Wales feels extra sympathy towards those who've got no job because in a way he's got no job ... He's 40, and he's not been able to take responsibility for anything, and I think that's his problem.' [21]

Prince Charles told his biographer that he found Thatcher 'formidable'[22] and he complained to the editor of the *Sunday Express* that she was 'a bit like a school ma'am' with a tendency to lecture.[23] Charles eventually became so disenchanted with Thatcher's Conservative policies that he sent a memo to the queen imploring her to do something before the prime minister ruined the country.

For once, the queen shared Prince Charles's views.[24] Lord Charteris, the queen's private secretary, told the historian Peter Hennessy that:

> You might say that the queen prefers a sort of consensus politics, rather than a polarised one … If you are in the queen's position, you are the titular, the symbolic head of the country, and the less squabbling that goes on in that country, obviously the more convenient and the more comfortable you feel.[25]

The queen, who came to agree with her son, shared her displeasure with Commonwealth leaders. 'Her Majesty was not at ease with Margaret Thatcher's policies,' said Robert Hawke, the former Prime Minister of Australia. 'She saw her as dangerous.'[26] Thatcher's willingness to accept high unemployment as a painful part of making British industry more efficient and her determination to tame the unions only sharpened social division, which the queen feared could rebound on the royal family. The monarchy had a vested interest in social harmony, continuity and consensus. Margaret told conservative aides that Her Majesty was not 'one of us'.[27]

The consensus that the queen so favoured was about to be broken in apocalyptic fashion as Margaret Thatcher prepared herself to face down Arthur Scargill. She even made secret plans to have 4,500 troops on standby ready to break the miners' strike, as official records declassified in 2014 reveal.[28] Whereas the first Thatcher Government would be dominated by monetarist economic reform and the Falklands War, the second would be overshadowed by the miners' strike, the longest in British history and one of the most bloody and tragic. Common belief during the 1970s and early 1980s was that trade union power was so great it simply couldn't be broken, and Mrs Thatcher had always believed this to be one of the least acceptable aspects of socialism.

Resistance from the miners' unions to any reform had pressured Ted Heath into the so-called 'U-turn' of 1972. The former prime minister had been forced to back away from free market principles, and the unions forced the country into a three day working week. It was a humiliation for both Heath and the Conservation Party.

Arthur Scargill, then a senior figure in the Yorkshire branch of the miners' union, had introduced the tactic of flying pickets, dispatching troops of militant strikers to the scene of any dispute, to devastating effect. Scargill was a socialist hero after helping to bring down the Tory Government in 1984. Miners were encouraged to chant his name and pledge loyalty to him personally rather than to the union. 'There's only one Arthur Scargill' was sung to the tune of 'Guantanamera'. It was the politics of a personality cult.[29]

For Thatcher, who had served in Ted Heath's Cabinet, the former prime minister's climb down was a shameful capitulation and an act of weakness. She wanted to show she was made of sterner stuff, and announced during the 1980 Brighton Conference that the 'the lady's not for turning'. Margaret spoke of, 'the enemy within' and was determined that Britain wouldn't, in her words, 'be made ungovernable by the Fascist left'. She knew Scargill was committed to increasing the political power of the unions, but public opinion was against their disproportionate leverage.

Thatcher sensed that the 'decent people' of middle England were outraged by their tactics. She had won to her side the aspirational working class who were skeptical about their union leadership. They increasingly viewed high taxation, inflation and government regulation as curbs on their upward mobility.[30] The country was ready for change. Thatcher waited for her moment and planned for it meticulously, ensuring that the coal stocks were built up, and the police prepared and equipped for the riots that were sure to come.[31] She made her goal explicit: she intended to destroy socialism in Britain. In return, Scargill made it his ambition equally clear: he planned to destroy Thatcher. And so the strike began.[32]

Scargill was never interested in the details of pay packets or in a pit-by-pit discussion of which coal mines were economically viable to keep open. He was determined to force the government, in Thatcher's contemptuous words, to pay 'for mud to be mined' rather than see a single job lost.[33] It cost £44 to mine a metric ton of British coal, while the rest of the world were selling it for £32 per ton. The Monopolies & Mergers Commission reported that some 75 per cent of British pits were making losses and the mining industry cost taxpayers £1 billion a year to subsidise.[34] For Thatcher, the coal industry represented everything that was wrong: waste, inefficiency, irresponsibility and unaccountability.

Under the urgings of a largely right-wing press, public sympathy now turned against the miners. To the astonishment of most people, including her party, she won the strike.[35] For the Tories, the defeat of the miners was essential revenge after the miners' humiliation of Heath. Norman Tebbit wrote that Thatcher had broken 'not just a strike, but a spell'.[36] Union power was broken in Britain for good.

Margaret Thatcher in a deep curtsy to the queen outside 10 Downing Street. (Photo by Tim Graham/ Getty Images)

The queen with her prime ministers in 2002. From left to right: Tony Blair, Baroness Thatcher, Sir Edward Heath, the queen, Lord Callaghan and John Major. (Photo by Terry O'Neill/Getty Images)

The Roberts family. From left to right: Muriel, Alfred, Beatrice and Margaret. (© Camera Press)

The royal family. From left to right: King George VI, Princess Margaret, Princess Elizabeth (the future queen) and Queen Elizabeth (the future queen mother). (Photo by Apic/Getty Images)

The queen with Margaret Thatcher at Claridge's in 1995 to celebrate her former prime minister's 70th birthday. (Getty Images)

Commonwealth leaders with the queen and Mrs Thatcher in London. Guests included Robert Mugabe of Zimbabwe. (© Associated Press)

The queen with Helmut Kohl, Ronald Reagan and Margaret Thatcher at Buckingham Palace. (© Associated Press)

Margaret Thatcher makes a speech in front of a crown logo. (Photo by Keystone/Getty Images)

The queen with Rupert Murdoch visiting the *Times* newspaper. (Photo by Popperfoto/Getty Images)

Michael Shea, the queen's press secretary. (Photo by Tim Graham/Getty Images)

Margaret Thatcher visits the site of the Lockerbie plane crash. (AP/Dave Caulkin)

The Thatchers with the Prince and Princess of Wales at 10 Downing Street. (Photo by Terry Fincher/Hulton Archive/Getty Images)

Mrs Thatcher in another one of her deep curtsies to royalty. This time with the Princess of Wales. (Image Collect)

The queen, Prince Charles and Lady Diana Spencer. (Photo by Fox Photos/Hulton Archive/Getty Images)

The Thatcher family in 1976. From left to right: Mark, Margaret, Denis and Carol. (Photo by Central Press/Getty Images)

Mark Thatcher, always his mother's favourite, found safe and well after going missing in the Sahara Desert. (Photo by Pierre Perrin/Gamma-Rapho via Getty Images)

The queen and Prince Andrew. Her Majesty has always got on better with her second son than with Prince Charles. (© Bettmann/Corbis)

Margaret Thatcher with the queen at the Lusaka Conference. (Photo by Anwar Hussein/Getty Images)

Margaret Thatcher greets the queen arriving at the Mandarin Oriental Hotel in 2004 to celebrate her 80th birthday. (Getty Images)

The queen with Tony Blair in the audience room at Buckingham Palace. He was her tenth prime minister. (Photo by Tim Graham/Getty Images)

For most hard-working miners their prime concern was not about a political battle between the left and the right, it was about their homes and families. In 1985, there were around 200,000 people employed in the industry; by 1995 it was down to 11,000, and vibrant mining communities were destroyed.[37] At the height of the strike in 1984, Arthur Scargill's wife, Anne, had presented to Buckingham Palace a petition signed by 20,000 women from mining communities appealing to the queen to support the coal miners. It read, 'We ask you, Your Majesty, to speak up on our behalf and help us to defend our families, our communities and sources of energy which can only grow in importance.' The petition also complained that the police had been used to:

> ... terrify us and to try to silence us ... As loyal and law-abiding citizens in this country, we never thought that violence, the denial of civil liberties, the day and night harassment, employed by police forces ... would enter our lives.

Mrs Scargill was later joined by her husband, Arthur, and some 15,000 women, mostly miners' wives carrying flowers, in a central London rally in support of the strike. They marched to 10 Downing Street, where they stood for a few minutes in what they called a 'silent protest'.[38] 'I hope the queen can help,' said one of the rally organisers, Martha Marshall, movingly.[39] But Her Majesty, who was on holiday at Balmoral, did not immediately see the petition.

The north versus south; old Tories versus Thatcherites; ethnic minorities versus police; strikers versus the police; rich versus poor; employed versus unemployed; Mrs Thatcher versus the Commonwealth and Mrs Thatcher versus everyone. Tensions were high all around. Britain, it seemed, had never been so divided.

From her holiday home in Scotland, Elizabeth was unimpressed by Margaret Thatcher's attitude regarding the unemployed and the underprivileged.[40] The rhetoric and violence of the miners' strike, which culminated in the terrible violence at Orgreave, when seventy-two police and fifty-nine miners were injured, were particularly shocking. Allegations were made on the BBC that Special Branch had infiltrated a spy, 'Silver Fox', right into Scargill's inner circle.[41] It all seemed very extreme.

The queen was more comfortable with previous Labour and Conservative governments who had secured industrial peace by consensus, even if that meant kowtowing to union demands. This new radical right with its subversive attitude to hierarchy, deference and consensus, seemed as big a threat as the republican socialists. Indirectly, Thatcherism wasn't kind to the royal family. Management of the royal finances, like those of other national institutions, were all coming under scrutiny: palaces, yachts, trains, holidays and retainers once taken for granted now had to be justified on a value-for-money basis.[42] It must have seemed as if it were only a matter of time before Thatcher tried to reform Buckingham Palace and its inhabitants.

By the mid-1980s, a royal whispering campaign started against Thatcher's regime. One of its manifestations was a long profile of Prince Charles in the *Economist*, which analysed his views and painted him as a hybrid of a 'one-nation' old school Tory and a moderate Social Democrat. The *Economist* was able to write with such great authority because of an off-the-record interview with the prince in which he discussed the key issues of the day. 'It was the manifesto of an SDP king,' said Simon Jenkins, who conducted the interview when he was the magazine's political editor. The prince clearly saw David Owen and his new party of Social Democrats as the potential saviours of Britain.[43]

The tabloid press was becoming increasingly intrigued by the notion that the country had two queens. Stories appeared throughout the decade that were both personal – such as the fact that Mrs Thatcher hated going to Balmoral – and political, with the two women disagreeing over the importance of the Commonwealth. It was a caricature that was too good an opportunity for the tabloid press to relinquish. In the satirical television show *Spitting Image*, the queen is shown throughout the series as relishing the opportunity to wind up Mrs Thatcher. The prime minister is always portrayed as having regal ambitions, wearing the imperial state crown and insisting her ministers call her, 'Your Majesty'.

In television soap land the battles of the two 'Dynasty Divas', Joan Collins (Alexis) versus Linda Evans (Krystal), fuelled this fantasy. They fought each other in the boardrooms of Denver and in one memorable fight they threw one other into a lily pond. Their rivalry became a hallmark of the series, and perhaps the tabloids wanted this fairytale to be replicated within the soap opera that the royal family was fast becoming. The queen versus Mrs Thatcher would be the ultimate cat fight. The press tried to extract clues from Buckingham Palace, and by 1985 began to have some success.

At the Commonwealth Conference in Nassau in the Bahamas in 1985, Margaret Thatcher and the queen found themselves at odds over the issues of economic sanctions against South Africa. Mrs Thatcher was loudly opposed to them; the queen was not. Edwina Currie feels there may have been a small undercurrent of racism towards the Commonwealth by Mrs Thatcher. Her views on South Africa would have been enormously shaped by Denis Thatcher, who had done a great deal of business there.[44] The head of the Commonwealth secretariat, Sir Sonny Ramphal, stated that, 'she [Mrs Thatcher] had worked herself into the position where people were beginning to identify her not with anti-sanctions but with pro-South Africa ... it was as though she was more opposed to sanctions than to apartheid'.[45]

The queen's position was different. She travelled to Nassau on the *Britannia* and remained on board throughout the conference. Many noticed the royal vexation, and when a group of delegates arrived late on the yacht, she drummed her fingers on the rail. Many of the delegates had made it clear to her that Britain was forfeiting its unique place in the leadership of the Commonwealth. Rajiv Gandhi, who had taken over his mother's position in India following her assassination, talked of the dangers of the whole institution becoming extinct. An identical message had been given to her by a succession of African leaders in their routine twenty minute meetings with her. The new Australian Prime Minister, Bob Hawke, was struck by the strained atmosphere. He said:

> I was well aware that you wouldn't describe the relationship between Her Majesty and her prime minister as one of extreme cordiality. In a formal sense there was a respect and acknowledgement of the role and importance of the other [but] it's fair to say that the queen didn't have a great affection for Mrs Thatcher.[46]

Although the Commonwealth countries voted 48:1 in favour of sanctions, Mrs Thatcher would not yield to secure unanimity. She remained in a self-righteous minority of one, fearing that any damage to the £2 billion in trade that took place annually between Britain and South Africa would affect employment in both countries. As Bernard Ingham explained:

> She [Mrs Thatcher] probably did as much by plain speaking to P.W. Botha [South Africa's President] as all the sanctions conceived to end apartheid. She did not think sanctions would work, given how often they are broken by supposed allies, and that if they did the very people who would be worst hit would be the proletariat.[47]

Early in the summer of 1986, Downing Street discovered, to the great annoyance of the prime minister's staff, that a senior unnamed courtier had made critical remarks about Mrs Thatcher's sanctions policy.[48] William Whitelaw, the deputy prime minister, also referred to a potential rift between the palace and Downing Street when briefing lobby journalists. The most explicit story was, however, published in *Today* in July 1986, and exposed the quarrel. It was based, allegedly, on apparently authorised information acquired by the editor from the palace press office and reported that the queen had urged Thatcher to agree sanctions against South Africa. 'She fears Britain's stand on trade sanctions could lead to a breakup of the

Commonwealth. The queen gave the prime minister a discreet warning during a private audience at Buckingham Palace.'

The main source of the story was the queen's press secretary, Michael Shea,[49] who gave the story to the newspaper as a reward for apologising (something tabloids are loath to do) for a false piece which claimed Princess Diana was pregnant. However, *Today*'s scoop was largely ignored.[50] The paper was not considered important and had little influence amongst London's opinion formers. Journalists, however, could clearly smell a story that warranted further scrutiny and realised that people inside the palace were talking.

Amid these rumours, on 20 July 1986, the *Sunday Times* blazed a trail when it exploded a bombshell article entitled 'The African Queen'. The feature was the joint work of journalist, Simon Freeman, and the paper's respected political editor, Michael Jones, and claimed that Elizabeth II was dismayed by the policies of Margaret Thatcher. The queen purportedly took issue with her prime minister's opposition to the Commonwealth's policy of using economic sanctions against South Africa to bring an end to apartheid. She was also concerned by Thatcher's rough tactics to break up the miners' union during the long and violent strike of 1984. It also claimed the queen was unhappy with her prime minister for granting permission to Ronald Reagan for United States' aircraft to refuel at British airbases before launching bombing missions against Libya the previous April.

According to the *Sunday Times'* report, the queen regarded Thatcher's approach to governing as, 'uncaring, confrontational and divisive'.[51] Altogether, the article suggested that the queen felt Mrs Thatcher was a menace to the consensus that, in her view, had served Britain so well in the post-war years. The queen feared that, because of the miners' strike, serious long-term damage would be done to the nation's fabric. This royal expression of vexation was not just a clash over economic sanctions for South Africa or anxiety that the Commonwealth might break up.[52] Her Majesty was even prepared to break with convention to make her displeasure public.[53] The British public was now transported back to the style of eighteenth-century politics with a so called 'Royal Party' that supported a stronger monarchy to counterbalance the office of prime minister.[54]

The timing couldn't have been worse, from Her Majesty's perspective or that of Mrs Thatcher's, or better for the newspapers. The article appeared just as the queen's second son, Prince Andrew, was about to wed Sarah Ferguson at Westminster Abbey. Margaret and Denis Thatcher were even VIP guests alongside Elton John, Michael Caine, Estee Lauder and Nancy Reagan. A week later, the Commonwealth Games were about to start in Edinburgh and the African states were boycotting it because of Thatcher's policies on South Africa.

Late on Saturday night before the story was published, senior royal advisors were dining at Boodle's, the Mayfair gentleman's club. At eleven o'clock, their assistants were dispatched to Victoria Station to grab early editions of the *Sunday Times*, just as the trucks were delivering them to the newspaper stands ready to be sold the following morning.[55] 'Sources close to the queen,' wrote Michael Jones and Simon Freeman, offered the *Sunday Times* readers an 'unprecedented disclosure of the monarch's political views'.[56] Stories claiming to represent royal opinion were always vague about their sources, but this one was precise and was based, as Jones and Freeman explained, on several briefings by the queen's advisors.[57] The *Sunday Times* stated, 'Far from being a straightforward countrywoman, a late middle-aged grandmother who is most at ease when she is talking about dogs and horses, the queen is an astute political infighter who is quite prepared to take on Downing Street when provoked.'[58]

The editor of the *Sunday Times*, Andrew Neil, upset both Mrs Thatcher and the queen in that one sentence. Both were furious that a major unwritten rule of the Establishment had been broken. Her Majesty hated to be pulled into the political amphitheatre because it would be damaging constitutionally. Margaret Thatcher knew it would hurt her to have a head of state as loved and respected as Elizabeth II denounce her policies.

If the story had been presented merely as inspired speculation it would have received scant attention, as rumours of the differences between the queen and her prime minister had been long-standing. In fact, the *Sunday Times* played down indications of a personality clash to underscore the disagreement with actual policy. What gave the account such effect was its detailed rundown of the queen's anti-Thatcher views and the claim from the journalists that they had an 'unimpeachable' source who wanted the comments to be published.[59]

A full-blown constitutional crisis was now on the horizon. The *Daily Mirror* took delight in rewriting the original story under the headline, 'Queen and Charles Loathe Thatcher'. The *Sun* delivered its verdict with the headline, 'Stop Your Meddling, Ma'am'.

More details emerged the following week, when the *Sunday Times* explained that its journalist had spoken to his source five times before publication; the article was also discussed with Downing Street and Buckingham Palace before going to print, and the palace had never asked for it to be withheld.[60] Michael Jones had called Bernard Ingham, Thatcher's press secretary, on Saturday, and read the news story over the phone to him for a Downing Street reaction. An angry Ingham informed Thatcher's private secretary, Nigel Wicks, who called Sir William Heseltine and told him the contents of the story.[61] Wicks called Mrs Thatcher who said, 'Don't say anything at all.' She was dismayed that this kind of thing could come between her and the queen. Ingram also spoke to Shea, who confirmed that he had spoken to the *Sunday Times*. Ingham wasn't entirely surprised:

> There was a feeling around Buckingham Palace that people were amused by Mrs Thatcher's passion. I lived to detect a certain snobbishness in the hangers-on who tended to ridicule this 'Joan come lately' and not least because of her apparently exaggerated deference to the queen. Note her very deep curtsies. I sometimes wondered whether she would ever get back upright in good order.[62]

Andrew Neil's team had done their homework. Bernard Ingham described his journalism as 'thorough and thoroughly commercial'.[63] Simon Freeman was an experienced news and features journalist assigned to investigate the potential rift developing between the queen and Mrs Thatcher over the Commonwealth. What he came up with was even better: now he had sourced information on a whole range of topics, from American planes using British bases to bomb Libya to the miners' strike. It was a hugely significant scoop because the queen's private thoughts on any issue are almost never publicly known. What made it doubly unique was that the source was the queen's press secretary, Michael Shea.[64] Shea had spoken off the record to Simon Freeman, which meant he could use the material, but not name him as a source. Freeman even read the article back to Shea and was corrected on some points, while having more details filled in regarding others.[65]

Before printing the story, Andrew Neil had phoned the paper's proprietor, Rupert Murdoch. 'Are you sure it's true?' Rupert asked. He wasn't surprised. Murdoch saw himself, like Thatcher, as an outsider. He told Neil, 'The Establishment hate Thatcher, and you can't get more Establishment than the royal family. But they're crazy to bad mouth her like this; it'll backfire on them.'[66] Murdoch also felt a fight between Thatcher and the queen wouldn't do Thatcher any harm, 'it will do her a lot of good,' he disclosed to Woodrow Wyatt.[67]

The account of the queen versus Thatcher dominated the news bulletins around the world for days, even knocking the royal wedding of Prince Andrew and Sarah Ferguson off the number one spot on ITV's *News at Ten* the day before the actual ceremony. The American networks were as preoccupied as the Commonwealth countries by a story involving two such high profile women. Arguably, an attempt by Buckingham Palace to distance themselves from Margaret Thatcher's hardline policies had backfired spectacularly.

Andrew Neil said:

> The palace was rumbled. It had overplayed its hand, its fingerprints were all over the story and it rushed for cover, rewriting history as it did so.[68]
>
> There was a whispering campaign orchestrated by the palace ... to do down the Thatcher Government. This began to appear in a whole host of stories done very subtly, never sourced to the palace ... that Mrs Thatcher was upsetting the royal family in general and the queen in particular.[69]

Thatcher's supporters, like Alan Clark, believed that the briefing 'must have been a put-up job to cut Thatcher down to size'.[70]

The hunt was now on for the source of the story, and a lynch mob was forming outside Andrew Neil's door. The Establishment was on the warpath, although in certain circles the Prince of Wales was suspected of being the leak.[71] Everyone seemed to be angry, and letters flooded into the *Sunday Times* from readers demanding Andrew Neil's resignation and threatening never to buy the paper again.[72] Michael Shea, who had lit the fuse, now dissembled and issued a statement that the story was 'entirely without foundation'. It was an act that obviously infuriated Andrew Neil, the *Sunday Times* editor, who found himself being trashed by the person who had fed him the story. In his biography, Neil stated, 'Why should I allow him to plant his bomb then print his denial of any responsibility for the explosion?'[73]

Various worthies and royalists were wheeled out to rubbish the story and condemn Neil. Faced with demands for authentication, Andrew Neil was forced to admit that the informant worked at Buckingham Palace.[74] This narrowed the field to the three potential courtiers. The queen's private secretary, Sir William Heseltine; her assistant private secretary, Robert Fellowes; and her press secretary, Michael Shea.

On 27 July the *Observer* pinpointed Michael Shea.[75] That evening Neil received a phone call from Charles Wilson, the editor of *The Times*. He explained that Monday's *Times* would be carrying a long letter from Sir William attacking the article and defending Michael Shea. 'It's an unprecedented intervention by such a senior courtier,' claimed Wilson, and it could only have been written with the queen's consent. That night Andrew Neil knew 'there was an Exocet heading my way in the morning'. Under the rules governing letters to *The Times*, he was not able to reply until after the letter had been published.[76] Meanwhile, two Establishment-supporting directors of Times Newspapers, Lord Drogheda, a well-connected figure in the palace and the press, and Lord Dacre, the famous Oxford historian who damaged his own reputation by authenticating the notorious fake Hitler diaries in 1983, started to lobby Rupert Murdoch to sack Neil. According to

Neil, a deal was even mooted that if he were fired then the palace would sacrifice Michael Shea.

The following morning, Andrew Neil woke up to read that his story has been dismissed as nonsense and that it was difficult to see how he could survive as editor. Sir William's letter disputed the account of the remarks that were published. As former royal press secretary, Ronald Allison explains this 'put Bill [Sir William] in a very difficult position which as you can imagine he didn't appreciate'.[77]

In his letter to *The Times*, Heseltine was forced to write that the queen is:

> ... obliged to treat her communications with the prime minister as entirely confidential ... After thirty-four years of unvarying adherence to these constitutional principles, it is preposterous to suggest that Her Majesty might suddenly depart from them ... It is equally preposterous to suggest that any member of the queen's household, even supposing that he or she knew what Her Majesty's opinions on government policy might be (and the press secretary certainly does not), would reveal them to the press.

He defended Michael Shea by explaining that:

> Although parts of the feature article 'The African Queen' were read over to the press secretary, other crucial parts were not; and no warning was given directly by the *Sunday Times* to the palace of the article on the front page or of the impact which the *Sunday Times* expected the articles to cause.

Neil, together with Michael Jones, sat down to draft a robust reply for the next day's *Times*, accusing the palace of 'playing with fire' and lacking the wit to blow it out before it burned them. Andrew Neil pointed out in his reply that 'for the first time' Buckingham Palace were admitting that Michael Shea 'was sufficiently involved with the preparation' of the article. He went on, 'We have said from the start that all of it was read, Sir William now says only parts of it. But when Mr Shea contacted me the day after publication he made no complaint that he had been duped'.

Andrew Neil's reply ended the crisis for him; perhaps the palace had expected him to roll over and surrender and were taken aback by someone daring to stand up to them. They clearly didn't relish a prolonged confrontation between Buckingham Palace officials, Downing Street and the Murdoch empire.

Andrew Neil was certain that Michael Shea was too cautious a man to act on his own. A graduate of Gordonstoun with a doctorate in economics from the University of Edinburgh, he had served for fifteen years as a diplomat before joining the palace in 1978 to run the press office. Neil believed that he must have felt his controversial briefings had the approval of at least some of the royal family and courtiers in the palace who were at least as senior as he was. As an ex-diplomat, he would have been too careful not to risk it otherwise.[78] The identification of the press secretary as the source raised several very serious constitutional questions. Michael Shea was the queen's official spokesperson. Ronald Allison, who held the post before him explains his duty:

> You represent the queen, you represent the royal family, you represent the monarchy ... If you express an opinion about something or other you ... will be held accountable as expressing the queen's opinion. So you don't express opinions about contentious issues.[79]

Shea had a strong working relationship with the queen and was known to be in contact with her two or three times a week. Questions were inevitably asked: How did he happen to be talking about such delicate issues? Was the queen herself in any way responsible for the disclosures?[80]

If so, she was breaking a lifetime of discretion. Lord Carrington insists, 'The queen ... has never said what she felt about anything.'[81]

A slightly alternative perspective is offered up by David Owen, a former Foreign Secretary, who suggests, 'She's [the queen] indiscreet to a point, but she doesn't cross a line ... she's very cautious, little asides that you might pick up that there's an edge in their relationship, that's maybe what Mike Shea picked up over the Commonwealth.'[82] As Foreign Secretary, Owen also accompanied the queen on the Royal Yacht *Britannia*. He remembers how she 'sort of kicks off her shoes, tucks her feet under her bottom and sits on the sofa and starts to mimic guests, is indiscreet, funny and completely different to the queen you ever see in any normal circumstances'.[83]

The *Guardian* journalist, Ian Aitken, expressed disquiet at the notion of the queen seeking to marshal public opinion in opposition to an elected government, even an objectionable one.[84] According to royal biographer, Nicholas Davies, the *Sunday Times* accurately summed up the queen's vision of 'one world' working towards the unification of black and white nations.[85] If Elizabeth had approved the story, in doing so she would have set herself up against Mrs Thatcher and arguably crossed over the constitutional line. Elizabeth believed fervently that South Africa should be punished for its apartheid policies, its suppression of free thought and imprisonment of government critics. The sanctions debate threatened her beloved Commonwealth, and she was determined to use her influence to prevent that. No other matter of policy throughout Mrs Thatcher's time in office proved so divisive to her relationship with the queen.

During the aftermath of the story, the Conservative Party's rating in the polls slumped by an astonishing nine points. There were some pained faces inside Downing Street as aides had to resist the temptation to hit back or even indirectly be seen to condemn the palace. The idea that the queen was vexed with Thatcher was the last thing they needed. The following Tuesday, at Question Time in Parliament, Mrs Thatcher had the humiliation of standing up in the House of Commons to answer the usual questions about her engagements for the day, which included the customary audience with the queen. At that moment, the Labour bench burst into braying laughter, and she just had to grit her teeth. The Left rejoiced at finding an ally at the palace[86] and seemed delighted by the embarrassment it caused Margaret Thatcher. Thatcher complained to Woodrow Wyatt. 'It's unfair on me. The queen doesn't have to fight an election. I do.'[87]

Meanwhile, in the *Sunday Telegraph*, journalist and 'Thatcherite High Tory' Peregrine Worsthorne thought the queen's displeasure had made an 'indelible impression on the public imagination', and that as a result, 'the prime minister's spirit may actually have been broken'.[88] For Thatcher, who had idolised the queen before she became prime minister, the rejection she felt was acute. In her memoirs, Thatcher glossed over the issue. She wrote:

> The press could not resist the temptation to suggest disputes between the palace and Downing Street, especially on Commonwealth affairs, I always found the queen's attitude towards the work of the government absolutely correct. Of course, under the circumstances, stories of clashes between, 'two powerful women' were just too good not to make up.[89]

However, her real inner feelings were revealed when Brian Walden went to interview her for the *Sunday Times*, some time after the row. Brian, an ex-Labour MP who was now a Thatcherite convert, had become very friendly with her. He noticed that she was a bit sniffy that he was there for the *Sunday Times*.

'Does the "Queen vs. Thatcher" story still rankle?' he asked.

'Yes, it does, Brian,' she replied, 'it hurt me very badly at the time.'

'But you know it was true,' said Brian. 'The palace was out to undermine you.'

Thatcher hesitated for a moment, then took off her glasses and pinched her nose, bowed her head and said sadly, 'I know, Brian, I know. The problem is the queen is the kind of woman who could vote SDP.'[90]

In the aftermath of the affair, Mrs Thatcher treated the reckless Michael Shea gently, at least superficially. Thatcher, the queen and Shea were all at Holyrood Palace, the queen's official home in Edinburgh while the story was still being reported. It couldn't have been a very jolly breakfast with press headlines everywhere about the queen's rift with her prime minister. Later in the day, the queen deliberately placed the press secretary between herself and Mrs Thatcher at table. Michael Shea apologised for what happened. 'Don't worry, dear,' the prime minister replied. Not much was said after that.

Thatcher didn't take it completely lying down; she told diarist Woodrow Wyatt that, 'We will have to see whether new arrangements are made to prevent such a thing happening again. I think they will be.'[91]

Following a decent interval, Shea was quietly dropped as palace press secretary, without much ceremony. He disappeared to write books and articles about spin-doctoring, and later took a corporate job at Hanson plc as director of public relations. He never received the customary knighthood that often comes with the job. His discreet memoirs about his time at the palace, *A View from the Sidelines* (2003), do not mention the affair. Thatcher's people later assigned the aristocratic William Whitelaw, who had links to grandees in the royal household, to tell the palace to ignore the dissident Tory wets.[92]

Downing Street may have been annoyed, but the Foreign Office was more conciliatory and over at the Commonwealth secretariat there was unashamed delight. 'I was very glad about the Thatcher row,' said Sir Sonny Ramphal. 'What Michael Shea was saying to the press, was what we knew to be the reality, and it needed to be said.'[93]

When Sir Geoffrey Howe made a visit to Zambia and faced the cameras for a televised meeting with President Kenneth Kaunda on 24 July, he found the leader full of venom towards Mrs Thatcher, whom he accused of 'kissing apartheid'. President Kaunda was only prepared to welcome the British Foreign Secretary because of his 'love and respect for Her Majesty the Queen'.[94]

The queen's rift with Thatcher rallied the black leaders of the Commonwealth to the monarch and encouraged them not to leave the organisation. She had, it seemed, protected her favourite institution from breaking up; if a battle had been fought behind the scenes, the queen had won it.

By 30 July, an *Evening Standard* poll suggested that the Tories were only one point behind Labour. The damage didn't last that long, as both women had moved quickly to brush such a potentially damaging disagreement quickly under the carpet. As Bernard Ingham said, 'I think the article damaged Mrs T only to the extent that it gave those who wanted to damage her something to play with … Otherwise, another short-term media sensation. They come around like clockwork.'[95] Rupert Murdoch told Woodrow Wyatt, 'I always said a row with the queen would do Thatcher a lot of good. You fought a civil war about this once.'[96]

Former Liberal Party Leader, David Steel, explained:

Michael Shea was a close friend of mine, so I am not impartial. He felt
shopped by Andrew Neil. He was a loyal servant to the queen and meant
wholly well, but was perhaps too indiscreet. I think Mrs T was furious and of
course it correctly showed that she was uncaring and confrontational which
was not helpful to her.[97]

Michael Dobbs, who also knew Michael Shea, points out, 'I think you have to be
able to distinguish between Michael Shea's opinion of Mrs Thatcher and the queen's
opinion of Mrs Thatcher. They weren't necessarily one and the same thing.'[98]

Many in the media made up their minds that the whole story was hyper-
bole. Woodrow Wyatt dismissed Shea as a 'megalomaniac'[99] and Tim Bell is also
dismissive, 'Michael Shea was a gossip queen. And he said things that he has no basis
of knowing; they're just inventions. The reason they do it is because they know
that nobody can deny it because nobody knows what happened between them.'[100]
David Owen is also suspicious of Shea, 'The household is full of gossip and people
purport to know what the queen's view is.'[101]

However, three years later, in October 1989, Andrew Neil had lunch with
former Cabinet minister and notorious Tory 'wet' Norman St John-Stevas (later
Lord St John of Fawsley). A loyal monarchist, he had publicly attacked the *Sunday
Times* during the queen versus Thatcher quarrel.

'Why did you attack me, Norman?' Andrew asked, 'When you must have known
the story was true?'

'Yes Andrew it was true, which is precisely why I had to deny it.' Then he added
with a smile, 'it was more true, Andrew, than you'll ever know.'[102]

When Michael Shea had joined the household he had found himself very close
to the pinnacle of the 'ultimate club', the British Establishment. To belong, you
must never repeat what the queen has said. You bow and hold your tongue. Royal
author, Graham Turner explains:

Once you are in that circle you see that preserving ring of silence that sur-
rounds and protects the queen ... When you join the household, Civil
Service or government you are never told that, but you just pick it up. You've
become part of the circle and accepted its norms.[103]

Michael Shea broke that rule.

8

UPSTAGING

Will someone tell that bloody woman to sit down?
Her Majesty the Queen.

The immediate aftermath of the *Sunday Times* articles was to shift the historical relationship between royalty and the Tory Party. Their support for the monarch would no longer be automatic, at a time when they were subject to more criticism than in any other time in their history.[1] Mrs Thatcher's relations with the queen were cooler for a period, and with Prince Charles they never improved. The strain took its toll on the queen, and as a result of the stress she allegedly had a heart check-up.[2] Only Mrs Thatcher's instinctive deference to the monarch held her back from a direct face-off. As an ex-*Sunday Times* journalist and biographer of Prince Charles wrote, 'The interesting thing about the House of Windsor plc is that they represented everything Mrs Thatcher loathed. It was a flabby, over-costed, ineffective, unproductive organisation that needed asset-stripping, cutting, chopping, perhaps even abolishing.' The prime minister never went that far.[3]

Margaret Thatcher was, 'too happy playing Elizabeth I to be disconcerted too long by Elizabeth II'.[4] To the many crowds that came out to see her, it was the prime minister far more than the queen who now embodied the nation. It wasn't just the stupid antics of the younger royals, it was the fact that the queen represented the old elite that didn't want to change; the aristocratic court with its outmoded pecking order full of wealthy Old Etonians and blue-blooded ex-Guards officers. She retained a tenacious adherence to royal practice and protocol which seemed increasingly out of step with reality. As David Owen points out, the queen is herself a 'product of the aristocracy'.[5]

When Ronald Allison, a former BBC correspondent, was appointed as palace press secretary, the *9 O'clock News* stated, 'Allison will become the only member of the royal household to be living in a three bedroomed semi-detached house in Twickenham'.[6]

The list of obsolete traditions and antediluvian customs was endless. At the state banquets, footmen wore gold-braided scarlet liveries, knee breeches and pink stockings. Guests processed from the music room to the ballroom at Buckingham Palace with the Lord Chamberlain and the Lord Stewart walking backwards in front of the queen. At Royal Ascot, admission to the Royal Enclosure was restricted to a social elite who were approved by the Lord Chamberlain. Over 120 grace and favour apartments scattered across the various royal properties remained in the gift of the queen and she gave them away to members of her household and family.

Criticism of the queen was growing and she looked rather extravagant. Her Majesty didn't pay taxes, and historians pointed out that her tax-free status was not a historic right; both Queen Victoria and Edward VIII had paid income tax. Even loyal royalists like the former Cabinet minister, Lord St John, whom Thatcher had sacked, argued that the tax exemption would have to become modified. There was the sense the monarchy was now an unaccountable vested interest with the royal wealth estimated to be anywhere from £100 million to £2 billion, depending on whether you included the Royal Collection and Palaces; and which newspaper article you read. The *Guardian* newspaper despaired, 'How can a sensible reckoning be made between the queen's rights and responsibilities?'[7] A perfectly legal application from the Balmoral Estate for a £300,000 Forestry Commission grant for fencing sat ill with the conspicuous display and luxury of the family who gathered at the castle every summer.[8]

By the mid-1980s Mrs Thatcher was a permanent part of the landscape, a national institution. There were now two queens in the hive, as Margaret demonstrated that the country could have a very plausible figurehead who was not a monarch, but an elected leader.[9] Around the prime minister grew something of a personality cult. To some she was the wicked witch of selfishness and privilege, for others she became a symbol of what women can do and what the British character can be. For a start she gave her name to an '-ism' as no previous prime minister had done and she exerted a hold on the national imagination that went far beyond politics. When elderly patients were asked by psychiatrists to name the prime minister, it was said, for the first time since Churchill they always got it right.[10]

While Thatcher set about remaking Britain in her own image, the queen sat on the sidelines watching her prime minister's 'manic sense of mission'.[11] With

Margaret adopting a more 'presidential style ... the British political system seems to have broken down ... Chances of really effective opposition are almost zero,'[12] wrote Thatcher's biographer, Hugo Young:

> In constitutional theory, at least, the British Prime Minister sits in Cabinet as the 'first amongst equals'. Although that has long been a fiction: the prime minister has always been far more influential and powerful than that. However, because of Mrs Thatcher's longevity in office and her dominating personality that power grew more pronounced. The press started writing about her 'reign' being an 'Elective Dictatorship'.[13]

Another constitutional axiom was that the monarch was a last-ditch defence against the possible dictatorship of any politician. Mrs Thatcher could not declare herself president while the queen was still on the throne.

By the end of the 1980s Margaret Thatcher was arguably the most powerful woman in the world, having gagged the media, booted out the critics in her own party and effectually vanquished the opposition. The prime minister was out to win her arguments, no matter how much she alienated people in the process. Usually she did both.

The leader of the Labour Party, Neil Kinnock, called her 'that appalling woman' and publicly complained that Mrs Thatcher was trickier to oppose because of her sex. For years, he was regularly humiliated at her hands and she wasn't above using her gender to embarrass him. When Kinnock demanded, 'How many Cabinet ministers has the Right Honorable lady sacked since she became prime minister?' Mrs Thatcher suddenly became the soul of feminine gentility, 'How very ungentlemanly of the Honorable gentleman. Cabinet ministers resign from time to time.'

The prime minister used the female card to manipulate not just the opposition, but her own court of male advisers with the skill of Elizabeth I. She was always proud of her looks and once defiantly said, 'you don't have to be aristocratic to have beautiful blue eyes'.[14] President Mitterrand said she had 'eyes like Caligula and the mouth of Marilyn Monroe'.

The grocer's daughter who had been the ultimate outsider had replaced 15 per cent of the British peerage by packing the House of Lords with her creations, even making three hereditary peers. She also controlled a majority of 100 in the House of Commons. By now, an inevitable question was being asked, 'Isn't that the way a *monarch* is supposed to be?'

Until now, the queen's qualms regarding Mrs Thatcher had been principally based on concerns about her policies; now their antagonism seemed more personal. After being portrayed as uncaring by the queen in the *Sunday Times* article, Mrs Thatcher embarked on a 'compassion programme' to Her Majesty's cost, usurping some of the monarch's roles. At any moment of national disaster Thatcher was quicker off the mark than the palace.[15] She broke with established protocol by rushing first to the scene of any tragedy. Normally, this was a role reserved exclusively for members of the royal family, and Buckingham Palace would always wait a few days so as not to impede the work of the emergency services. Thatcher wasn't troubled by such misgivings. No accident was safe from her swift and ministering presences.[16]

In the spring of 1987, when a British cross-Channel ferry, the *Herald of Free Enterprise*, sank outside the Belgian port of Zeebrugge, Mrs Thatcher set out immediately, but not before telling her staff that the royal presence, in this case the Duke and Duchess of York, was not allowed to upstage her own.[17]

The prime minister and her husband, Denis, arrived in royal, or perhaps presidential, style at the crisis centre in a military helicopter after flying over the wrecked ferry. She visited two hospitals where British survivors were being cared for. She met a young teenager who was rescued from a ledge in the dark, he had been forced to listen to the cries of passengers struggling in the water 20ft below him until rescuers smashed through the glass with axes and pulled him to safety. 'You must tell everyone to pray for the others,' he said to the prime minister.

'They are,' she replied. 'They already are.'

Calling the press around her after talking privately to survivors, Mrs Thatcher said many were still dazed and unable to recollect clearly what had happened. 'Sometimes the wound to the mind is more difficult to heal than the wound to the body,' she said, speaking slowly and softly.

Just as Mrs Thatcher's motorcade sped away, another motorcade arrived with Prince Andrew and his wife, Sarah. The Duke and Duchess of York then visited survivors in the intensive care unit upstairs. Royal biographer, Nicholas Davies, writes, 'Knowing how sensitive the queen felt on such occasions, the prime minister's actions indicated to what depths their relations must have sunk to treat Elizabeth with such disdain and disrespect.'[18]

Whenever there was an accident or terrorist attack, Mrs Thatcher always dropped everything to go at once. When the IRA bombed Harrods at Christmas in 1983, she and Denis were attending a carol service at the Festival Hall, but left at the interval. Downing Street briefed that 'the royal family couldn't be relied on to go'.[19] When the queen ordered her advisors to investigate this upstaging, they reported back, 'If Mrs Thatcher can arrive within hours, why can't the royals?' When the queen discussed the issue with her prime minister, Mrs Thatcher just ignored her and ordered her staff to make sure no member of the royal family arrived before her. Their frosty relationship now turned to ice.[20]

The biggest and most damaging mistake for the royal family occurred when Pan Am flight 103 was blown up over Lockerbie on 21 December 1988. The bomb that brought down the airplane killed all 259 aboard and eleven people from the town of Lockerbie. Mrs Thatcher had swiftly visited the site.

The queen failed to send anyone to the Lockerbie memorial service, and the entire family was exposed by the Murdoch press as being on a series of very expensive holidays. The queen was pictured horse riding, Prince Diana was sunbathing in the Caribbean, Princess Anne was skiing, and so on. The service, held at Drysdale Parish Church, was attended by Margaret Thatcher. 'Where are the royals?' asked the *Sun*, above a picture of a weeping Pan Am stewardess and an inset of photos of nine royals and what they were doing instead. 'Fury as family snubs Lockerbie memorial,' the *Sun* continued.[21]

Other tabloids followed suit in their condemnation of the Windsors. *Daily Express* columnist Jean Rook wrote, 'At a time of national mourning, we naturally and rightly turn to our queen for the lead … Broken-hearted Britain watching TV need to see their equally grieving monarch.' Buckingham Palace stated that the queen doesn't attend memorial services or funerals, and that it was a personal decision for other members of the royal family to attend.[22] Then, to the indignation of the general public, Buckingham Palace announced that Prince Philip would fly to Japan for the funeral of Emperor Hirohito.[23]

The people of Lockerbie, in particular, felt affronted by the royal family. The queen had ignored the advice of Sir Robert Fellowes to go to the crash site immediately, partly because of her horror of ambulance chasing and her fear of getting in the way. A fortnight later, she came up to Fellowes while he was with several other people and said, 'You were right about Lockerbie and I was wrong. I wished I'd gone there earlier.'[24] Five weeks after the crash, Prince Charles eventually visited the town, listened and talked to relatives of the eleven people killed there, and laid an elaborate floral tribute at the town hall. He inspected for himself the crater gouged by the fallen Boeing 747 in the Sherwood Crescent neighborhood, where all of Lockerbie's victims lived. It was an attempt to redress the mistake. 'I thought it was a bit late in the day for Charles's visit,' said Anne McPhail, speaking to a reporter, 'but now I feel better about it. You see, we all make mistakes. You can always rectify them, can't you?'[25]

Although Charles's brother, Prince Andrew, the Duke of York, had come to Lockerbie the day after the crash, he had offended people with ill-judged remarks that seemed to show more concern for the American bereaved than those of Lockerbie. 'I am pleased that the Prince has come to make amends for his brother,' a bystander said, as Charles toured Lockerbie.[26] Despite these belated efforts, it was a public relations disaster for the royal family, who looked lazy and inept.

The Thatcher PR push went on as Margaret continued to try to win over those who felt she was getting too harsh and too powerful. During the mid-1980s Mrs Thatcher had never looked more energetic or hard-working. It was rumoured she lived on vitamin C, coffee and royal jelly, as befits a queen bee.[27]

One misguided piece of thinking led to the prime minister's appearance on the children's BBC1 show *Saturday Superstore* in 1987, where she reviewed the new singles releases. She expressed concern that Pepsi & Shirley's 'Heartache' didn't have a strong enough melody, while the Style Council's 'It Didn't Matter' also failed to impress her. It was a surreal moment of broadcasting history. Refusing to compromise her style and presentation, she talked down to everyone, or as Keith Waterhouse neatly put it, 'As if my dog had just died'.[28]

Saturday Superstore, however, was just a minor setback. Overall, a more polished Margaret emerged during this period. She had entered Number 10 as a rather menopausal looking 53-year-old, who said, 'No one I know of has a glamourous life. I don't think it exists.' After a lifetime of hard work and sober effort, Margaret Thatcher now had the flush of someone intoxicated with power. It was a look that suited her and with that security came the courage to express her femininity more openly. At 60, she had never looked better.[29] Her appointment diary for 1984 shows she visited a hairdresser 118 times in the space of twelve months. Five of the sessions were on consecutive days in June when the coiffured prime minister hosted world leaders at an economic summit in London.[30]

In 1987, poised for the momentous trip to Moscow that would see her seal her friendship with Mikhail Gorbachev, Mrs Thatcher called in the chief designer of Aquascutum for a warm coat, on the recommendation of her personal assistant Cynthia Crawford, nicknamed 'Crawfie', who acted as her *de facto* lady-in-waiting and was a close confidante.[31] Designer Marianne Abrahams padded out her shoulders and pulled up her skirts. Crawfie revamped her entire wardrobe and evolved a system with each outfit being given a name, 'Gdansk Green' worn at a Polish shipyard, 'Wogan Burgundy' which she wore on television for the Children In Need charity appeal presented by Terry Wogan, and 'Sapphire Blue' for the Party Conference, and so on.

Mrs Thatcher arrived in Moscow looking a million dollars in a glamourous fur hat. Like an 'Aquascutum tsarina,' said journalist Piers Brendon.[32] On Russian television, she spoke with an awesome frankness and championed nuclear capitalist democracy, using the phrase 'nuclear security'. She took part in royal-style walkabouts, visiting the monastery at Zagorsk where she lit a candle. She was cheered by crowds in Georgia and kissed by a young man. With Gorbachev beside her, it became the 'Maggie and Mikhail Show', they exchanged views frankly, interrupted each other like old friends and clearly enjoyed each other's company. She saw herself as part of a triumvirate, alongside Reagan and Gorbachev, that ended the Cold War and acted as a political interpreter between the other two leaders. Politically she was in Reagan's camp, but she was strongly drawn to Gorbachev's intellectual strength.[33]

Margaret's trip to Moscow couldn't have been better timed. Mrs Thatcher launched the 1987 election in May off the back of her visit to Gorbachev at the end of March, using her international prestige to fuel her domestic political success. She won, albeit with a reduced majority, meaning she could look forward to four more years in power. At Buckingham Palace, Her Majesty waited for the third time to invited Mrs Thatcher to form her government.

Royalty, it seemed, was no longer the public face of Britain aboard. As the queen's former press secretary, Ron Allison, pointed out, 'When she [Thatcher] toured abroad in some places they thought they were seeing the queen, which is a mistake they wouldn't have made if the PM had been a man. And she didn't do very much to disabuse them of this [laughter].'[34] 'The Chinese got confused at the differences between the two women after their subsequent visits. 'Which was which?' said Edwina Currie, 'Buckingham Palace felt upstaged by Mrs Thatcher.'[35]

There were mutterings at the palace. Diarist and politician, Alan Clark, picked up on these bad vibrations. He wrote, 'Mrs Thatcher's personal charisma and glamour and the deference that was accorded on the global stage ... were certainly bitterly resented.'[36] In response to pressure from the palace, the Foreign Office sent out instructions that the prime minister should not be greeted with the National Anthem when she landed on foreign soil. 'I'm afraid there were periodic attempts to humiliate her,' wrote Clark, 'to cut her down to size.'[37]

In 1988, an invitation for the queen to visit Moscow arrived. Mrs Thatcher wasn't about to share the limelight, and it was her turn to cut Her Majesty down to size and she vetoed the trip. Thatcher's irrepressible press secretary, Bernard Ingham, held one of his regular discreet briefings for a select group of political correspondents. The 'government sources', or rather Bernard Ingham, claimed that a major barrier would be the 'butchering' of the Russian royal family, the Romanovs, after the 1917 Revolution. Czar Nicholas II was a first cousin of Britain's King George V, and the czarina was a granddaughter of Queen Victoria. This was political humbug. The *Guardian* scoffed that Ingham was merely trying to put a gloss on a political decision.

Ingham was also reported to have said it would be wrong for the queen to visit Moscow until Gorbachev had improved human rights in the Soviet Union. In a veiled reference to the reported tension between the queen and her prime minister, George Robertson, the Labour Party foreign affairs spokesman, called it, 'sad and sour' for Thatcher to veto a visit that 'could only encourage Gorbachev's policies on reform … The queen is being made a scapegoat for Mrs Thatcher's obsession with dominating the scene.'

Even some of Thatcher's own supporters were surprised. 'My own view about people with rather bad records in human rights is that they should be exposed to the beauty of a free society,' commented a former Lord Chancellor, Lord Hailsham, in a BBC interview. 'The more you can expose them to it, the better things are likely to be.' Peter Temple-Morris, another Conservative MP, said a royal visit to Moscow would be, 'A tremendous thing to happen … the big fear in the Soviet Union is that Gorbachev's reforms will fail. A visit by the queen would be a marvellous encouragement to the Russian people.'[38]

The golden rule of Buckingham Palace is never upstage the queen. After decades on the throne, the queen was starting to look dull and less glamorous, outshone by the younger Princess Diana and a more queenly Mrs Thatcher with her new wardrobe, bigger hair and more expensive jewellery. Historian Dr Daniel Conway thinks:

> Margaret Thatcher always thought she had to keep up appearances, to use that phrase. Because she came from a lower middle-class background. Because she was a woman in a man's world. Particularly, I would say, in the company of the queen.
>
> She used her appearance to accentuate her power and to make statements … I also think … towards the end of her period of office, her dress could signify her hubris, and her inappropriate presidentialism, or even being like the monarch … I've got pictures of Margaret Thatcher going on tours, receiving flowers, meeting children, and they're quite strange in a way, it's quite unusual, and I can't think of another prime minister that would have done that in the same way … I think she viewed herself as someone who embodied the nation, and was there to save the nation. And so, inevitably, she became increasingly regal and monarchical. I'm sure there must have been some tension with Buckingham Palace.[39]

Prince Charles, waiting on the sidelines, was impatient for his chance to be king. Palace courtiers began talking of QVS, Queen Victoria Syndrome, when a fickle public grew tired of an aging monarch and the extended royal family.[40] Prime

Minister William Gladstone wrote about Queen Victoria after she hid herself away at Balmoral after the death of her husband Prince Albert, 'The queen is invisible, and the Prince of Wales is not respected'.[41]

There were other points of similarity. Like Queen Victoria, Queen Elizabeth II was becoming the butt of populist humour. When she came to the throne in 1953, it was forbidden to represent the queen on stage, and any caricature of her could not be published. By the early 1990s, she was constantly being lampooned, nowhere more brutally than the television puppet satire, *Spitting Image*, which attracted enormous audiences every Sunday evening. The *Times* described her puppet as 'a dotty granny presiding over a loony soap opera'.[42] Mrs Thatcher, although depicted as a hectoring harridan, was inhumanly immune to criticism. John Lloyd, *Spitting Image*'s producer, said, 'The more you mock her, the stronger she becomes'.[43]

By the end of the 1980s, the Windsors were fighting amongst themselves. A disdain developed in the relationship between Prince Charles and the queen. The queen felt her son was too extravagant and she was apparently very critical of Prince Charles taking the royal train with boxes of crockery and silver up to Scotland for lavish dinners. She 'raised her eyebrows quite frequently'.[44]

Meanwhile, Princess Diana was rapidly morphing from 'Shy Di' into a global icon. While the Prince and Princess of Wales were at war privately, a vigorous campaign was started by Prince Charles to rival his wife's high profile. This saw him busy himself with community projects and strongly-worded speeches, which often backfired and irritated Mrs Thatcher by implying criticism of her regime. One case in point was his role as president of Business in the Community (BITC), a body dedicated to business regeneration in the inner cities, where his speeches linked unemployment and urban neglect with social ills. In Bernard Ingham's opinion, Charles sailed 'presentationally at least, a bit close to the wind at times'.[45]

On 25 March 1988 at Kensington Palace, there was a fascinating encounter between the Prince of Wales and Margaret Thatcher. It was the prime minister who called on the prince, but in actual terms it was he who came to her 'cap in hand'. He had arranged the meeting in the hope that he could win back favour, and even gain some concessions from the prime minister which his mother had so far denied him. Would it be possible, he asked, to preside over the state opening of Parliament in his mother's absence? Margaret agreed, but if he did so it would only be as a lord commissioner and he could only read the queen's speech (written, of course, by the prime minister) from the bench in the chamber rather than from the actual throne. Charles even asked for another title that would give him greater significance in the running of state affairs, he even bizarrely suggested Prince Regent. However, this title would only be relevant if the queen had ceased to be able to perform her usual functions, and his mother was very much in control of her senses. The prime minister had no choice but to turn him down.[46]

The prime minister had little more time for Prince Charles than his mother did. David Owen said:

> I think that sometimes he [Prince Charles] certainly was out of control when he was younger, in that he didn't understand that he simply couldn't have a view. I mean he was virtually SDP, and he used to send me speeches and things to look at and I would say 'fine I agree with every word of it, but unfortunately, the prime minister doesn't, therefore you can't say it'. He got rather fed up with it, so he didn't send his speeches to me for, and I was very glad.[47]

As Michael Dobbs points out, the prince was 'walking a tightrope between his conscience and the constitution, but then I suspect most modern heirs might find that'.[48]

For his part, Charles had never warmed to the prime minister and complained that she was 'a bit like a school ma'am' and, like many, felt she was the shrill governess who had risen above her station.[49] Yearning for real responsibilities, he schemed to become Governor-General of Australia, but Thatcher dismissed this. The one real job that was mooted seriously by the prime minister for the prince was the distant prize of becoming Britain's last Governor of Hong Kong before it reverted to Chinese sovereignty in 1997. The role would have mirrored that of his great-uncle Lord Mountbatten, who had been the last Viceroy to India before independence. In the event, the job was seen to be too delicate after the Tiananmen Square massacre in 1989 for someone as forthright in their opinions as the Prince of Wales can sometimes be.

Later that year, stories were circulating that the queen might retire, as had Queen Juliana of the Netherlands in 1980. One poll in 1990 showed nearly half the population supported such an idea, and it was predicted inaccurately that the queen would use her Christmas broadcast to declare her intention to step down on 6 February, the fortieth anniversary of her accession.[50] The rumour was nonsense. The queen took the unprecedented step, during her Christmas broadcast, of reminding viewers that she was mindful of her coronation oath to be queen for life. Allegedly these words upset Prince Charles, and the queen and her son were not on speaking terms for some time. It was unlikely that Mrs Thatcher would ever have countenanced the removal of a 'wet' queen in favour of an even 'wetter' Prince of Wales.

Buttressed now by a third successive election victory, Mrs Thatcher had an unbreakable faith not only in her rightness but in her righteousness, something both colleagues and members of the royal family found tedious. The prime minister began to feel that attending the queen once a week was a waste of time, and she seemed to find the queen's world increasingly petty and irrelevant. In military matters, for example, Margaret worried about actual military capacity and real issues of defence. Whereas, it seemed to her that Her Majesty was only interested in historic cap badges and mascots, and the survival of cherished military regiments with which the royal family had strong connections. Mrs Thatcher concerned herself with real issues like ending the Cold War. In contrast to every other engagement in her diary, Mrs Thatcher now only read the agenda for her weekly meetings with the queen at the last minute, in the car on the way to the palace.[51]

A frost between the palace and Downing Street had set in. If the queen dreaded Mrs Thatcher coming to the palace, Mrs Thatcher loathed the annual prime ministerial trip to Balmoral, the queen's country estate in Scotland.[52] In the remote highlands there could be no question of upstaging, this was the queen's home turf. Balmoral, with its dark pitch pine, tartan curtains, tartan carpets, tartan wall hangings and tartan-covered furniture, projected an atmosphere that the prime minister found sheer purgatory. Charles Powell, her chief advisor, said that she only went 'out of loyalty'.[53] A handwritten thank-you letter exists in the Thatcher archive from Margaret to Lady Moore, the wife of the queen's private secretary, Sir Philip Moore, in which she writes, 'Whatever the difficulties, you always cope magnificently', and refers to Balmoral as a 'different world'.[54]

A later prime minister, Tony Blair, vividly described his first Balmoral weekend as a 'combination of the intriguing, the surreal and the utterly freaky', fortified by 'rocket fuel' cocktails and breakfast, lunch and dinner 'out of Trollope or Walter Scott'.[55]

Ron Allison points out, 'Everything is done to make the visitor feel absolutely as at home possible ... but the queen doesn't regard it as her duty to entertain you 24/7. She'll see you at luncheon out on the shoot. And then you're left to your own devices.'[56]

For the queen, Balmoral represents a continuum dating back to Queen Victoria. Guests, including relatives who call her Lilibet and longtime friends, still bow and curtsy when they greet her in the morning and when she retires at night. Her Majesty spends ten weeks over the summer at her Scottish castle. There, she follows a routine rooted in the Victorian era, and everyone is expected to fall into line with boarding school schedules rather like a summer camp. However, it is a camp on a very grand scale. Built under Prince Albert's supervision, the white stone castle resembles a German schloss. Here, the highland life is the closest she gets to 'normality' and a sense of genuine freedom. When the queen goes into the nearby village shops, she stands in the queue; she completes household chores in remote cabins and dresses in well-worn old clothes.[57] At the castle itself, as many as 120 staff look after only six members of the family. Guests, when invited, are normally limited to fourteen or sixteen.[58] The household servants, trained in discretion, appear only when required, aware that to be seen or heard without a purpose would be to intrude. Dinner for guests at Balmoral is served at 8.15 p.m., and guests don't know until the last minute whether it will be black tie and gowns indoors, or sweaters with trousers or skirts outside. Meals are frequently accompanied by music played by three Scottish pipers.[59]

Many staff are housed in temporary Nissen-type huts that were erected for the servants during the Czar of Russia's visit to Queen Victoria in 1882, although since then heaters have been installed. The queen doesn't mind spending money at Buckingham Palace, as long as it is done discreetly, because the government pays, whereas she doesn't like to spend much at Balmoral because the money comes directly from her purse.[60] 'In fifty years she hasn't spent anything on anything,' claims David Owen.[61]

Among the characters who also serve the queen at Balmoral are the 'Edinburgh women', extra staff who are needed to help with the house parties. These Edinburgh women come year after year, a busload of them, mostly widows, large jolly ladies for whom the ten weeks working for royalty is the treat of the year. They are housed in the castle itself, two to a room. At the end of the summer, they're invited to the Ghillies Ball, the highlight of the holiday, where the royal princes make a point of dancing with as many of them as possible. It's a strange and unique world, unseen anywhere else except, perhaps, on the television series *Downton Abbey*.

The obligatory annual prime ministerial visit occurs one weekend in September, when they're expected to join in this tartan rustication. In theory, the appointment is in the calendar to allow the queen and her prime minister to discuss matters in an informal setting. In reality, it has often been the backdrop to two very different worlds clashing head on.

Mrs Thatcher used to arrive early, just as she did with the audiences at Buckingham Palace. Often she stayed beforehand with Sir Hector and Lady Laing at their Scottish home on the Findhorn. Once, she had to kill time, so the official car was stopped up in the hills and she got out, tottering up and down the highland road in high heels. Locals who drove past gave her some shocked looks when they realised who she was.[62] When Mrs Thatcher got to the castle in her new tweed suit, she was ill-prepared for country walks.

'Does the prime minister like to walk in the hills?' asked one royal guest.

'The hills? The hills? She walks on the road!' replied the queen.[63] It was left to the ladies-in-waiting to get the prime minister out of her heels and into hush puppies.

At dinner the prime minister upset royal etiquette by refusing to withdraw with the other women after dinner. The queen circumvented such extraordinary behaviour by holding a less formal barbecue which didn't require such traditional dining customs.

These 'informal' events were organised by Prince Philip and took place in one of the cabins or summer houses on the 49,000 acre estate. A royal barbecue consists of many steaks, sausages, chops and all kinds of salads that are prepared in the Balmoral kitchens. They begin with the prince setting off in a Land Rover with a special trailer, kitted out with all cutlery, glasses, plates, food and drink. By the time the guests arrive, the prince has the barbecue going, and the queen is laying out the knives and folks. One guest called it a kind of 'virtual reality' where the queen and her husband play at being normal. They also witnessed Margaret struggling with the ultra-rare meat Prince Philip cooked, and watching uncomfortably as the queen carried out menial tasks. The prime minister kept trying to help, only for the queen to hiss, 'Will someone tell that woman to sit down?' The story is demonstrative of their relationship, an overtly deferential prime minister and a monarch irritated by it.[64]

After one trip, Mrs Thatcher sent the monarch a pair of washing-up gloves, after watching her clean the dishes with her bare hands.[65]

It didn't get better after dinner. In the evenings, the royal family has a long tradition of playing drawing room pursuits, such as charades, or sometimes vigorous games such as 'Kick the Can' (a form of hide-and-seek) and 'Stone'. Guests, even prime ministers or private secretaries, as well as members of the household, are expected to join in.

Other aspects of Balmoral life bemused Mrs Thatcher, such as the queen's strict 11.15 p.m. curfew in the evening, far too early for a workaholic prime minister, who survived on five hours sleep a night. When Denis Thatcher suggested to his wife it was time to retire to bed, she apparently replied with a puzzled, 'Bed? What we would do up there?' It caused considerable royal giggling when the Thatchers left the room.[66]

Horse riding, fishing, shooting and dog walking are the main pastimes, but Mrs Thatcher didn't do 'pastimes'. 'Mrs Thatcher wouldn't have understood the concept of leisure,' said Edwina Currie. 'The queen did: she rode, spent time in the country and walked her dogs. Leisure was an anathema to Mrs Thatcher with her childhood.'[67]

Each morning, an immaculate Land Rover draws up outside the front of the castle to take shooting guests to the edge of the moor or up the mountain.[68] When someone shoots a stag, it is gutted on the hillside and its disembowelled carcass is strapped on the back of a pony and carried down the hill to the castle larder for skinning.[69] Such carnage is part of country life, and the queen is matter of fact about it. She was once photographed strangling pheasants, which caused a minor scandal.[70] None of these country pursuits appealed to the prime minister.

When one of Mrs Thatcher's aides was bitten by one of her dogs, the queen got very cross with him, blaming him because he had trodden on it, and it had nipped him. There was zero sympathy, and she made it very clear that the dog was the injured party.[71]

Courtiers spoke of the difficulty of finding 'something to do in the afternoon' with Mrs Thatcher. Thankfully, this was often mitigated by her insatiable appetite for her official boxes.[72] The official red boxes also offered an escape for the queen. A senior civil servant who went to Balmoral with Mrs Thatcher was amazed to see the queen dealing with correspondence when dinner was over. 'When the meal had been cleared away,' he recalled, 'She brought in a huge basket of letters from the public … She was plainly more interested in reading them than in making small talk.'[73] Both women used work to avoid each other.

Lady Mary Coleman, niece of the queen mother, confided in diarist Woodrow Wyatt that everyone at Balmoral had been beastly to Mrs Thatcher when she had been a guest there. Lady Mary had been at a Balmoral house party for three days when the prime minister arrived. Many of the aristocratic guests asked her silly questions about what she was going to do about unemployment, and Lady Mary felt the queen was horrid to her. The prime minister had been talking about the Falklands, and the queen said sharply in a loud voice, 'I don't agree with you at all,' and Mrs Thatcher went red and looked very uncomfortable. Lady Mary felt the queen was trying to put Mrs Thatcher in her place, knowing that she was unaccustomed to the upper-class society of which the court consists.[74]

Denis Thatcher survived much better in these circumstances, making jokes and laughing, deliberately being oblivious to the queen's unpleasantness.[75] An equerry was assigned to play golf with him and the queen routinely took the prime minister for tea at Birkhall, the Scottish retreat of the queen mother. Unlike her daughter, the queen mother was an ultra-Thatcherite who would happily talk to anyone about the shortcomings of communists or left wingers inside the BBC. The queen mother first invited the prime minister to Birkhall shortly after her election victory in May 1979, when she gave her a silver brooch which Mrs Thatcher always treasured. She remained an ardent admirer because both women shared a belief in the greatness of Britain.[76]

The queen mother sang Thatcher's praises to diarist Woodrow Wyatt, a confidant of both women. He wrote, 'She [the queen mother] adores Mrs Thatcher and thinks she is very brave and has done tremendous things.' The queen mother had a habit of raising or lowering her glass in dinner table toasts. For those of whom she disapproved, such as some socialist politicians, she would propose a toast of 'down with' while lowering her glass out of sight of the table. For those she favoured, the toast was more traditional, with the glass held up. For Mrs Thatcher, the glass was always high.[77] 'Margaret had a signed photograph in her front room of the queen mother,' said Jeffrey Archer, 'So their relationship was very strong indeed.'[78]

On the final day of the Balmoral trip, the prime minister and her husband usually left at 6 a.m.; Mrs Thatcher couldn't get away fast enough.[79] Margaret was always impatient to do something that she considered 'useful' on the trip north to Scotland, such as visiting Tory officials in Edinburgh or perhaps squeezing in a meeting of north-east Scottish Conservatives. This time-management was noted with wry amusement by palace officials, who had worked all their lives at a more 'well-bred' pace.[80]

Thatcher had always been irritated by the number of staff surrounding the royals. At Balmoral, the Thatchers had personal attendants assigned to look after them and unpack for them. One year, Margaret returned to Downing Street in a fury, flung open the freezer, and defrosted shepherd's pie for her guests. The frugal Mrs Thatcher constantly worried about saving government money. When she moved into Number 10, eager to avoid an expenses row over refurbishment work, she even provided her own crockery and ironing board. At Chequers, the prime minister's official country home, she always insisted that heating for the indoor swimming pool was kept off, except for special occasions for guests.[81] It was a more prudent attitude to public funds than many royals displayed at the time.

9

MOTHERHOOD

You're an awful mother!
Carol Thatcher

There were several similarities between family life at home with the Windsors and Thatchers. Both were Victorian in their outlook, and neither were very tactile or demonstratively affectionate; it is unlikely either set of parents ever read the fashionable advice of Dr Spock. The hugs and kisses policy favoured by Princess Diana in later years was never on the agenda. As a result, both the Windsor and Thatcher children suffered similar problems growing up in the spotlight.

Mrs Thatcher would be hurt by her daughter's remoteness, and the damage caused by her son's financial and political scandals. Elizabeth II would witness the harm inflicted on the monarchy by a succession of failed marriages, and come to regard her son and heir, Prince Charles, as a fool. Although both women had immense authority over their children, both failed to use it sufficiently. The queen and the prime minister, particularly in the instances of their favourite children, Mark Thatcher and Prince Andrew, would protect and indulge their respective failures at considerable damage to their reputations.

During the 1980s, 1 million women joined the workforce, yet the burden of childcare was still seen as women's work, even if you were the queen or prime minister. Modern society would confirm that sexism was still prevalent by pointing the finger of guilt for any failings amongst their children at the two mothers, rather than the children's fathers. Such critics ignored the fact paternal influence is equally as important as the maternal one.

After her father's death, Elizabeth struggled to make room in her life for her family. When she became queen, she knew she had to reach a compromise with her husband. While she would be the head of state, he would become the head of the family effectively making Philip, who had abandoned his successful naval career to support her, the boss at home. It was a division of labour, with Philip acting as paterfamilias, which produced mixed results. The prince had to grapple with the prejudice of the royal courtiers who viewed him as a foreign upstart from a minor German-Danish royal family, the house of Schleswig-Holstein-Sonderburg-Glücksburg. Sir Alan Lascelles, his wife's aloof private secretary, snubbed him, describing him as, 'the matrimonial nigger in the woodpile'.[1] Philip now vented these frustrations on his eldest son.

Elizabeth had been an almost obsessive-compulsive child, methodical and tidy, and in her new role she was always zealous about answering her mail, making speeches and working through her official boxes. As the sovereign, she knew she had to reign, to travel, make state visits, consult her prime minister, deliver speeches, cut ribbons, wave to the crowds, accept salutes, bestow honours and keep smiling. It became easy for her to shut herself off in the office rather than have a row with her husband or children. She was now always queen first, wife second and mother third.[2]

Publicly, she was the perfect wife and mother, as the pictures of her with her handsome blond husband and her two young children, Charles and Anne, which appeared in newspapers and magazines demonstrated. She had learned valuable lessons from her shrewd mother who, as queen, had authorised books such as *The Family Life of Queen Elizabeth*, and arranged photo spreads called 'Our Little Princesses at Home' and 'Playtime at the Royal Lodge' to foster the idyllic royal family image. Now her daughter recognised the value of good press in keeping the monarchy popular. Posing for family photographs was part of the job, and she got on with it.

Before Charles's birth, Elizabeth promised, 'I'm going to be the child's mother, not the nurses'.[3] As a mother, she never lived up to that promise, and with such distant parents Charles grew up largely bereft of normal parental interaction. Philip assumed there was little he could contribute in these early formative years, and Elizabeth was busy putting duty first and trusting the staff they had employed to get it right. This neglect produced a young boy prone to forlorn self-analysis and self-pitying traits. 'Royalty regards their children like cattle,' wrote John Gordon in the *Daily Express*, after learning that Elizabeth had stayed in bed when Prince Charles was rushed to London's Great Ormond Street Hospital for an emergency appendectomy at midnight.[4] When the 7-year-old Princess Anne had her tonsils removed, it was her nanny who took her to the hospital and stayed the night at her bedside[5] while the queen remained at home.[6]

Elizabeth was simply adopting the aristocratic, upper-class style of child rearing from the 1920s and 1930s. She delegated her maternal role to two Scottish-born nurses, Helen Lightbody and Mabel Anderson, who imposed a rigid daily regime. Charles only saw his mother for thirty minutes in the morning, and again in the early evening when she would try to clear two hours in her day. During the royal bath time, she sat on a gilt chair with a footman behind her and watched one of the staff bathe her son. 'She didn't put her hands in the bath water,' Charles said, 'but at least she watched.'[7] Passing by her office one day, the little boy urged his mother to come and play. 'If only I could,' the queen said, as she shut the door against him.

Daily Mail columnist Lynda Lee-Potter wrote, 'Her dislike of physical contact is almost a phobia. By her inability to demonstrate love for her children, the queen has made it difficult for them to give affection in return. She is a stoic and, like her mother, has a ruthless streak.'[8] Given the habits of her class, she knew no better. She grew up more able to form relationships with dogs and horses than with people. Maternal attentions were rationed to sporadic sessions that fitted in around her schedule.

This is a precise mirror of earlier generations of the royal family. Lord Harewood, the queen's first cousin, wrote that the whole of his family bottled up their feelings and avoided discussing awkward subjects. They never talked of love or what they meant to each other, only duty and behaviour.[9]

Charles was 3 years old when his mother became queen. Although not invested as Prince of Wales yet, he became Duke of Cornwall, Duke of Rothesay, Earl of Carrick and Baron of Renfrew, Lord of the Isles and Great Steward of Scotland. He was given, at this young age, a car and chauffeur, a detective, Sergeant Kelly, and a footman, Richard Brown, whom he once 'knighted' with a table knife. 'Why haven't you got a Richard?' Charles once asked a well-born playmate.[10]

There was also a formidable code of etiquette for any child to master, as he was often dressed up to meet distinguished visitors and had to learn to bow before kissing his great-grandmother, Queen Mary. In public, Elizabeth treated Charles with a chilly formality.

The boy's third Christmas in 1950 saw his father still stationed in Malta with a naval command. His mother chose to spend the holiday alone with her husband and left her children in the care of nannies. When Prince Charles was due to celebrate his 5th birthday in London, the queen and Prince Philip decided to stay at Sandringham, even though nine days later they were to leave Britain on a six month tour of the Commonwealth in November 1953 without him.

'The queen and her husband,' the *Daily Telegraph* reported, 'Have endeared themselves to the British peoples by a devoted family life, and their separation from their children at an age when children especially need their parents has been a real privation.'[11] When the family was finally reunited in May 1954, when her little boy came to greet her the queen told him, 'No, not you dear,' and addressed the various waiting dignitaries first. Then she just shook the 5 year old's extended hand.[12]

It was a 'miserable childhood', Prince Charles recalled later. One of his saddest recollections was growing up alone. He said that his father was rarely present for his birthdays and missed the first five. Instead, his father sent him notes. Charles's much loved uncle, Lord Mountbatten, said, 'Loneliness is something royal children have always suffered and always will. Not much you can do about it, really.'[13]

If Charles found his mother tough and unsentimental, his father could be brutish. Prince Philip, the Duke of Edinburgh, was determined that his son should grow up to be a 'man's man' and tried to instill vigour into his weak-chested and flat-footed son, who was uncertain riding a horse, queasy on a boat and afraid of the dark. Ignoring Charles's screams, he threw his 3-year-old son into the palace swimming pool to teach him to swim. Cut out of state affairs, Philip asserted his role as head of the family. When Philip rebuked his son, he often made the boy cry.[14] Charles found his father a bully and complained to friends that there were two kinds of father: the first instills self-confidence in his children by offering praise when merited and withholding criticism when possible; 'The second is the Duke of Edinburgh,' he said.[15]

Philip viewed his son as spoilt, something he took upon himself to correct.[16] As a result, father and son further withdrew from each other.[17] Prince Philip was determined to make his son as unemotional as he appears to be, but had limited success. Philip's preoccupation with manliness bordered on prejudice. Interior designer, Nicholas Haslam, recalls how Philip refused to allow his son to be shown round the newly decorated Porchester House. 'We don't want him knowing anything pansy like decoration.' However, with so many women, including his grandmother, looking out for him, he was the subject of considerable feminine influence. Philip burst out one day, 'Nothing but nannies, nurses and poofs!' referring to the household staff, who were largely homosexual.[18]

Eventually, Philip sacked one of Charles's nannies, Helen Lightbody, because she encouraged his 'softness',[19] and he later sent this sensitive boy to school at Gordonstoun, a remote, spartan establishment with an unusual emphasis on outdoor and physical pursuits. It was to be one of the most unhappy episodes of his son's life; it had all the comforts of a juvenile remand home with unpainted walls, bare boards and naked light bulbs, and resembled an army barracks. 'Well, at least he hasn't run away yet,' Prince Philip replied when asked how his son was surviving under the tough regime. Charles always loathed the place. 'It's absolute hell,' he wrote home.[20] His status as heir to the throne did nothing to endear him to the school bullies. He was not, and never could be, one of the more popular boys. Many ostracised him; he was hit with pillows and punched at all hours of the night. For him, the entire place was a 'prison sentence' and his parents rejected his pleas to be taken away from the school.

Charles's only escape during this incarceration were his frequent visits to the queen mother at Birkhall on the Balmoral estate, where she overindulged him with cakes and affection, which he guzzled. Both parents created an 'affection gap' that helped to forge a strong rapport between grandmother and grandson. This bond developed into the most intimate of the prince's relationships within the family, and became for him an all important source of love and encouragement. The queen mother viewed him, like she did her late husband George V, as someone to be nurtured, not forced.[21]

The prince's shy, retiring and artistic characteristics, which were understood by his grandmother, only confused Elizabeth and Philip. At Windsor, the young Charles once discovered a collection of drawings by Leonardo da Vinci, which held him spellbound. When he told his family about it, they were bemused, leaving him feeling squashed and guilty, as if by choosing the library rather than horses he had in some way let them down.[22] As Charles grew up, he communicated with his parents by letter or internal palace memorandums delivered by footmen. Few topics were felt suitable for face-to-face confrontation. Neither of his parents saw that any great harm was being done to a sensitive boy.[23]

At Cambridge University, where Charles won a place because of his birthright rather than his examination grades, he stood out, wearing tweed jackets and brogues amongst the scruffy student body protesting against the Vietnam War. He changed his course several times, and achieved a very average second-class degree. This was followed by a spell in the army, and then a spell in the navy. Since then there has been no career, and it has made him a dabbler with this and that. His sycophantic friends have assured him that he is 'an intellectual' and he happily gives opinions on subjects such as global warming, Carl Jung, modern architecture, gardening, inner cities, herbalism, orthodox medicine, yoga, Eastern philosophy, reincarnation, spiritualism, vegetarianism, green issues and low energy light bulbs.[24] The queen saw many of these interests as silly, and called him a fool. The Duke of Edinburgh called him an 'intellectual pillow',[25] bearing the mark of the last head to make an impression on him.

Philip's belittling of his son continued into adulthood. When Lord Mountbatten died following the IRA bomb explosion, the Prince of Wales was deeply upset and left the lunch table to be alone. When he returned to the table, his father embarked on a course of baiting Charles until he just walked out. Both guests and staff in the room found it distressing. Shortly after his marriage to Diana Spencer, everyone present at a shooting party heard Philip shout at the prince, in front of guests too, 'Move your bloody arse!' He felt his son was lagging behind. The prince never answered back and just walked off.[26]

One of the questions often asked by people who know the royal family is, 'What went wrong?' and the extent to which the queen can be blamed for her oldest son's unhappiness.[27] Prince Charles's life has become one large 'what if?' The British constitution defines no precise role for the heir to the throne. Its unwritten rules state clearly what the Prince of Wales should *not* do, but there is little guidance about what to do in the years he has to wait to take up the top job. History has seen monarchs-in-waiting becoming rivals to their parents, acting as unofficial leaders of the opposition, barely disguising their eagerness to take over. Some have become playboys, leading lives of self-indulgence, and others make themselves useful through their charitable work.

It has not been a particularly distinguished office to date.[28] While waiting to become king, the prince regent (later George IV) committed bigamy, Edward VII liked actresses so much he was nicknamed 'Edward the Caresser' and Edward VIII conducted numerous affairs with married women and even married one – Wallis Simpson – losing his throne in the process.

The fact that the queen and Prince Philip were not hands-on parents left the door open for other influences. Charles fell very much under the charms of Lord Mountbatten, which Lord Charteris believes 'was extremely bad news'.[29] Mountbatten advised him that he ought to sow his wild oats before marrying an aristocratic virgin. He had his granddaughter, Lady Amanda Knatchbull, in mind as a future queen.

Charles took his advice and became something of an indulgent playboy during the 1970s. His parents were worried, and there was endless discussion about finding the prince a real job. Even Mountbatten became concerned, telling *Time Magazine* that his great nephew was always 'popping in and out of bed with girls'.[30] These amours were just carnal, and are thought to have run well into double figures, but failed to provide the emotional satisfaction Charles desired.

There were also outbursts of volcanic princely tempers and fits of foot stamping over tiny matters such as a valet forgetting to put out his favourite comb.

'The life he'd led,' said Lord Charteris, 'was bad preparation for marriage', as his eventual bride, Lady Diana Spencer discovered. The queen griped in private that her children were 'rotten pickers' when it came to choosing marriage partners, but she had never guided them in the right direction.[31]

The prince also became very absentminded with his official duties and lazy with his official boxes. At the memorial service for former Australian Prime Minister, Sir Robert Menzies, at Westminster Abbey, he read the wrong lesson. Menzies' widow didn't comment, but it was very clear what everyone felt about such negligence.

Mountbatten finally wrote to Charles warning him that he was 'beginning on a downward slope which wrecked your Uncle David's life'. By this he meant Edward VIII, the Duke of Windsor, who was called 'David' by close family members, and whose sybaritic behaviour led to the abdication.[32]

There was talk about Charles going to work at the Cabinet office, or being appointed as an ambassador somewhere. Prime Minister James Callaghan tried to find Prince Charles real employment. However, he was snubbed by, what an aide called, 'this arrogant young man'.[33] As Lord McNally recorded, 'Beyond a general look around Whitehall, the prince did not display very much enthusiasm for doing a specific job.'[34] The queen and prince completely failed to get to grips with the situation. The so-called 'Firm' had never become a functional family unit.

Both the queen and her husband found an easier relationship with their daughter, Princess Anne. Anne shared an almost identical upbringing as her brother, as they were brought up together in their six-room nursery complex on the second floor of Buckingham Palace. Of all the queen's children, Anne is the most secure and self-sufficient. She was never obviously distressed by her parents' long absences, although one nanny, Helen Lightbody, showed preference for Prince Charles, as did the governess they later shared, Catherine Peebles (known as 'Mipsy').[35] When Anne and Charles were sent for their lessons in the palace schoolroom, the princess was ignored as Miss Peebles became possessive about Charles. He could do no wrong in her eyes and she hated leaving him, even when he was spending time with his mother. She wept for days when he was sent away to school.

When left only with Princess Anne, two other 5-year-old girls, Susan (Sukie) Babington-Smith and Caroline Hamilton, both granddaughters of senior courtiers, were brought into the palace to share Anne's lessons. However, there was never any great enthusiasm for education from any of those involved.

When Miss Peebles died in her room at Buckingham Palace, there was a question mark over her death as her body remained undiscovered for several days. Charles was inconsolable, Anne said later the only emotion she felt was a 'sense of guilt because I could not grieve as sincerely as my brother'.

Eventually, Anne was sent to Benenden boarding school and the palace schoolroom split up. Sukie Babington-Smith stated that she felt it was done deliberately:

I'm quite sure it was laid down by the queen and her advisors that we should be split up, and I'm equally sure it was the right thing to do, even though at the time it seemed rather brutal. We never wrote to each other after leaving the palace; we didn't even have a farewell party.[36]

It seems a very harsh way to treat little girls who had spent all their waking hours together. When she arrived at Benenden, the princess proved able but not academic and decided not to go to university, pursuing instead a career with horses that led her winning a gold at the 1976 Olympics in Montreal.

The mother–daughter relationship has always run reasonably smoothly, largely because both women have such a strong bond through horses. All her life, the queen has been absorbed by horses and doesn't tire of discussing the most arcane details of horsemanship. In spite of this, there is a curious formality about all relationships within the royal family, which is difficult for an outsider to understand. Even though the princess's apartments are only minutes from the queen's at Buckingham Palace, they can spend weeks without seeing each other. The princess would never dream of walking into her mother's sitting room without an invitation. If she wanted to see her mother, she would ring the royal page first to see if it were convenient. Meetings are set up through intermediaries, never directly from mother to daughter.

When Princess Anne and Tim Laurence went to speak Michael Mann, the Dean of Windsor, about their wedding, the dean asked her, 'Have you spoken to your mother?'

Anne replied, 'You know how difficult it is to talk to Mummy about these things. Auntie Margaret always says that the only time to see her is when she's on her own, and the dogs are not there, and then she's usually too tired.' It took Anne three weeks before she could nail her mother down to a date.[37]

Her relationship was more relaxed with her father. Princess Anne was far more to his taste than the son he regarded as rather wimpish.[38] Anne was extrovert, self-confident to a fault and temperamental like her father. She has always been her father's favourite. Athletically gifted, she was also sharp and quick, with a mastery of detail, and like him, she didn't suffer fools. She was a female clone of daddy, and easily coped with her father's tough love and bullying with her lacerating wit and thick skin.[39] They were on the same wavelength and closely resembled each other. Prime Minister Tony Blair wrote, 'She is a chip right off the old man's block. People think Prince Philip doesn't give a damn about what people think of him, and they are right. Anne is exactly the same. She is what she is, and if you don't like it, you can clear off.'[40]

Life in the Thatcher household was much more bourgeois. Nevertheless, Margaret, like the queen, had to juggle work and motherhood, which took enormous stamina. The Thatchers planned to have children, one of each sex, so it was a dream come true when, on 15 August 1953, Margaret gave birth to twins by caesarian section, a boy and a girl, at Princess Beatrice Hospital in Chelsea.

Denis never felt the need to 'fill the gap' to become a house husband, and he was little help in bringing up the children, Mark and Carol. He viewed his role as like that of a Victorian father who earned the money and left the domestics to his wife. It was typical that when the twins were born Denis was watching cricket at the Oval. When he saw them for the first time, he said, 'My God, they look like rabbits. Put them back.'[41]

Denis had no intention of having his life disrupted by their arrival, and when Margaret came home, they leased the flat next door, where the children lived with their nanny.[42] Somewhat bitterly, Carol noted in her memoir, 'I don't think they [her parents] can have relished being in charge on nanny's day off.' Indeed, their mother's (and father's) absence meant Mark and Carol depended on their nanny/housekeeper, a devoted and extrovert older woman called Abby, who became their virtual mother. 'Shh,' she would whisper to the twins. 'Your mother's working.'[43] Like the Windsor children, their family was quite a formal one. There were no nicknames and neither Margaret nor Denis romped with their children much. In some ways, Margaret resembled an affectionate teacher. 'She never shouted at them,' said her sister Muriel, 'it was all sweet reason. I could have screamed at her sometimes for being so reasonable. Her attitude all the time was to teach the twins interesting things. Everything she did with them was teaching.'[44]

Carol recalled, 'When it came to being a mother she gave Mark and me the opportunity to make up our own minds. That meant anything from being allowed to choose wallpaper in our bedroom [which Mrs Thatcher always decorated herself] to church being an option each Sunday.'

Denis believed that Margaret overcompensated for her absence by excessive fussing and worrying about the twins. Mark was the favourite; as a mother she pampered him, fetched and carried for him and seldom corrected him. Edwina Currie feels, 'Carol was put aside in favour of Mark. She [Mrs Thatcher] was very much a 1950s housewife at heart and Mark was the eldest son. Mrs Thatcher was a victim of her own old-fashioned upbringing in a way.'[45] It's a view shared by Lord Carrington, 'She loved Mark, and rather neglected … what's her name?'[46] Diarist Woodrow Wyatt observed, 'A different note comes into her [Thatcher's] voice when she speaks about Mark.'

Despite her own strict Methodist upbringing, she was curiously conciliatory towards Mark, despite his mischievous and disruptive behaviour. Mark told biographer Murray:

We weren't brought up very strictly. It was a sort of back scratching operation. If I did things she expected of me as far as work was concerned and behaved in a reasonably civilised fashion, it was fairly easy going. If I misbehaved or did something idiotic, then it was trouble.

Although he may have been a 'mummy's boy', she was not soft with him. When he complained that he wanted to drop out of skiing because of the freezing climate, she refused to allow it.[47] Margaret developed a more awkward relationship with her independent-minded daughter Carol, who was always less obviously needy.[48] 'I don't remember her being a tough disciplinarian, definitely not a shrieker,' said Carol. 'If she ever smacked me I don't recall it.'

Carol never forgot that, when she won a prize on sports day, her parents weren't there. Like many affluent hard-working parents, the Thatchers overcompensated for their absence with riding lessons and skiing holidays.[49] Margaret wanted her children to have the opportunities she had never had, and to give them an upbringing as different as possible from the puritanical severity and starkness of her own; although that didn't stop her claiming that it had been good for her. Mrs Thatcher said once, 'There was not a lot of fun and sparkle in my life. I tried to give my children a bit more.'[50] Carol said, 'She had such a strict upbringing herself that she was conscious that ours would be different. But nor did I grow up in one of those homes where people climb into bed with their parents on Sunday morning.'

Although Mrs Thatcher mythologised her father in later life, she saw very little of him after she left home for university. When she took Denis to meet his prospective in-laws, he and Alfred Roberts found that had they nothing in common. After the wedding, they rarely went back to Grantham. When her mother died in 1960, Alf remarried a local farmer's widow called Cissie Hubbard. 'I suppose that's a good thing,' Margaret said, 'She's a nice homely little woman.'[51] Growing up, Mark and Carol hardly saw their grandfather, and they were 16 when he died.[52]

In her memoir, *The Path to Power*, Lady Thatcher wrote, 'To be a mother and housewife is a vocation of a very high kind. But I simply felt that it was not the whole of my vocation. I knew that I wanted a career.'[53] Jonathan Aitken, a Tory MP who dated Carol, explained, 'The prime minister also had guilty feelings about her children. She worried that she'd worked so hard at her political life that her career was damaging her life as a mother.'[54] It is a dilemma countless women with ambition face. Carol examined the same issue in her memoir, *Below the Parapet*, saying, 'My mother's political ambitions, and the single mindedness with which she pursued them, eclipsed our family and social life. No woman gets to the top by going on family picnics.'[55]

The Thatchers decided that boarding school would be best for the children, partly because it was Denis's preference, but also to separate the two of them, who were not getting on. Their mother called them 'mortal enemies'.[56] Carol herself does not look back on their relationship with any feeling, 'The two of us used to bicker about small things'.[57] Mark was 8 and Carol was 9 when they were sent away to school. Both were so used to their mother being away at work that neither were afflicted with homesickness.

Of the two Thatcher children, Carol has always been the public favourite, handling the extraordinary public pressure of living under their mother's shadow with a considerable degree of verve and guts. But she was often prickly in her parents' presence and happy for them to be the butt of her jokes. She once embarked on a shopping quiz, asking Margaret, 'Let's see if you know what inflation is doing to food prices. How much is a pint of milk? How much is half a pound of margarine?' When she failed several of the questions, Margaret became annoyed. It may not have gone down well at the time, but a few weeks later 'Thatcher's shopping basket' became a weapon of election propaganda as the Leader of the Opposition (as she was then) unveiled her groceries on television with emphasis on their price rises under Labour's inflation. Margaret could spot a good idea when she saw one.[58]

Carol escaped the early Thatcher limelight by heading off to Australia after completing a law degree at University College, London. She became a journalist on the *Sydney Morning Herald* and worked for a television current affairs programme, before returning to London to work on her mother's first election campaign in 1979. Although Margaret wasn't as close to Carol as Mark, her former boyfriend, Jonathan Aitken, feels Margaret loved her every bit as much. In the winter of 1978, Carol was given a fifteen day holiday in the Swiss resort of Verbier by her parents. Jonathan planned to join her there for a long weekend. Unfortunately, his return flight clashed with a vote in the House of Commons, so Margaret switched the voting dates, and the three-line whip was dropped to allow Carol to spend the weekend with her new boyfriend in the Alps.[59]

When he returned to Westminster, Mrs Thatcher was quick to ask, 'Did you two have fun? Come into my office and tell me about it then.' The young MP found himself sitting in a chair across from his boss while she kicked off her shoes and asked about the weekend. She said that she was worried about Carol being out in Verbier by herself, but added, 'You won't tell Carol that I was worrying about her, will you? She will think I'm being overbearing.'[60]

When Jonathan and Carol's affair ended, Carol was very hurt and Margaret angry. Eventually, the ice thawed towards Aitken, largely due to his support of the prime minister during the Falklands.[61] However, the break-up could not have helped his political career much.

Carol's down-to-earth and vigorous, if slightly eccentric, personality is in direct contrast to the moody, devious and untrustworthy image of her brother Mark, the so-called 'international businessman'. Carol never had a good word to say about Mark, seeing him as someone whose hands were outstretched to receive an over-large slice of the inheritance cake.[62] She felt a rivalry that her brother was closer to her mother than she was; although it was her choice to keep her distance.[63] She has said publicly, 'I always felt I came second of the two. Unloved is not the right word, but I never felt I made the grade.' In the mid-1990s, when Carol was 43 and Mark was married to his first wife, Diane, and lived with their children in South Africa, Carol vented her feelings of discontentment and inferiority. 'Mark was married to a beautiful girl, has two fabulous children and various mansions scattered around the world. I'm an ancient spinster of no fixed abode living in a rented holiday flat in a ski resort. I still don't measure up awfully well on the Richter scale.'[64]

Without a doubt, Mark had a better connection to his mother emotionally. In the early days of the Falklands War, Mark was always by her side, together with Denis. They were an indefatigable pair. Evidence of Mark's support is found in the private archive of personal notes he wrote to his mother. They are simple messages, 'I love you' or 'I am so proud of you'. At the time, he was living in a spare bedroom in the prime minister's flat over 10 Downing Street. He was 28 years old, the same age as many of the soldiers.[65]

Mark Thatcher had relatively little money until his mother became prime minister. He used her decade in power to build up a large fortune estimated to be worth $40 million.[66] This wealth was widely perceived to have come about simply because he was the prime minister's son, rather than because of any inherent business ability. He has been pursued from Britain to Texas and South Africa by lawsuits and tax investigations, and has acquired a tarnished reputation. There have been allegations, but never proof, of mother and son colluding to win overseas contracts.[67] Margaret had always been deaf to criticism of him, convinced that Mark was a financial genius, 'Mark could sell ice to the Eskimos and sand to the Arabs,' she once claimed,[68] and she has repeatedly scolded the media for infringing on the lives of her family.[69]

Whatever Margaret's faith in Mark's business judgement, it didn't stop her worrying about him. It also didn't stop Mark wanting to prove to her that he could succeed: the classic case of a son favoured by his mother, who didn't have the ability and skill to meet her expectations.

Even as a little boy, Mark basked in his mother's reflected glory. 'My mummy's a member of Parliament,' he boasted to his schoolmates. When he was sent up to Harrow, he found himself out of his depth socially and academically. The school rivals Eton as a training school for the Establishment; its alumni included Winston Churchill. His classmates soon spotted his 'inferior' petty bourgeois background, which they deemed 'below-stairs'. Mark was teased and mimicked mercilessly, but instead of laughing off the jibes he adopted a pompous stance,[70] becoming brash and arrogant.[71]

Margaret, who had battled so hard against the Tory elite in her party, now, it seemed, wanted to turn her son into a member of it, but again the Establishment managed to diminish her, even without trying. When she arrived at Harrow to talk to her son's housemaster, Mark Tindall, he was interviewing new domestic staff, so Mrs Thatcher waited patiently outside his office. When he opened his study door and noticed her sitting in the corridor he said, 'You must have come about the new under-matron vacancy.' Margaret was not amused, considering she had just been promoted to the Cabinet as Secretary of State for Education.[72]

At Harrow, Mark flourished at sport but was regarded as a bit of a dunce, gaining only three O levels and mediocre A levels. Despite the lack of promise, he stayed on to study for the Oxbridge exams and told friends he had won a place at Keble College, Oxford, much to their surprise.[73] Instead of taking up such a coveted place, though, he headed to a job in Hong Kong fixed up by his father,[74] and when that didn't work out, he found work with the accountancy firm Touche Ross, where he failed his Intermediate and Part One accountancy examinations. It took him three attempts to pass before quitting the city for good.[75] After a spell of unemployment, he secured a job in a Manchester jewellery shop as a sales manager.

All Mark wanted to do was motor racing, and when his mother became prime minister in 1979, he started looking for sponsorship to fund his obsession to become a driver. Behind the scenes, his mother secretly urged his friends and business associates to discourage his racing career. A meeting with porn baron Paul Raymond at the Windmill Theatre in Soho was arranged where the two of them discussed plans for starting a new *Men Only* British Racing Team.[76] Subsequently, Mark won other sponsorship and drove at Le Mans in 1980 and 1981, crashing both times.

When Mark got lost for six days in the Sahara during the Paris–Dakar rally in 1982, it became an international embarrassment for his mother. At the height of the drama, nine aircraft from Algeria, France and Britain were involved in the search, as well as Algerian land forces. Denis flew out to Africa, while Margaret remained in London in a state of high anxiety for the entire period. Reporters who caught her off-guard at a London hotel found her crying quite openly, when there was still no news.[77] It was the first time she had ever shown emotion in public.[78] One political colleague pointed out, 'When he got lost in the desert, everybody hoped he would never be found, but then, she was very upset'.[79] When he was finally found, he claimed to be 'simply staggered' by all the publicity, 'Why all the fuss?' he remarked.[80] The prime minister insisted on paying £2,000 personally towards the cost of the search, although an unpaid 11,500 dinar hotel bill, one third of which was for drinks, caused some diplomatic embarrassment. Mark's composed attitude led cynics to claim that he was far from lost and knew exactly the publicity implications of what he was doing. He had, after all, made news headlines around the world.

Mark had been quick to recognise the enormous financial opportunity that presented itself when his mother became prime minister, and set up a company called Monteagle Marketing. He received $40,000 for advertising tennis wear in the US and $50,000 for promoting whisky in Japan. In April 1981, at the peak of her early unpopularity and when she could ill afford any bad publicity, Mark joined his mother during an official visit to Oman where a £300 million contract was up for grabs to build a new university. Mrs Thatcher squeezed the Omanis to award it to a British firm. Mark was part of the deal promoting the construction firm Cementation International.

What Mark Thatcher brought to the table was nothing other than his family connections, and when Cementation won the contract, his firm received a commission reportedly in six figures. Two years later, the *Observer*[81] uncovered the story, alleging Mark received £350,000. The prime minister faced a succession of written questions in the House of Commons that forced her to start preparing a thirteen page draft to respond. She was going to say of her son, 'He is under no obligation to reveal to me the details of his business or personal affairs. Like most parents, I know only what I am told.'[82] In the event, this statement was never delivered. However, in answer to written questions Margaret insisted that she had never spoken about Cementation to anyone in Oman while she was there battling for British industry,[83] and therefore, questions about whether or not she knew that Mark was representing the firm were 'irrelevant'.[84]

It is highly possible that the Omanis thought they were being encouraged to give business to the British Prime Minister's son. Mrs Thatcher must have known that the potential existed for Mark to profit if Cementation won the contract, though that is not necessarily to say that she should, therefore, not have lobbied for them. In the Middle East, the fact that the prime minister's son could be an intermediary was not unusual. Most Arab countries are run by families, so Mark, in a sense, might have been perceived as a kind of 'crown prince' and his involvement wouldn't have raised any eyebrows.[85]

However, the allegation that Mark Thatcher was enriching himself on the back of his mother's patriotic salesmanship did not go away.[86] In 1984, on the advice of Sir Bernard Ingham,[87] who viewed Mark as an election liability, the prime minister's son left the UK to move to the United States to work for Lotus and British Car Auctions. In 1987, he married Diane Burgdorf,[88] and it was around this time he became inexplicably wealthy.

At the time Margaret Thatcher, as prime minister, was playing an instrumental role in the so-called Al-Yamamah deal, the name for a series of enormous arms sales by the United Kingdom to Saudi Arabia that was paid for in the delivery of crude oil. Just a few steps behind her was her son Mark, who had friends in the arms business like Wafic Said, a key player in the negotiations for Al-Yamamah. 'Wafic was using Mark,' said Adnan Khashoggi, the international arms broker, in an interview.[89] 'His value was his name, of course, and whenever Wafic needed a question answered, Mark could go directly to his mother … He would pick things up unofficially.'[90] Mark's role was as an unofficial conduit for negotiations and information.

Various journalists have estimated that Mark Thatcher made £12–20 million for helping with the Al-Yamamah arms deal. The evidence is only circumstantial, since the investigation of the Al-Yamamah deal by the National Audit Office was never published.[91] Alex Sanson, former Managing Director of British Aerospace, Dynamics Division, talked to the *Mail on Sunday* and was quoted as saying:

> Mark Thatcher was trying to cash in on the [Al Yamamah] deal … in the arms business we had many people, royal hangers-on. We called them 'Black Princes' and sometimes they had to be bought off … Thatcher was acting in the same way, as a kind of British Black Prince, but it was surely not the proper role for the British Prime Minister's son.[92]

In November 1992, Ken Livingstone, then a Labour MP, claimed in the House of Commons that Mr Thatcher had acted as a fixer on the so-called 'Supergun' project. Livingstone alleged that Mark was promoting the sale of South African artillery at a time when Britain had an arms embargo on South Africa. He also claimed that Mark was a friend of arms manufacturer, Carlos Cardoen, who supplied Saddam Hussein with chemical weapons technology. Mark Thatcher was just indignant, saying 'This is the thanks I get for being a good British businessman.'[93]

Back home in Dallas, the more public face of Mark Thatcher, was presented through a burglar alarm company called Emergency Networks.[94] In Texas, as in Britain, Mark Thatcher wasn't a very popular figure and his American affairs came under investigation by the Texas courts in 1995. He was sued by his business partner for alleged conspiracy involving 'mail fraud, wire fraud, tax fraud, deceptive trade practices, perjury, theft and assault'.[95] Eventually, he settled out of court for $500,000 but he still faced another $4 million case being brought against his Grantham company (which traded in aviation fuel) by the American Fuel Corporation, as well as charges of tax evasion. After a family summit, his mother was reported in the *Sunday Times* to have cleared his debts of $700,000.[96]

Now *persona non grata* in the USA, Mark moved to Cape Town in South Africa where his reputation followed him.[97] However, in 2005, he still managed to surprise everyone when he was suddenly charged with involvement in an attempted coup to overthrow the President of Equatorial Guinea. He pleaded guilty, receiving a suspended sentence and a fine of 3 million rand (£265,000). Soon after that, his wife Diane divorced him and returned to the United States. Meanwhile, Mark settled amongst the British expat community in Spain.

Mark Thatcher made few friends amongst his mother's closest colleagues. Sir Bernard Ingham felt his mother indulged him.[98] One political colleague explained confidentially:

> He tried to involve her, you see … he used to go to the ambassador of wherever it was and say, 'Make sure that this company, that I'm going to get the job.'
>
> And the blessed ambassador said, 'I can't possibly do that'.
>
> 'I'll tell my mother.'
>
> And so, he did tell his mother, and she used to ring me up and say, 'The ambassador in Kuwait's no good', or something.
>
> And I'd say 'But you've never been there – you've no idea.'
>
> And she said, 'Well, Mark tells me …'
>
> He was a thoroughly bad egg.[99]

The queen found herself facing similar problems with one of her children, Prince Andrew who, like Mark Thatcher, was a walking calamity. The queen's undisguised preference and affection for Andrew stands in contrast to her cool relationship with Charles. Andrew was born twelve years after Charles, with whom she never properly bonded as a child. Charles was born just before she became queen, and she was arguably overwhelmed by her new responsibilities. With Andrew things were different, she had gained a great deal of self-confidence and was ready to be a better mother, juggling her private and public roles more adeptly.

Right after Andrew's birth, she wrote to Lady Mary Cambridge, her cousin. 'The baby is adorable,' she wrote. 'All in all, he's going to be terribly spoilt by all of us, I'm sure.' The spoiling never stopped, and Andrew learnt how to play to it. He always greets 'mummy' in the same way, bowing from the neck, kissing her hand, and then kissing her on both cheeks. She adores him.[100]

With both her two youngest children, Andrew and Edward, the queen was more indulgent. Although still not inclined towards hugging and kissing, she showed a more playful streak and allowed them to race their pedal cars along the gilded Grand Corridor of Windsor Castle with its twenty-two paintings by Canaletto.[101] Like many second sons of great families, Prince Andrew comes across as arrogant. He was once handsome, but he hasn't aged well, and is described by one associate as 'a man with a fat bottom who laughs at his own jokes'.[102] One minute women are having their bottoms pinched, the next minute he is reminding them to call him 'Your Royal Highness'.[103]

In 1984, during a royal tour to Los Angeles, he was called a brat for turning a spray hose filled with water based paint on the press during a tour of a housing project. The British Consulate paid $1,200 damages to the American photographer whose Nikon camera was damaged, and issued an apology. The incident drew headlines like 'Vandal Andy', 'Hooligan Prince' and 'A Royal Squirt', from the press. A Los Angeles television commentator reported that Andrew's 1984 trip to California was 'the most unpleasant British visit since they burned the White House in the War of 1812'. Prince Andrew feebly said that the paint gun went off accidentally. No one believed him.

Mrs Thatcher was so appalled that she commissioned a confidential report from public relations specialists in the London office of Saatchi & Saatchi, on how to improve Prince Andrew's image. Saatchi's was the firm that had helped get the prime minister elected in 1979. Mrs Thatcher's report was sent to an indignant queen, who refused to read it. She allegedly remarked, 'I hardly think I need advice from that frightful little woman'.[104]

Fighting a brave war during the Falklands crisis, and facing considerable danger on an equal footing with his compatriots without being given any special treatment impressed the British public, and on the strength of that Prince Andrew got away with a lot.

After retiring from his active naval career in 2001, and following a divorce from his debt-ridden wife in 2002, he was appointed a special trade envoy for Britain. It was a bad appointment. Like Mark Thatcher, Prince Andrew isn't particularly bright, and he was as much a walking PR disaster for the queen, as Mark was for the prime minister. Like Mark Thatcher, the prince also seemed happy to use his new role to enrich himself, and as with Mark's middleman facilitator role, 'trade envoy' was a vague job description and a recipe for trouble.

With such a profligate (now ex-) wife, Andrew has always complained that it was hard to live on his yearly stipend of £249,000 from the queen, and portrayed himself as a poor relative, which explains why he and his ex-wife, 'Fergie', always seemed to be scavenging for money. One of the perks of being a special envoy is the prodigious travel expenses worth hundreds of thousands of dollars a year. This fact earned him the nickname 'Air Miles Andy' from the press, and criticisms from the National Audit Office for taking a helicopter just 50 miles to lunch with Arab dignitaries.[105]

The prince always travels with a team of six, including equerries, secretaries, protection officers and a valet who carries a 6ft long ironing board and claims, 'no one knows how to iron His Royal Highness's trousers like me'.[106]

Many of Andrew's endeavors on behalf of British trade look questionable when scrutinised:

He was accused of hosting a Buckingham Palace lunch for Mohamed Sakher El Materi, the billionaire son-in-law of the now deposed Tunisian strongman, Zine El Abidine Ben Ali; he allegedly accepted a gift of a gold necklace worth £20,000 for his daughter, Princess Beatrice, from a convicted Libyan gun smuggler (although a Buckingham Palace spokesman said to the press that it never comments on private gifts made to members of the royal family);[107] and there was also the story of the trip Andrew made in 2008 to Libya, where he met Muammar Qaddafi. In addition, it was reported that Andrew had flown to Sharm el Sheikh with David 'Spotty' Rowland, a controversial British businessman who provided £40,000 to help pay the Duchess of York's debts.

While in Egypt, Andrew dined with Nursultan Nazarbayev, the President of Kazakhstan.[108] It was Nazarbayev's billionaire son-in-law, Timber Kulibayev, to whom Prince Andrew sold his Sunninghill estate in Surrey. The house, a wedding gift from the queen to Andrew, had once derisively been nicknamed 'South York', for its resemblance to the American ranch home (Southfork) of the fictional Ewing family in the soap opera *Dallas*. The property had been languishing on the market for almost five years with a £12 million price tag. Andrew had met Timber Kulibayev through his role as the government's trade ambassador. Kulibayev paid £15 million, and there has yet been no adequate explanation as to why anyone would pay £3 million over the asking price.[109]

A diplomat in Bahrain, Simon Wilson, explained to the *Daily Mail* how Andrew had earned the nickname 'His Buffoon Highness' for his foreign dealings. This stemmed from his childish habit of doing exactly the opposite of what had been agreed. He appeared to regard himself as an expert in every matter, which Wilson put down to an inferiority complex. This article was followed up by a second where a former ambassador, Sir Ivor Roberts, revealed how he was forced to send in his people to clear up the mess after the prince offended people. Sir Ivor stated, 'I would never have thought of him as the natural choice to be trade envoy in the first place. If the net result is negative, you wonder whether he should be in that position.'[110] In the House of Commons, Chris Bryant MP, a former Foreign Office minister said:

Isn't it especially difficult to explain the behaviour of the special ambassador for trade who is not only a close friend of Saif Gaddafi, but is also a close friend of a convicted Libyan gun smuggler Tarek Kaituni? Isn't it about time we dispensed with the services of the Duke of York?'[111]

The final straw came when the *Mail on Sunday*, which had decided to investigate the private life of Prince Andrew, interviewed a young woman named Virginia Roberts. Ms Roberts claimed that a billionaire friend of Prince Andrew, Jeffrey Epstein, had initiated her into prostitution and flown her to London, when she was just 17 years old, to spend time with Prince Andrew. Ten years on, Virginia had decided to tell the *Mail on Sunday*.

The newspaper had evidence to support the allegations, including flight logs from Epstein's two private jets and a damaging photograph showing Prince Andrew with his arm around the teenage Virginia. Standing just behind them in the picture was Ghislaine Maxwell, daughter of the late newspaper tycoon, Robert Maxwell,[112] who worked as Epstein's fixer.[113] According to Virginia, Ghislaine recruited her as Epstein's 'sex slave' when she was 15 years old and arranged for her to see Andrew three times. Both Prince Andrew and Ghislaine Maxwell denied the allegations.[114] The FBI investigated Jeffrey Epstein and, as the result of a plea bargain, he escaped the more serious charges, like statutory rape, that could have sent him to jail for life. Epstein served thirteen months in prison and Prince Andrew was never subpoenaed.[115]

Only a week before this story became public, another damaging photo surfaced in different tabloid, the *News of the World*, showing Prince Andrew strolling in New York's Central Park with Epstein. These two photos capped months of negative press coverage which had started when Andrew's ex-wife, Sarah, Duchess of York, was secretly filmed by an undercover reporter posing as a businessman. Sarah was caught on video demanding $821,000 in return for business access to her ex-husband, who was still at the time Britain's Special Envoy for International Trade & Investment. The Duchess was heard saying on camera, 'You'll get it back tenfold. That opens up everything you would ever wish for. And I can open any door you want. And I will for you.' It was shocking and depressing to watch. Under a torrent of criticism, Sarah apologised, but what was so damaging was her claim on the tape that Andrew had advance knowledge of her extortion.

Despite the shabbiness of the allegations and the amount of stories that were stacking up against Prince Andrew, the Buckingham Palace press office issued denial after denial. They defended his trips abroad. They dismissed the notion that he had advance knowledge of his ex-wife's business negotiations. They stated that the sale of Sunninghill was, 'A private sale between two trusts. There was never any impropriety.' On his role as trade envoy, they insisted, 'His Royal Highness is massively highly valued by the people who matter most, leaders of British companies'. Prominent businessmen, like Terry Hill, the chairman of Arup, praised Andrew's role in promoting British business interests, 'He's knockout attractive to overseas clients'.[116]

However, the prince's critics were vocal. Tom Porteous, UK director of Human Rights Watch, said Prince Andrew was making the UK 'look stupid'.[117] Kaye Stearman, of the Campaign Against Arms Trade, said that the prince had become a 'sort of cheerleader and door opener for the arms industry'.[118]

Prince Andrew was forced to resign his trade envoy role, but then the queen intervened and invested him as a Knight Grand Cross of the Royal Victorian Order for 'personal service' to the sovereign. It was a symbolic act of support, and almost overnight the press criticism evaporated.[119] Mummy had come to the rescue and the critics were silenced.

Ms Roberts' claims against Prince Andrew have since been thrown out by a US judge. However, Prince Andrew's reputation has suffered enormously and his friendship with Epstein brought the monarchy into disrepute.

Another royal prince who seemed lost was Prince Edward, the queen's youngest son, who was overshadowed by Andrew while growing up.[120] He initially followed the traditional route of royal princes, a career in the armed forces, by joining the marines. This kind of military service was supposed to validate male members of the royal family. However, after ninety days in uniform he resigned. His departure horrified the queen, who implored him to reconsider, and his sister feared he would be branded a quitter, while his father shouted at him to pull himself together. The young prince allegedly broke down and cried for hours. But the next day he resigned his commission. The headline in the *New York Post* ran, 'The Weeping Wimp of Windsor'.

Prince Philip wrote to the marine commandant expressing his dissatisfaction, and when it was published in the press, the queen sued and won damages, but by then everyone knew of Philip's dashed expectations. When Edward decided to work in the theatre and joined Andrew Lloyd Webber's production company as a production assistant, he was ridiculed. Columnist Taki Theodoracopulos complained in the *Spectator* that Edward was 'paid out of the public purse to pursue a theatrical career and assorted bachelors'. The press snidely insinuated that he was homosexual, and this passed into popular gossip. The innuendo even made it into the hit movie *Priscilla, Queen of the Desert*, when one transvestite asked another transvestite, 'Can the child of an old queen turn out all right?'

'Well, look at Prince Charles.'

'Yes, but there's still a question about Prince Edward.'

It wasn't just the media that made fun of the prince. In a lecture at the Smithsonian, historian David Cannadine stated, 'the queen is worried that Edward is not divorced'. Writer Christopher Hitchens said in an interview, 'Gay friends of mine refer to Prince Edward as Dishcloth Doris.' This forced Gore Vidal to correct Hitchens, 'He's Dockyard Doris.' When a *Daily Mail* gossip columnist wrote that the prince had a 'touching friendship' with a male actor, Edward finally responded, snapping at reporters in New York saying, 'I am not gay.'

The rumours only died down when Edward started to date Sophie Rhys-Jones, although their romance was disparaged early on by one newspaper as 'arranged for public consumption'. The queen, however, extended a protective hand to her youngest son's reputation by letting it be known she had given permission for Sophie to spend nights with Edward in his apartment at Buckingham Palace. When the Archdeacon of York scolded Her Majesty for allowing the couple to live in sin, the queen simply ignored the pompous cleric.

The queen and Mrs Thatcher were both part of that first post-war generation of working mothers. They both avoided family responsibilities by hiding behind their work ethic. Had either woman taken half as much trouble with the rearing of the children as they had about breeding horses or Cabinet reshuffles, both the Windsor and Thatcher families would have probably ended up in far less of a mess. It was always too easy for the mothers to say, 'I've got these red boxes full of documents from Whitehall. That is my constitutional duty as queen or prime minister, and I'd rather read them than risk confrontation with my children or husband.' Neither woman spent anything like enough time on their families. Getting the right work life balance right can be hard, but it totally eluded both the queen and her prime minister.

10

DOWNFALL

Oh dear, she's going to feel sorry for the poor again!
Margaret Thatcher

Margaret Thatcher was toppled, not by any election defeat, but by an internal *coup d'état*. At Buckingham Palace, there was genuine shock at witnessing the assassination of the rival 'queen' by her 'courtiers'. If anything, there was a sense of pity for Mrs Thatcher when she was forced out of Downing Street by her own Cabinet. As a gesture of goodwill, the queen even invited Margaret to a horse racing meeting. However, Margaret was in no mood to accept.[1]

This political execution of a sitting prime minister had been in gestation for months, as colleagues found Mrs Thatcher increasingly dictatorial, egocentric and out of touch. For some time, her relationship with voters had been damaged by the recession, backbench MPs were worried by the poll tax riots, and her own Cabinet were frustrated with her management style. Hardcore Tory supporters were anxious about the recession, as thousands of businesses were going bankrupt every week. As Edwina Currie pointed out, 'You can't be a party of economic prosperity and not deliver it.' When Currie visited Margaret to explain that local businesses were suffering because of the downturn caused by recession and high interest rates, she found a highly unsympathetic prime minister, whose opinion was that the business weren't working hard enough. 'Megalomania had set in and she simply wasn't willing to listen.'[2]

Backbench MPs with seats in marginal constituencies, whose jobs were, therefore, at stake, had been poisoned by the reform of local government funding, and the new 'poll tax' which was blasted for being unfair, as every adult had to pay the same charge whether they lived in a council flat or a country mansion. 'As far as people were concerned,' said Tim Bell, 'This woman who had constantly said she would reduce their taxes ... had suddenly put their taxes up, and they didn't understand. They didn't understand the argument.'[3]

Riots broke out in Trafalgar Square; shops were looted, and over 300 people were arrested. In one incident, rioters seized knives and crossbows from a camping equipment shop. One eyewitness said, 'This was a class war. Expensive cars were attacked and set alight, and anyone smartly dressed was abused or attacked.' Such scenes showed the depth of hatred for the new tax reforms.[4]

The final straw was Mrs Thatcher's poor relationship with her own Cabinet. By now Margaret was increasingly ignoring Cabinet advice and becoming dangerously self-sufficient, even isolated. She clearly preferred the counsel of special advisers such as Alan Walters, Tim Bell, Charles Powell and Bernard Ingham. Members of her Cabinet were seen as rivals, and she wondered apprehensively who might have designs on 'her crown'.

Lord Whitelaw had counselled her about the danger of not getting on with her two most senior Cabinet colleagues, Foreign Secretary Sir Geoffrey Howe and Chancellor of the Exchequer Nigel Lawson. Whitelaw told her that if she alienated them she would risk everything. She did, and she lost.[5] What William Shakespeare called the 'insolence of office'[6] had, by now, firmly set in.

The pro-European Geoffrey Howe became the central object of her loathing as his ponderous and convoluted presentation irritated her. Publicly she was rude, belittling and treating him as a 'doormat and punch bag'.[7]

'She did treat him very roughly, very roughly. And in public, with other people there ... Henry Kissinger and people like that. And he [Geoffrey] put up with a lot,' revealed Lord Carrington.[8]

Margaret had also taken a distinctly female dislike to Geoffrey Howe's wife, Elspeth, who became the personification of a familiar adage in Westminster, 'Margaret is bad with wives'. The tension with Lady Howe, however, went far deeper. Elspeth was a feminist in her sympathies, sharp-tongued in her humour and fiercely supportive of the idea that her husband could be the next prime minister.[9] John Biffen compared their relationship to that of 'two wasps in a jam jar'. Jonathan Aitken commented on the 'bitchiness' between them, with Thatcher dismissing Elspeth's 'equal opportunities' mindset.[10] 'Everybody disliked Elspeth Howe, and she was a real busybody and very much wanted to promote Geoffrey's career. If she wanted to interfere that much she should have stood as an MP like the rest of us,' claimed Edwina Currie.[11]

This intense rivalry became centred on the Foreign Secretary's two official residences, No. 1 Carlton Gardens and Chevening, a grand stately home in Kent that had once been the country seat of the Prince of Wales. Both properties rivalled the prime minister's official homes in Downing Street and at Chequers. It was also much more fun at Chevening, as the Howes were far more easygoing hosts than the Thatchers. It helped convince Mrs Thatcher that the Howes were using the house to hold court[12] and she demoted Sir Geoffrey to the inferior Cabinet posts of Leader of the House of Commons and Lord President of the Council. He was also given the meaningless title of deputy prime minister to soften the blow publicly, although Bernard Ingham belittled its significance at his morning lobby meeting the following day. What made the demotion even worse was that she replaced him as Foreign Secretary with the unseasoned John Major, who gained Chevening as his official residence. Howe took the surprise demotion and loss of the house as a personal insult.[13]

Nigel Lawson thought that he had the right, as Chancellor of the Exchequer, to be in charge of economic policy. However, his enthusiasm to join the European Exchange Rate Mechanism (ERM) and his policy of shadowing the deutschmark was arguably contrary to Mrs Thatcher's wishes. As interest rates increased and recession hit, Thatcher turned to her economic advisor, Sir Alan Walters, who contradicted the chancellor's opinion. Lawson felt that his authority was being undermined and demanded that Mrs Thatcher fire Walters. It was an ultimatum the prime minister rejected, and her chancellor resigned. In yet another promotion for John Major, he was moved from the Foreign Office to replace him. Thatcher was then forced to succumb to John Major's advice to join the ERM. Sir Geoffrey Howe only discovered this fact while visiting Balmoral for a privy council meeting, where the queen informed the rather startled deputy prime minister, who hadn't been consulted or kept in the loop.[14]

Margaret became increasingly irritated by the men around her, viewing the Cabinet as a rather idle, sleepy lot. 'If you want anything said, ask a man. If you want anything done, ask a woman.' Her greatest strength, that ability to be independent of the men around her, now became her greatest liability. Nigel Lawson commented, 'One of the qualities that men tend to have ... from the sort of background that most of the cabinet came from is clubbability. They're extremely clubbable. And there's a kind of men's club atmosphere. She had no element of clubbability in her at all.'[15]

Thatcher was becoming increasingly hostile to Europe. When the eleven other European powers pushed for greater integration, Britain stood alone. 'People who get on a train like that deserve to be taken for a ride,' she vented, adding that the train appeared to be heading for 'cloud cuckoo land'. In the House of Commons, Margaret blazed for ninety minutes at the dispatch box dismissing the European single currency as 'totally and utterly wrong' and asserting that the European

Commission was 'striving to extinguish democracy and planning to take us through the back door to Europe'. She shouted 'No! No! No!' to Europe.[16]

In Howe's view, this was the 'language of the battlefield rather than of the partnership',[17] and he felt it would needlessly antagonise our friends in Europe. It was apparent in Cabinet that week that the rift was deepening, as Margaret obnoxiously took Geoffrey Howe to task over the poor preparation of the legislative programme with a blistering put-down. 'Why aren't their bills ready?' she demanded. 'Isn't it the Lord President's responsibility to see that this kind of thing has been done?' The rebuke continued on for several minutes. Geoffrey believed that it was bad manners to 'reproach officers in front of other ranks',[18] and that afternoon he resigned. He wrote in his biography, 'Far from being the last straw, this final tantrum was for me the first confirmation that I had taken the right decision.'[19]

Having lost a second Cabinet minister so soon after Lawson meant that the prime minister was forced to reshuffle the Cabinet again. Margaret even tried to persuade Norman Tebbit to come back, but he declined because he had to look after his wife, paralysed during the Brighton bombing in 1984. Three days after Margaret Thatcher died, a remorseful Tebbit bitterly informed the House of Lords, 'I left her, I fear, at the mercy of her friends. That I do regret.'[20]

On 12 November, Mrs Thatcher delivered a speech at the Lord Mayor's Banquet in the London Guildhall. In it she used a cricketing metaphor that would later rebound spectacularly, to describe her current beleaguered status:

> I am still at the crease, though the bowling has been pretty hostile of late, and, in case anyone doubted it, can I assure you there will be no ducking of bouncers, no stonewalling, no playing for time. The bowling's going to get hit all around the ground.

The following day, Geoffrey Howe made his formal resignation speech in the House of Commons. He claimed her attitude to Europe and the single currency had undermined both the Chancellor of the Exchequer and the Governor of the Bank of England. He also seized the opportunity offered by her cricketing metaphor, 'it is rather like sending your opening batmen to the crease, only for them to find, at the moment the first balls are bowled that their bats have been broken before the game by the team captain.' The last line of the speech proved the most savage, he declared that the time had come 'for others to consider their own responses to the tragic conflict of loyalty with which I have myself wrestled for perhaps too long'.

As Mrs Thatcher sat and listened to the speech, she remained composed. This was an open invitation for her long-standing rival Michael Heseltine to challenge her for the leadership. She felt particularly bitter, and said Howe would be remembered from this point on, not for his work as a government minister, but for this 'final act of bile and treachery'.[21]

One Tory MP, recalling the remark by Denis Healey that being attacked by Sir Geoffrey was like being savaged by a dead sheep, said, 'The dead sheep has turned out to be a Rottweiler in drag.'[22]

On 14 November, Mrs Thatcher received the official notification that Michael Heseltine was contesting her leadership. Margaret was far from secure, and she badly misjudged her campaign to be re-elected as leader, putting it in the less than capable hands of Peter Morrison, her parliamentary private secretary. He was a disaster: lazy, overweight, with a drink problem and predisposed to sleeping in the afternoon. Peter sweepingly accepted every pledge of support and stated that the prime minister would get 220 votes, making it an easy win.[23]

However, Margaret had no understanding of her crisis. She made a bad decision to attend the non-essential Conference on Security and Cooperation in Europe (CSCE) summit in Paris on the very day of the leadership vote, when she should have devoted the time to winning over the Tory backbench MPs. It was hubris again, as Mrs Thatcher wanted to be on the world stage in Paris and not scrabbling around for votes. She had grown remote from domestic politics. Her attitude was, 'Tory MPs know me, my record and my beliefs. If they were not already persuaded, there was not much left for me to persuade them with.'[24]

When news of the final vote came through, it was not good. Margaret had to achieve a simple majority plus 15 per cent, a total of 208 votes. She had received 204 votes compared to Michael Heseltine's 152. She was four votes short, which meant there would have to be a second ballot.

Her first thought on hearing the news was to ring Denis from the British Embassy in Paris. Mr Thatcher was quick to offer his support. 'Congratulations, Sweetie Pie, you've won; it's just the rules,' he said, but there were tears in his eyes. He listened sympathetically to her insistence that she would be fighting on to win on the second ballot, but he didn't believe a word of it. When he put the phone down, he said, 'We've had it. We're out.'[25]

That night there was a ballet performance at the Palace of Versailles, socially the crowning point of the conference. Mrs Thatcher sent a note to President Mitterrand to say she would arrive late because of events back home. However, Mitterrand wanted to honour her at such a difficult moment and delayed the performance. As she made her extraordinary regal entrance in a black velvet ball gown with a Tudor style collar, she looked every inch the queen as the other presidents and prime ministers applauded her. Her hauteur was obvious, but behind the scenes the word 'coup' was used. Many of those heads of states and world leaders attending found it surprising that an elected leader could be overthrown by a minority rebellion in their party whilst out of the country.[26]

That night in her room, she sat until dawn talking to Crawfie. Cynthia Crawford remembered:

> She wasn't all right, she wasn't going to sleep and we decided to have a drink, and then we just stayed up all night and talked about every aspect of her life; her childhood, her father, her mother, getting married to Denis, having twins and her political career; and we just never went to bed, and then about half past six we just sort of got ready for the day.[27]

When she arrived home in London, Mrs Thatcher immediately went to Buckingham Palace, where she sought an audience with the queen and informed her that she would be standing in the second ballot. When the prime minister returned to her room in the House of Commons, a procession of her Cabinet ministers and loyalists came to see her one by one. While each gave her his backing, they also said she couldn't win. She risked being humiliated by her party in the second ballot and splitting the Conservatives. Denis advised her, 'Don't go on, love'.[28]

Cecil Parkinson explains that Margaret had been expecting somewhere around 264 votes, based on Peter Morrison's calculations:

> So I think she got a great shock on that, when the result was announced ... she was having to cope with the surprise of that, and she was suddenly saying to herself, hey, you know, have I been properly informed about how the party feels?[29]

Her next step was to find out what her Cabinet was thinking. Parkinson feels this consensus approach was her big mistake:

> She asked her Cabinet to tell her what she should do. That was totally out of character. If she had got the Cabinet together and said, 'You are only here because I asked you, invited you to join, now I need your support,' I think she would have won, I think she would have won the next ballot comfortably. But she tried to lead by following ... and it lead to her departure.[30]

Edwina Currie also points out, 'She was getting tired and didn't realise it or want to acknowledge it, hence her irritation and impatience.'[31]

Early the following morning, Mrs Thatcher made it known that she had finally resolved to resign, and plans were made for a second audience with the queen. A statement was prepared for the Cabinet, which she read from a paper in front of her, but after five words, 'Having consulted widely among colleagues ...', she broke down.[32]

'For God's sake, you read it, James,' said Cecil Parkinson to the Lord Chancellor, Lord Mackay. The prime minister shook her head and tried again and eventually she managed it:

> Having consulted widely among colleagues, I have concluded that the unity of the party and the prospects of victory in a general election will be better served if I stood down to enable colleagues to enter the ballot for the leadership. I should like to thank all those in Cabinet and outside who have given me such dedicated support.[33]

The prime minister also sent messages to presidents Bush and Gorbachev and to the European heads of government. Then she went to Buckingham Palace for the final audience with the queen. She returned from the palace 'highly emotional, with tears in her eyes'.[34]

'She's a very understanding person,' Thatcher said later. 'She understood ... the rightness of the decision I was taking ... It was very sad to know that was the last time I'd go to the palace as prime minister.'[35]

The queen mother, who had always been a Thatcherite, was deeply upset by Thatcher's departure, calling her 'very patriotic' and expressing hope that she would come to stay at Balmoral after she left office. She told diarist Woodrow Wyatt, it was 'desperately unfair, and an appalling way to do things'.[36]

Mrs Thatcher's last speech to the House of Commons as prime minister was arguably her best. Boosted with a vitamin B6 injection, she ripped apart Neil Kinnock's motion of no confidence tabled against the government as 'windy rhetoric ... just a lot of disjointed opaque words'.

The mood of the house was in overdrive after the high drama that had taken place. When asked if she was going to continue her fight against a single currency and central bank, Dennis Skinner, the Labour MP for Bolsover, shouted, 'No. She is going to be governor!' That was a turning point, and Margaret rode the wave of laughter.

'That's a good idea,' she agreed. 'I had not thought of that,' turning the humour to her advantage. 'But if I were, there would be no European central bank accountable to no one, least of all national Parliaments … So I shall consider the proposal of the Hon. Member of Bolsover. Now, where were we? I am enjoying this.'[37]

The House was also enjoying the electric performance, and most of the Tory MPs were cheering. She spoke of helping Eastern Europe escape from totalitarian rule and ending the Cold War. She focused on the past conflict in the Falklands and the coming conflict in the Gulf.[38] Hypocrisy ruled, as many of those cheering had just voted her out.[39] One Tory MP, Michael Cartiss, leaped to his feet shouting, 'Stay on then. You can wipe the floor with this lot.'[40] Labour MPs shouted at their Conservative colleagues, 'Judases!'[41]

Jonathan Aitken pointed out, 'There is little doubt that if the leadership ballot could have been reinstated that afternoon she would have won by a land-slide.'[42] Many Tory backbenchers had a look of 'what have we done?' on their faces. The *Daily Mail* captured the mood with its headline, 'Too Damn Good for the Lot of Them'.[43]

Leaving Chequers was an emotional wrench. She and Denis were in tears as they stood in the gallery overlooking the great hall for the last time.[44]

Returning to Downing Street, it was clear that the momentum in the leader-ship election was moving towards John Major. Margaret publicly supported him, and canvassed support on his behalf. When the news came through, it said that he had won 185, compared to Michael Heseltine's thirteen. Most newspapers identi-fied the new prime minister as a Thatcherite, largely because he grew up in Brixton and went to a grammar school. However, as Edwina Currie knew, 'he was more complex and more of a pragmatist than that'.[45]

Mrs Thatcher's last day in office was Wednesday, 28 November. With the help of Carla Powell, Crawfie and Joy Robillard (her constituency secretary) she super-vised the moving out of 10 Downing Street. Padding around in her stockinged feet, she filled tea chests and mobile wardrobes. No longer occupied with the decisions of government, she spent the day deciding 'whether to wrap knickknacks in two layers of paper or whether one would do'.[46] When she went to check her office for one last time, she was shocked to discover that she had been locked out.

At the staff leaving party she declared, 'Life begins at 65!' and she was presented with a first edition of Kipling's poems and a high frequency portable radio. Her pri-vate secretary, Andrew Turnbull, said that the gift had been chosen, 'So wherever you are in the world. You can continue to be cross with the BBC.'[47]

Anyone who viewed a television set that evening will remember the footage of a weepy Margaret Thatcher in the back of the car being driven away from Downing Street, as she said goodbye to what had been her home for over eleven years. It was the end of an era, not only for Margaret Thatcher and the Conservative

Party, but for Britain. According to her driver Denis Oliver, as Margaret and Denis were driven to their new home in Dulwich, so troubled were her feelings that she did not speak a single word to her husband on the entire fifty minute journey.[48]

A compulsive workaholic, Mrs Thatcher had lost a job she loved and had no other interests outside of politics. She was now stripped of her main reason for living. The former prime minister had defined happiness in an interview to *Woman's Own* as, 'Having a very full day, being absolutely exhausted at the end of it, but knowing that you have had a very full day.'[49] Now that was over.

There were other losses too; not just the Downing Street flat and Chequers. Mrs Thatcher was forced to hand back the many priceless gifts given to her during the seventy-seven official foreign trips she had made during her premiership. Many were from the Middle East, and included a heavy silver coffee pot from the Sultan of Oman, which perched on the sideboard of 10 Downing Street, and a jewelled desk set from Abu Dhabi. There were also jewels fit for a queen. A pearl necklace from Prince Khalid of Saudi Arabia, a glittering gold bracelet encrusted with diamonds and rubies from the Sultan of Brunei (the *Times*, 18 February 1994), and a stunning necklace worth £200,000 from Sultan Qaboos of Oman, created by Asprey.[50] It was this last item that Mrs Thatcher had become particularly emotionally attached too, and it had been presented to her during her controversial trip to Oman in April 1981. She was dazzled by the platinum necklace set with diamonds and sapphires, and she often wore it on state occasions. One Omani diplomat remarked, 'it was more of a collar, actually, than a necklace and gave her the appearance of having won "Best of Breed" at Crufts.'[51]

Under government rules, Mrs Thatcher was not allowed to keep any gifts valued at over £125, so they languish in a vault in 10 Downing Street, available for the use of future prime ministers and their spouses.

The ex-prime minister was equally annoyed by another aspect of Whitehall housekeeping. The Cabinet secretary sent her the standard letter sent to all former prime ministers asking for the return of all government documents in her possession. She refused, with an invective that was severe even by her standards.

She also unleashed her outrage on the government whips for not finding her an office within the Palace of Westminster. Alastair McAlpine, the Conservative Party Treasurer, lent her his house in Great College Street. She used the house as a base for her secretariat and for receiving visitors in its tiny first floor drawing room. The atmosphere inside these new offices was of administrative chaos, combined with a Mrs Thatcher struggling emotionally with losing the premiership.

There were compensations. On 9 December, it was announced that the queen had awarded her the Order of Merit, the highest honour in the sovereign's gift. It is limited to just twenty-four individuals, and Mrs Thatcher filled the vacancy created by the death of actor, Sir Laurence Olivier. Controversially, Denis was created a baronet, a title that could be inherited by Mark Thatcher. He was now Sir Denis, and Margaret became Lady Thatcher.

In 1992, she was also created a life peer, although she was never made a hereditary countess, a title that had been mooted in the press and by political colleagues. For some time, there had been speculation that she had indicated that she would accept the title Countess of Finchley, after the parliamentary constituency she had represented for thirty-two years. This would mean her son Mark would have become Earl of Finchley on his mother's death.[52] Many of her party viewed this as crass and graceless and attributed it to her being a complete snob.[53] However, such titles were just empty trappings compared to the real power she had enjoyed as prime minister and the title of countess was never bestowed.

As prime minister number eight left office, the new premier, John Major, kissed hands at Buckingham Palace as the queen's ninth incumbent. At 49, he was the first prime minister to be younger than the head of state. The queen soon discovered in him a less tense and more congenial visitor than Mrs Thatcher. There was never any hint, during his six and a half years in office, of the agitation that existed between the queen and Mrs Thatcher. The new prime minister found his audience with the queen hugely enjoyable and helpful. Far from regarding them as a chore, which his predecessor had done, he looked forward to them. It was, he felt, marvellous to share all his hopes and fears with someone who had enormous experience, but who was totally apolitical. There was nothing, John Major said, that he couldn't talk to her about, knowing that the only eavesdroppers were the queen's corgis.

Although Thatcher's prime ministerial days may have been over, her days as an MP were not, and from the back benches she continued to make her views known. This made her unsuitable for any of the big international jobs at NATO, the World Bank, United Nations or within the diplomatic service. John Major would have loved to have kept her occupied abroad, but as he wrote in his memoirs there 'was no credible job to offer her'.[54] As Edwina Currie points out, 'There are very few jobs for ex-prime ministers or presidents, look at Clinton or Blair. What do you do with them?'[55]

At times, Lady Thatcher's determination to remain visible made things uncomfortable for her successor. Deep down, she still considered John Major the protégé whom she had promoted too rapidly, and treated him as an unfledged deputy whose job it was to carry on 'her work'. On leaving office she had declared, much to his discomfort, 'I shall be a very good back seat driver'. In the event, she even had to be dissuaded from sitting immediately behind Major at his first Prime Minister's Questions.[56]

Margaret came to hate John Major's pursuit of consensus politics, his lack of absolute principles and his constant attempts to distance himself from her and her policies. She couldn't help but sabotage her successor, and lacked the self-discipline to stop grumbling about him, 'What a silly little man!', 'How petty!', 'How stupid!' and 'The boy from Coldharbour Lane'. Using a Scottish accent, she mocked him as a 'puir wee bairn'.[57]

However, close colleagues of the former prime minister, such as Tim Bell, felt that 'she didn't do anything to interfere with John Major's life. John Major's life was made difficult for him by his own character and by the fact that he had a very small majority.'[58]

Thatcher's anger was again unleashed when she opposed the Maastricht Treaty, despite the fact that John Major achieved considerable success in securing an opt-out from joining the single currency for Britain. Had Margaret still been in command, she would in all likelihood have been pleased with this result.[59] Nothing that Major did was right for her, and it was difficult to fight back. Edwina Currie remarked, 'When John Major responded to her insults it just escalated … She could never forgive the Cabinet. Had she been defeated at an election, she would have become Leader of the Opposition and been able to legitimately attack the rival party. Once she was ousted she came to view her own party as the Opposition.'[60]

After the 1992 general election Margaret was elevated to the House of Lords as Baroness Thatcher of Kesteven. However, she worked overtime to undermine John Major, and it was without precedent to have a former Conservative prime minister in the Upper House inciting Conservative backbench MPs in the House of Commons to rebel against her successor's key legislation. John Major focused on her bad behaviour almost obsessively,[61] 'I want her isolated! I wanted her destroyed!' he demanded.[62]

The Baroness's scorn wasn't just directed at her replacement prime minister, but also his wife, Norma. In 1994, she saw photographs of Norma Major wearing the beloved necklace, which had been a gift from the Sultan of Oman, during a banquet for the Polish leader Lech Walesa given by the queen at Windsor Castle. She flew into a rage and telephoned John Major instructing him that the jewel was a private gift and a personal favourite. She demanded that no one else wear the necklace again. Major backed down and agreed that his wife wouldn't wear it again, although under Cabinet Office rules the necklace could be used by the incumbent prime minister and his wife. One MP wryly commented, 'Thatcher obviously believes that diamonds really are forever.'[63] It is said that when Margaret Thatcher visited Oman six months later to drum up funds for her new political organisation, the Thatcher Foundation, she asked if a replacement necklace could be provided. The sultan was 'visibly shocked' by the request, and he courteously brushed it aside.[64]

Lady Thatcher's angriest tirades were directed against her former Cabinet colleagues, whom she now vilified as 'spineless, gutless Judases'.[65] When asked if she ever forgave her Cabinet colleagues for forcing her resignation, Bernard Ingham replied, 'I hope not'.[66]

The wounds inflicted on the Tory party by her traumatic overthrow didn't heal during the entire seven years John Major spent in office.[67] Her former colleagues were unforgiving and when they lost the 1997 election in the worst defeat in the party's history they sought to blame her, ignoring their mistakes and a whole series of sleaze scandals.[68] Although she described herself as the 'matriarch of the Conservative Party', she behaved like its 'disgruntled mother-in-law', failing to realise the party needed to move out of her long shadow. When the Tories elected Iain Duncan Smith as leader, he asked her not to attend the 2002 Party Conference. It was the first conference she had missed since 1946.[69]

While Margaret felt aggrieved at being out of the limelight, Her Majesty found herself forced to endure too much publicity and public scrutiny. Elizabeth II came to regard this new post-Thatcher era as her crisis years, as scandal after scandal hit the house of Windsor. For someone who believed in quiet dignity, privacy and duty, such a public washing of the Windsor dirty linen was unbearable, as the whole world discovered that Prince Charles had gone back to his old mistress, Camilla Parker-Bowles. Princess Diana had an affair with James Hewitt and leaked what royal life was like to Andrew Morton. The *Daily Mirror* obtained photographs of a topless Duchess of York having her toes sucked by an American named John Bryan, who was supposed to be her financial advisor. Finally, the *Sun* published the excruciating transcripts of a telephone conversation between Charles and Camilla containing their absurd sexual banter, especially Charles's wish to be reincarnated as a tampon so he could live inside Camilla's trousers.

This atmosphere of decadence created by the queen's children led the editor of the *Sunday Times*, Andrew Neil, to write a highly critical editorial that resonated throughout the media. The impression took hold, and it never went away, that vast public funds were being wasted on the royal family, and that it was time for the queen to pay taxes on her substantial private income.[70]

The 'new Establishment' which had grown up under Mrs Thatcher could no longer be relied upon to give the queen their unwavering support. Many now regarded the monarchy as a peripheral impediment to Britain's development. Tom Nairn, in his acclaimed book *The Enchanted Glass: Britain and its Monarchy*, feels it was Thatcherism that was the culprit in this new anti-monarchist sentiment. In her determination to reverse decline, Margaret Thatcher fostered a new society based on enterprise culture, thus replacing gentility and class with something new. Unlike the rest of her party, she was irreconcilably impatient, not just with socialism, but also the old Establishment, which she viewed as an obstacle preventing the energetic citizen from forging ahead. She had always felt there was a dynamic American-style society waiting to be released inside the declining British one. The Tory Party had always spoken about 'setting the people free', but the old club rules of the post-war consensus had effectively put a stop to that, until her arrival.[71]

Columnist and arch-Thatcherite, Julie Burchill, identified royalty as a tranquiliser. She wrote:

> It makes a population stolid and fatalistic, undynamic, unbelieving in meritocracy, the kiss of death to a country, to see a group of people, undereducated … inbred, possessing neither intelligence nor beauty … ruling all it surveys. Only the deeply dull drop-out countries of the world have monarchies, countries for whom a major victory means coming second in the Eurovision Song Contest: Spain, the Netherlands, Great Britain … monarchies are not the hallmark of classiness, but a brand of lack of confidence.[72]

A.N. Wilson, a historian and journalist, also felt that Thatcher's legacy undermined the royal family. Thatcher, not the queen, had become the grand, national icon. Britain had been shown that we could have an alternative, elected, national figurehead. Thatcherism, in its purest form, opposed all hereditary privilege. No matter how deeply Mrs Thatcher curtsied to the queen, that fact couldn't be ignored.[73] For years, Elizabeth Windsor and her family had been cosseted, but during the 1980s Murdoch exposed them, and the current household was struggling to work with the changes.

When the final disaster of 1992 struck, the fire at Windsor Castle, the public mood of antipathy to royalty took both the queen and her new prime minister, John Major, by surprise. The fire started when a number of rooms at Windsor Castle were being rewired, and a spotlight ignited a curtain in the Private Chapel and the fire spread. Nine state rooms, including the magnificent St George's Hall where the queen had entertained President Reagan on his state visit in 1982, were destroyed. Then Heritage Secretary Peter Brooke announced that the estimated £60 million cost for restoration would be paid for by the taxpayer.[74] However, to the astonishment of the queen and John Major, the *Daily Mail* led an angry populist crusade against the plan, fuelled by amassed disgruntlement with the behaviour of the young royals. They demanded the queen pay for the refurbishment and start paying taxes.

Four days after the fire, the queen made a speech at a luncheon at London's Guildhall in which she described the past year as her '*annus horribilis*'.

Six days after the Windsor fire, John Major made the surprise announcement that both the queen and Prince Charles would voluntarily pay tax on their private incomes. The queen would also reimburse the government for the Civil List payments made to minor royals such as Prince Andrew, Princess Anne and Prince Edward, as well as covering their official expenses. The queen also agreed to finance the reconstruction of Windsor Castle by opening the state rooms at Buckingham Palace to the public during the summer months when she was at Balmoral. The queen accepted these reforms, although the queen mother was secretly furious.[75]

For his part, John Major had been very reluctant to agree to the reforms and was privately indignant about the public's response to the restoration of a national monument like Windsor Castle. His hand had been forced. Journalist Auberon Waugh pointed out in the *Spectator*, 'There seemed to be a general feeling that the royal family had been around long enough; there were too many of them.'[76]

However, the scandals that had occurred so far were just the tip of the iceberg. On 9 December 1992, John Major stood before the House of Commons to announce the separation of the Prince and Princess of Wales. Prince Charles went on to further shock his parents by appearing in a television interview with journalist Jonathan Dimbleby in which he confessed to his adultery with Camilla. The queen was dismayed, and worried that Charles had provided Dimbleby with diaries, letters and official papers for his book about the prince.

John Major was concerned as well, telling Woodrow Wyatt that he might use the Official Secrets Act (a law that prevents publication of state secrets) to stop any ministerial documents being used. Charles complied when the queen asked for the return of the confidential papers, but their relationship became even more strained.[77]

The last straw came in 1995, with Diana's appearance on the BBC's current affairs programme, *Panorama*. It was Diana's ultimate revenge on her estranged husband and his family. The princess totally undermined him by saying he would find the role of king 'suffocating' and that the 'top job' would bring 'enormous limitations to him, and I don't know whether he could adapt to that'. As for his confessed affair with Camilla, Diana memorably said, 'There were three of us in the marriage, so it was a bit crowded.' The other line that stuck with her besotted public was her wish to be 'the queen of people's hearts'. She had finally gone over the heads of her 'enemies' in the Establishment and put her case to the people.

Over lunch in Mayfair, the queen's Lord Chamberlain, Martin Charteris, a man at the heart of the old Establishment, told Woodrow Wyatt that Diana was 'very dangerous' and that a divorce was now 'inescapable'. After consulting both John Major and the Archbishop of Canterbury, the queen wrote to the Prince and Princess of Wales to agree an 'early divorce ... in the best interests of the country'. The marriage was dissolved on 28 August 1996.

During these tense times, the queen was fortunate to have a prime minister with a more tranquil temperament than Mrs Thatcher. John Major relied on her as a confidential sounding board as he faced his dramas, and she depended on him to work through complicated family matters. Their Tuesday audiences became 'mutual support sessions', according to royal biographer, William Shawcross. 'Major knew that the scandals were devastating for her.'[78] Years later, Major said, 'People don't realise quite how strong she is. I think the way she behaved in those years has saved the monarchy from far worse problems than it otherwise might have faced.'

When Major was defeated in the May 1997 general election, it was Tony Blair's turn to go to Buckingham Palace. Her Majesty was direct, 'You are my tenth prime minister. The first was Winston. That was before you were born.'[79] The queen relaxed more when Cherie Blair came in and chatted about moving the children into Downing Street. Mrs Blair was a known republican. 'Contrary to popular belief,' Blair asserted, 'Cherie always got on well with her.' Her refusal to curtsy amused rather than offended the queen, who is said to have remarked, 'I can almost feel Mrs Blair's knees stiffening when I come.'[80]

Blair wrote in his memoirs:

> I am not a great one for the Establishment. It's probably at heart why I'm in the Labour Party and always will be. I always felt they preferred political leaders of two types: either those who were of them ... or the 'authentic' Labour people ... who spoke with an accent and who fitted their view of how such people should be. People like me were a bit nouveau riche, a bit arriviste, a bit confusing and therefore suspect.

Margaret Thatcher, with all her elocution lessons and self-improvements, could have echoed those sentiments completely.

Three months later, on 31 August 1997, after unwisely dispensing with her official police protection, Diana's car crashed into a concrete pillar in a Paris traffic tunnel while being pursued by the paparazzi. They had wanted to get pictures of her together with her new boyfriend, playboy Dodi Fayed. Diana had damaged the monarchy greatly while she lived, but her death shook it as never before.

The queen was at Balmoral with Prince Charles and Princes William and Harry. Public anger grew after Diana's death, as the Windsor family remained hidden and silent on their Scottish estate, trying coming to terms with the tragic news and its effect on the two young princes. In contrast, the new prime minister, Tony Blair, was more sensitive to the mood of the nation and told his press officer, Alastair Campbell, 'This is going to unleash grief like no one has seen anywhere in the world.' In a public statement, the prime minister dubbed her 'The People's Princess'.

Meanwhile, a mounting wave of criticism grew and by the end of the week it had reached dangerous levels of hostility. The police were panicked into requesting the presence of the army in the background.[81] There was a gathering hysteria in London. 'Do they care?' and 'Where is the queen when the country needs her?' the *Sun* asked. The anger of the crowds was further provoked by the failure to fly the royal standard at half-mast over Buckingham Palace. Traditionally, this is only used to indicate if a sovereign is in residence, and after some pressure, the queen was persuaded to allow the Union Jack to be flown there at half-mast as a symbol of mourning.

On the evening before Diana's funeral, encouraged by Tony Blair, the queen gave a live televised broadcast about Diana. She sat at a window through which the grieving crowds outside Buckingham Palace could be seen. On the actual day of the funeral as the gun carriage carrying Diana's coffin passed, the queen bowed her head, the only other time she does this is at the Cenotaph in Whitehall, at the annual remembrance services for soldiers killed in wartime.

A total of 2,000 guests were invited to the service at Westminster Abbey, an extraordinary mixture of people representing the range of Diana's life, charities and friendship. Amongst the crowd inside the abbey was the former prime minister, Margaret Thatcher, looking solemn and sympathetic.

The death of Diana, Princess of Wales, subjected the queen to her greatest public humiliation, when she was forced to yield to public opinion, fuelled by a hostile media, to come back to the capital. The queen was bullied by the press. There was also another, more damaging, disagreement going on behind the scenes, between the queen's office at Buckingham Palace and Prince Charles's at St James's Palace, as the Prince of Wales tried to distance himself from the criticism the queen received during those fraught days. The two palaces were totally at odds with each other.[82]

Tony Blair's first traditional visit to Balmoral took place the day after Diana's funeral:

I was shown up to see the queen in the drawing room, which was exactly as Queen Victoria had left it. I was just about to sit down in a rather inviting-looking chair when a strangled cry from the footman and a set of queenly eyebrows raised in horror made me desist. It was explained that it had been Victoria's chair and that since her day no one had ever sat in it.[83]

Like Margaret Thatcher, the new prime minister and his wife were unused to the culture of the country house weekends which Balmoral typified. Blair found it unnerving and totally alien and, in private conversation that weekend, both the queen and her new prime minister were nervous.[84] Blair said:

> I talked, perhaps less sensitively than I should have, about the need to learn lessons … at points during the conversation she [the queen] assumed a certain hauteur; but in the end she herself said lessons must be learned and I could see her own wisdom at work, reflecting, considering and adjusting.

A surreal end to a surreal week, he concluded.[85]

The monarchy and New Labour had a mixed relationship. In the early days of his premiership, Tony Blair neglected the audience and squeezed it out of the agenda, until the palace said it had to have higher priority.[86] When Blair moved the audience to Wednesday evenings instead of Tuesdays, the queen expressed her 'surprise' at this break with tradition.[87] The Blairs also committed several faux pas, and the new prime minister didn't seem to understand his constitutional role as head of government vis-à-vis the queen's as head of state. Blair's idea of his position was much more akin to being president of the United Kingdom. Mrs Blair even accepted the title of 'first lady' bestowed on her by the press, although no such thing existed in British practice. There was also one toe-curling moment of acute embarrassment when Cherie claimed, in a 'leak too far', that they conceived their youngest child, Leo, at Balmoral. The queen survived the Blairs, and the Blairs survived (and even multiplied) at Balmoral, which they came to dislike almost as much as Margaret Thatcher had.[88]

By contrast, Gordon Brown and his wife, Sarah, were genuinely thrilled about their first visit to the queen's Scottish home and were determined they show due decorum, in contrast to Tony and Cherie's first stay. Gordon was delighted to have been driven around the Balmoral estate by the queen in her Ranger Rover and to witness her grapple with collapsed fence posts. His spin doctors were constantly on the lookout for stories that could prove his monarchist credentials, such as leaking the story that Gordon had thwarted Tony Blair's attempt to scrap the Queen's Royal Flight when he was Chancellor of the Exchequer.

As prime minister, Gordon Brown was always diligent and obliging in his audiences with the queen. He was unusually nervous too, particularly when reforms to betting duty meant that Her Majesty might grill him on its effect on her beloved horse racing, a subject he knew little about, but in which she had considerable expertise. He swotted up on the subject so as not to be caught out.[89]

In one incident, Gordon became furious with his press team for leaking a story to the *Sun* about the design of a new 50p coin to mark the anniversary of the Victoria Cross. Gordon was advising the queen that he was unhappy with a design showing one of the soldiers apparently about to be shot in the back. Although the story earned suitable praise for Gordon, he phoned Damien McBride, his press officer, at five o'clock that morning and screamed, 'How can you do this to me? This is the queen. THE QUEEN!' The leak had offended Gordon's sense of constitutional propriety because it revealed his dealings with the queen.

With David Cameron's election as prime minister in 2010, the queen again has an old Etonian, and fellow aristocrat with several royal connections, inhabiting Number 10. His Tory political views are far closer to the governmental consensus she favours. This is not surprising, as Cameron is a lineal descendant of King William IV, by his mistress Dorothea Jordan, through their illegitimate daughter Lady Elizabeth FitzClarence, which makes the prime minister a fifth cousin of Her Majesty.

11

AFTERMATH

Home is where you go when you've nowhere else to go.
Margaret Thatcher

The queen's relationship with Mrs Thatcher seemed to go through four stages:

At first, there was suspicion of her because she was a woman who achieved power on her own merit. Second, there was a fear that her policies were threatening the concept of consensus politics, to which Her Majesty was closely attached. Third, there was irritation at her grandiosity and constant upstaging of the monarchy, and finally, there was a relief after the storm, because the 'other queen' had finally moved on.

Mrs Thatcher was a British icon, and so was the queen. Not merely had they been at odds over political questions and the style of government, in a sense they were rivals for the same job. While in office, Thatcher had taken on both the role and the persona traditionally fulfilled by the monarch alone.

Indeed, Thatcher's regal stance could be unnerving. At a Christmas party, Lady Annabel Goldsmith whispered to the guest standing next to her as Margaret walked in, 'For God's sake remind me not to curtsy, that's what I did last time!'[1]

However, the most notorious example of this was the infamous royal 'we' she used when she emerged from 10 Downing Street to announce the birth of her grandson. Historian Peter Hennessy has written how history at its most cruel can be reduced to a single one-liner, and if so, Thatcher's defining phrase must surely be 'we are a grandmother'.[2] The British people, as much as the queen herself, disliked the royal position being usurped in this way, and they were uncomfortable that a prime minister should be so powerful as to feel able to do so. Television journalist and host Richard Madeley was the first to ask her why she had said this. The Iron Lady explained that her husband Denis, who disliked the public limelight, wouldn't come out to be with her on the steps of Number 10 as the new grandfather. Wanting to make sure she included him, she became tongue-tied and came out with the words that appeared so affected. Not everyone believed the explanation.

By the end of Mrs Thatcher's time in office, the queen had come to accept Thatcher's dominant presence. She invited her to the races and the queen mother paid her the compliment of asking her to stay at her Scottish home, Birkhall, on the Balmoral estate. Margaret never took up either invitation. She never liked country life and certainly didn't want to make the same mistake as Harold Wilson.[3] After Wilson had left office, the queen did not want to see him, although she had been fond of him when he was in power, not least for increasing her own Civil List payments. She had become bored with his bragging. 'She thought he was absurd,' stated Lord Charteris, 'Rather like Toad in *Wind in the Willows*.'[4] What Wilson forgot was that the queen has reigned for a long time, so none of her prime ministers are as special to her as she is to them.[5] Nevertheless, the queen did attend the ex-prime minister's 70th birthday party at Claridge's as the guest of honour in 1995.

Margaret Thatcher's exit from 10 Downing Street was something of a personal tragedy: she found herself on the political scrapheap and out of the game. What hurt her most was the fact she was no longer indispensable to Britain – and she couldn't even begin to imagine a new role for herself, let alone actually occupy one. 'She wasn't interested in reinventing herself … she would never have changed,' said Tim Bell. 'She was a resolute woman … unshakeable.'[6] As Charles Powell observed, 'it was the exercise of power she was built for, and without that she felt life lacked purpose. A dreadnought is out of place in a fishing fleet.'[7]

She became more like an empress in exile than a retired prime minister. To combat her sense of impotence, she was determined to underline her gravitas and to let the world know she still mattered. She said, 'It had come to an end … But what I did didn't come to an end.'[8] She always dreaded retirement, and still believed that she had a lot more to do. Margaret had always insisted that she would not retire until she had found a worthy successor to her ideas, something she never achieved. She was now airbrushed out of Tory Party history by the undistinguished grey men she had previously chosen to surround herself in order to make herself shine all the brighter.[9]

The day Margaret Thatcher left office, Woodrow Wyatt rang her in her Dulwich home and found her 'coming down to earth with a bump'. Although Denis and Margaret had bought a neo-Georgian house in south London, after over a decade at Downing Street and Chequers, the new Lady Thatcher had long outgrown suburbia. There were other problems associated with not living 'over the shop'.

Deprived of the Downing Street office staff, the ex-prime minister had to make her own phone calls and had no idea how to use a push button phone, so she had to get advice from the police officers stationed in her garage.

Unhappy in Dulwich, Lady Thatcher borrowed a luxurious duplex flat in Eaton Square, Belgravia, owned by Mrs Henry Ford. It was grand and central. Baroness Thatcher, sitting under a portrait of Queen Isabella of Spain, held lunches there and complained bitterly how the wheel of fortune had turned against her.

The Thatchers eventually bought a four storey Georgian house, with too many stairs, at 73 Chester Square, just around the corner from Eaton Square. She filled her sitting room with prized possessions, including an extensive collection of porcelain. There was also a large portrait of her by American artist Nelson Shanks and, on another wall, a painting of Downing Street by Nick Ridley. Among the rows of snuffboxes and china was a silver-framed photograph of her looking rather overdressed, with the queen and the queen mother at Balmoral.

There was little consolation from family life. After the Thatchers had left Downing Street, Mark and Denis didn't get on. Mark was often extremely rude to his father in front of Margaret and sometimes even in public. Lady Thatcher always sided with her son. While Denis gave her emotional support, Margaret turned to Mark to manage her financial and speaking affairs. He became her business advisor, literary agent, tour operator and chief fundraiser. She signed up to the Washington Speakers' Bureau for a reported fee of $50,000 a lecture, a fee second only to Reagan's. In the short term, this enabled her to enjoy the admiration of her global fan base.

She occupied herself with frenetic travels and speechmaking, sometimes startling well-intentioned questioners by pummelling them into the ground as though they were Neil Kinnock at PM's Questions. Controversially, she also became a consultant to Philip Morris, the giant tobacco corporation, in a deal worth $1 million over three years. Advising them how to break into troublesome foreign markets, she upset the anti-smoking lobby in the process. The irony was that she disliked smoking, and while she was prime minister had actively sought to protect vulnerable teenagers from tobacco companies.[10] The job attracted much negative press comment.

Margaret spent time writing her memoirs. 'I think the first thing she wanted to do was to get down on paper her history,' said Tim Bell.[11] Meanwhile, Mark tried to secure a publishing deal. Obviously, every publishing house in the world was interested and a multi-million pound advance on royalties beckoned. In his memoirs, Alan Clark wrote dismissively, 'Mark has been winding her up', as he had claimed a book deal was worth $20 million.[12] There was a general agreement that Mark was becoming a bit of a 'problem'.[13]

Instead of striking a deal within weeks of leaving office, Mark procrastinated and missed the big opportunity. The legendary American super-agent, Irving 'Swifty' Lazar, said publicly, 'The son is the fly in the ointment. The son thinks he can be an agent. He's decided he knows about publishing, and he's an amateur.'[14] Mark was negotiating at the time with newspaper tycoon Robert Maxwell, who owned Macmillan Publishers. Mark wanted as much as $10 million, and Maxwell was offering $8 million. Despite Mark Thatcher and Robert Maxwell eventually agreeing a 'handshake contract' the deal collapsed, which was just as well, as five months later Maxwell died.[15]

With the negotiations going so slowly, a family friend and bestselling novelist, Jeffrey Archer, brought in respected literary agent, George Greenfield, to advise. By now, Mark was talking to Marvin Josephson, a New York literary agent. Within days of Josephson signing Thatcher as a client of his company, International Creative Management Inc., publishers were finally invited to bid and the deal went to Rupert Murdoch's HarperCollins publishing house for £3.5 million.

Michael Sissons, a knowledgeable literary agent in London, summed it up best:

This was unquestionably, the most saleable autobiography of our times … So the project initially had enormous value, and to see that frittered away was immensely depressing. The value just seemed to fade because of the bad publicity, the indecision and the aura that Mark Thatcher's involvement gave it.[16]

Despite, rather than because of, Mark's intervention, within two years of leaving office Margaret was placed 134th in the *Sunday Times* 'Rich List' with an estimated wealth of £9.5 million. The memoirs, entitled *The Downing Street Years*, received a good reception from the critics, although she told the book buyers at Hatchards that she would have preferred the title 'Undefeated!'[17]

A BBC documentary, *The Downing Street Years*, was also filmed. She came across as angry and bitter. 'It brought out the very worst of her,' said Lord Carrington. 'I mean, she was horrid about everybody, and to everybody. And she wasn't like that … she was the kindest person. But the one thing she didn't want to be was to be thought of as kind … she wanted to be the Iron Lady.'[18]

Another missed opportunity as a result of Mark Thatcher's management was the Thatcher Foundation, set up with the intention of preserving Lady Thatcher's legacy, and promoting her ideas around the world. The ambition was to raise $20 million initially, and Margaret asked Mark to handle the financial affairs and act as chief fundraiser. Margaret Thatcher had always been generous to big business and now, in Mark's mind, it was payback time and the new foundation provided an opportunity for big business to be generous to Margaret.

At one fundraising meeting, he read out a list of high-powered CEOs who had made their money during the 1980s boom and asked each one how much they were donating. When enlightened about the amounts, he was dismissive, 'Chickenfeed. My mother made them. Now they have to pay up.'[19]

Just before her trip to the Far East, he telephoned a Hong Kong millionaire tycoon and told him, 'It's time to pay up for Mumsie.'[20] When one leading industrialist offered to raise £7 million for the Foundation, Mark was dismissive. 'That's not good enough,' he sniffed.

However, when complaints were reported back to mother, mother paid no attention, until some of her close friends and admirers briefed the *Sunday Times*. The result was a front page story on 21 April 1991, with the headline, '"Mark is Wrecking Your Life", Friends Tell Thatcher'. The article contained a disparaging assessment of his inept leadership.

Eventually, the Thatcher Foundation moved into a fine Georgian property in Belgravia at 35 Chesham Place, where her private office was arranged to look like the study at 10 Downing Street. Mark Worthington, a former researcher to Tory MPs, served as her aide and gave her political briefings each day. He did his best to create the impression of relevance, and those wishing to visit called him for an appointment.[21]

There was an old leather-covered desk, and a high-backed chair by the fireplace where she would look at her papers with the help of a magnifying glass (she refused to wear reading glasses out of vanity). The offices were very feminine, filled with flowers and plants, and Mrs Thatcher wore a heavy scent, usually Chanel No. 5, which filled the air. All around the room were memories of past glories, busts of Ronald Reagan, Winston Churchill and Denis. Two watercolours of Chequers, a portrait of her by Russian artist, Sergey Chepik, and some amateur paintings of the Falklands campaign hung on the walls.

Her favourite books were kept in a glass-fronted bookcase. Selected for inspiration, they included mostly political volumes or histories, such as *The Rise and Fall of the Great Powers* by Paul Kennedy, Ronald Reagan's *Speaking My Mind* and Barbara Tuchman's book on the Holy Land, *The Bible and the Sword*. She would often read a large print version of the *King James Bible* to check her scriptural quotations. She was very annoyed when Denis threw out Reagan's autobiography by mistake (or so he claimed).[22]

Despite its elegant offices, the Thatcher Foundation never fulfilled its potential. Some grants were awarded, including a scheme to educate students from the Eastern bloc in English public schools and a fund for Russian librarians to spend eight weeks in Washington.[23] However, fundraising was scuppered by Mark

Thatcher's insensitive approaches to sympathetic businesses. Its greatest achievement was arguably the collation and distribution to universities of the complete public statements of Margaret Thatcher on CD-ROM.

Margaret's moods were dark; the ex-prime minister often broke down and cried. Almost unhinged, she started to drink Scotch, largely because it was less fattening than a gin and tonic. With Denis pouring the drinks, as he now always did, she found her glass filled with quadruple shots of spirits. Fearful about gaining weight, she cut down on what she ate at lunch and the alcohol went straight to her head. Painfully, she had to have major dental work carried out and was forced to wear cumbersome plates, so she often slurred and hissed at guests. Naturally, people thought she was intoxicated as she could become loud, argumentative and unpleasant to those who crossed her.

She was, by temperament, belligerent.[24] Her increased deafness and her mental decline made her conversation repetitive and impossible to understand. Again, many blamed the Scotch. Much of her unsteadiness was also caused by her determination to keep wearing high-heeled shoes, not, as gossips suggested, by too many whiskies.[25]

Denis, ten years older than Margaret, gave up his company directorships but kept up with his rugby, cricket and his boozy lunches. He spent much of his time carefully checking his bank statements and reading biographies. Although he had pressed his wife repeatedly since she left Downing Street to retire and look after him at home, she couldn't give up work. Ever the loyal husband, he joined her on foreign tours and was physically not always able to keep up with the demanding schedules. He refused to take taxis because they were too expensive, and Margaret tried to make him take the official car, which she wasn't officially allowed to do unless they were travelling together. Once, when he was jumping onto a bus in Piccadilly, he fell off, smashing his watch.

For seventy years, Mrs Thatcher's health had been extraordinarily good. However, during a speaking engagement in Chile in 1994 she suddenly lost consciousness and slumped forward onto the lectern. She quickly recovered, and apologised, very embarrassed about what had happened. It was probably a first, very minor, stroke.

The most obvious sign of her delicacy was the loss of short-term memory. If she had a script, she could deliver an impeccable professional performance, but without one, repetitions would creep in. During a holiday with Denis to Madeira in 2001, she suffered a second minor stroke, and sometime early in 2002 she had a third. Afterwards, it was announced that she would do no more public speaking.

The more time Denis and Margaret spent together, the more spiky relations became. Margaret's forgetfulness and repetitiveness proved an irritation.

By the time Denis's health collapsed, their marriage was going through a difficult patch. The hours they spent together dragged a little. When Denis was diagnosed with pancreatic cancer, he was admitted to the Chelsea & Westminster Hospital, where, surrounded by family and friends, he died with Margaret holding his hand on 26 June 2003. His funeral took place in the chapel of the Royal Hospital, Chelsea, after which he was cremated.

Margaret was devastated with grief. Denis had always been her best friend, as she had never made time in her life for other friendships to grow. They became much closer in Downing Street than they had ever been in the earlier part of their marriage.[26] Denis and Margaret, whose relationship was often rather formal and a bit stiff, had loved each other perhaps more than they ever knew. For months she couldn't work, sleep or function. Behind the Thatcher facade of success was a lonely woman who lived only for her work, and Denis had been her one link to normality. 'Denis dying,' explains Tim Bell, 'had an enormous impact on her because he was absolutely her rock through everything, and he was fantastic at the job.'[27]

'I think she would have found it very much more difficult without him. I think he is a huge component of the story,' said Michael Dobbs.[28]

New losses, like that of Ronald Reagan who died of pneumonia in 2004, sharpened her pain. Each year, until his withdrawal from public life, she had attended and spoken at his birthday party. He had wanted her to perform a eulogy at his funeral, the first time a foreigner had been asked to do such a thing for a former president. Margaret constantly worried about whether she could do him justice. Eventually, Reagan's death coincided with her own ill health, and she recorded it in advance in London and listened to herself in Washington Cathedral, before attending the final interment at the Reagan Library in California with Nancy, family and friends.

Her family provided little consolation for her in old age. She rarely saw her grandchildren, Amanda and Michael, and saw little more of her children. Her childhood had never been that affectionate and such patterns tend to be repeated. She was never the sort of granny to knit socks or get stuck into Lego. Mark and his family now lived in South Africa and seldom came to Britain. Carol spent most of her time in Switzerland in an on–off amour with a ski instructor called Marco Grass. She and her mother had never gone shopping together nor enjoyed girls' days together at the spa. Carol had neither the academic talent nor the ability to make money, traits that Lady Thatcher respected. There was little intimacy, as it had never been a close-knit family, and as a consequence Mark and Carol spent little time in their increasingly frail and forgetful mother's company.

'Look, you can't have everything,' an elderly Margaret Thatcher said some years ago, in a revealing interview in *Saga* magazine:

It's been my greatest privilege being prime minister of my country ... Yes, I wish I saw more of my children. We don't have Sunday lunch together; we don't go on holiday skiing anymore. But I can't regret. And I haven't lost my children. They have their lives. I took a different life.[29]

Carol published an affectionate biography of her father, Denis, which drew a devastating picture of Mrs Thatcher's remoteness as a mother. 'As a child I was frightened of her,' Carol revealed.[30] If anything, the emotional wounds between matriarch and belligerent daughter festered rather than healed after Margaret left Downing Street.[31] After one clash with her mother, Carol stormed out of the family house, then Chester Square in Belgravia, shouting, 'Lady Thatcher, you were a great prime minister, but you are an awful mother!'

Nevertheless, Margaret became extremely proud of Carol's success in the television reality programme *I'm a Celebrity, Get Me out of Here!* Friends vetted some of the less tasteful incidents, including the moment when Carol was filmed urinating by her camp bed, but she was glued to the screen for the parts she saw, including the final, and was delighted by her daughter's courageous victory. Lady Thatcher had no objection to a bit of vulgarity, particularly when Carol turned her triumph into financial success with several television and book offers.

This new harmony didn't last. Carol's second book, *A Swim-on Part in the Goldfish Bowl*, revealed intimate details of Margaret's 'dementia', as Carol referred to it. Carol disclosed in that memoir the exact moment she realised there was a problem. Over lunch with friends in 2000, Lady Thatcher inexplicably confused Yugoslavia with the Falklands. 'I almost fell off my chair,' said Carol. 'Watching her struggle with her words and her memory. I couldn't believe it. I had always thought of her as ageless, timeless, and 100 per cent cast iron damage proof.'[32]

It was wrongly assumed that the former prime minister was in an advanced state of Alzheimer's disease. People thought that she had retired completely and couldn't be invited to private functions. There were even discussions in the press about whether someone with mental health problems could vote in the House of Lords. For several days, Lady Thatcher's staff kept the information from her, but in the end she had to know. When she read it, she was shocked at seeing, in print, facts about her condition. Margaret was deeply wounded that her daughter could behave in such a fashion.[33]

Worse was to come when a political scandal engulfed her son, now Sir Mark Thatcher, after he had succeeded to his father's baronetcy. Mark was placed under house arrest in South Africa and charged under the country's anti-mercenary laws for his involvement in a failed political coup in Equatorial Guinea. After plea bargaining, he was convicted and given a four year suspended sentence as well as a fine of about £240,000 ($370,000). Margaret put up £100,000 of the bail money to get him released from police custody and helped with his fine. On his arrest, his wife Diane divorced him and left with her two children, Amanda and Michael, for her native United States. She perhaps summed it up best when she said, 'Mark was given one of the best seats at the banquet of life, and he's blown it.'[34]

Mark's convictions mean that he cannot live in the United States, and he now lives in Europe and has remarried. Carol was openly contemptuous of her mother's decision to bail him out, and the entire episode deepened the two women's estrangement. In December 2005, it was widely reported that Margaret had a fainting fit while at her hairdresser. A stroke caused it. Mark rushed to his mother's hospital bedside. Carol, although in London, stayed away. She also absented herself from Chester Square during the following Christmas, alienating herself from her mother as much as her brother.

There were less woeful times as well. In October 2005, Lady Thatcher celebrated her 80th birthday with a party at the Mandarin Oriental Hotel in London's Hyde Park. Attended by 650 guests, *Times* journalist Andrew Pierce called it 'the ultimate 80s revival night'.[35] The queen and Prince Philip were guests of honour, along with Tony Blair and most of her 1980s Cabinet colleagues, minus Lord Heseltine.

The red carpet was rolled out for Lady Thatcher's arrival, and she appeared dressed in a navy blue cocktail coat and a Camilla Milton silk chiffon dress. The party would be one of the last big public events that she would host. Guests included Joan Collins, Dame Shirley Bassey, June Whitfield, P.D. James, Terry Wogan, Lord Lloyd-Webber, Sir Jimmy Young, Jeremy Clarkson, Princess Alexandra and President Cossiga of Italy. There was a rare appearance from John Profumo, who had retreated from public life in 1963 after lying to the Commons over his relationship with Christine Keeler. Jeffrey Archer, who was jailed for perjury, also attended. His wife, Mary Archer, said, 'Lady Thatcher may appear to be the Iron Lady, but her friends saw a warm, kind and thoughtful person who does not desert you when you are not in vogue.'

Even Sir John Major, who accused Lady Thatcher of undermining his premiership, made a surprise appearance, a sign that their feud was over. Geoffrey Howe also seemed to have been forgiven. He said, 'Her real triumph was to have transformed not just one party but two, so that when Labour did eventually return, the great bulk of Thatcherism was accepted as irreversible.'

However, the quote of the night went to Joan Collins who said, 'She is the Iron Lady, and I want to be just like that when I grow up.'[36]

Cecil Parkinson also attended:

I think one of the most poignant moments of Margaret's eightieth birthday, was when the queen took Margaret under her wing that night. She was holding her arm and escorting her for quite a part of the evening. And that was a real sign of concern and friendship to me ... The queen did care about her, as a person, and respected her and wanted that evening to be a great success for her.[37]

In 2008 she was admitted to hospital for tests after she felt ill at the House of Lords. After that, there were only rare public appearances. Lady Thatcher was spotted watering the roses in the Temple Gardens in London's legal district, hunched and frail in raincoat and scarf under the watchful eye of her police protection; it was a weekly routine she liked to perform until she got too delicate even for that. There was another sighting of the former prime minister sitting on a park bench in London enjoying the sunshine in March 2011, patting a playful dog.[38]

At Christmas 2012, suffering abdominal pains, she was rushed to the hospital to remove a growth in her bladder. It wasn't a difficult operation, but when she was released from the hospital she couldn't manage the stairs at Chester Square. Instead, she moved into a luxurious suite at the Ritz Hotel where she received round-the-clock nursing. Reading the papers, she noticed a large picture of Meryl Streep, playing her in the film *The Iron Lady*. 'How elegant!' was the response. However, it was unclear whether she was paying tribute to the actress or herself. Margaret never saw the film, and those around her kept her shielded her from the fact that it focused on her dementia.[39]

In contrast to Lady Thatcher's deterioration, the queen and the royal family started to make a comeback in public opinion. Edwina Currie pointed out, 'The queen and Buckingham Palace finally got their act together, just as Mrs Thatcher went into decline.'

The opening of the state apartments at Buckingham Palace following the fire at Windsor Castle had been very successful. Similarly, the queen's golden wedding celebrations, after the death of Diana, showed Her Majesty was able to listen to criticism. At a lunch hosted by Prime Minister Tony Blair, dubbed a 'people's banquet', she acknowledged the difficulty royalty experienced in reading public opinion. 'But read it we must,' she said.[40] Buckingham Palace stressed the queen's continuity, adaptability, permanence and endurance, and words like glamour and mystique were dropped from the vernacular.[41]

Amongst the staff at Buckingham Palace, there was a new sense of urgency and purpose. The queen had stated in her memorable speech, made the evening before Diana's funeral, that there were 'lessons to be learned' and that was now taken up as a mantra. Taking the public's temperature became an obsession at the palace.

There was a choreographed change of style. Before the Diana tragedy, if the queen visited a school, she would stand in the doorway and listen to the teacher. Now she made a point of sitting down with the children. Buzzwords such as 'listening', 'modernisation' and 'informality' were used. There were changes to royal protocol. Bowing and curtsying to royalty became optional, and unoccupied royal residences automatically had a Union Jack hanging over them, to be lowered to half-mast should the need arise.[42]

Even Camilla Parker-Bowles was rehabilitated. For years, the queen refused to receive her. It was said on this issue that 'the Head Lady is not for turning'.[43] To her, he could either become king and put Camilla aside, or marry her and reconsider his future. It sounded liked the ultimatum given during the abdication crisis to the Duke of Windsor. However, members of the family like Princess Margaret's daughter, Lady Sarah Chatto, and key palace courtiers like Sir Michael Peat, recognised that the queen would appear hard-faced and out of touch.[44] Finally, the queen met Camilla at Highgrove, a necessary gesture if there was to be any hope of building a better relationship with Charles.

There were setbacks. At the ceremonial decommissioning of the Royal Yacht *Britannia*, after forty-four years in service, photographers caught the queen crying. Some tabloids picked up on the fact that, by comparison, she had wept no tears at Princess Diana's funeral.

Prince Charles also remained a problem. His detractors dismissed him as a privileged crank, and his handwritten letters regularly landed on the desk of government ministers. Newspaper reports in August 2013 revealed that the prince had held thirty-six meetings with Cabinet ministers since Britain's coalition government came to power in 2010. Rupert Murdoch's *Sunday Times* alleged that Prince Charles had placed 'moles' at the heart of Britain's government and that he was interfering in the political process. A recent rash of articles has proposed bypassing the Prince of Wales in favour of the shiny younger royals: King William and Queen Katherine would certainly sparkle. Such leapfrogging is unlikely to occur, however, as Charles has recently taken on many of his mother's officials roles, including the state opening of Parliament and presiding at the Commonwealth Heads of Government Meeting in Sri Lanka, in 2013.[45]

The film *The Queen*, starring Helen Mirren, which dealt with the aftermath of Princess Diana's death, did a great deal to boost Elizabeth II's reputation. When the actress stood up to received her Oscar for her performance, many agreed with the sentiments of her speech:

... for fifty years and more Elizabeth Windsor has maintained her dignity, her sense of duty and her hairstyle. She's had her feet planted firmly on the ground; her hat on her head, her handbag on her arm and she's weathered many, many storms. And I salute her courage and her consistency.

In 2013, the British Social Attitudes Survey showed that the monarchy emerged as the only institution to gain in popularity. It did so because it stands for continuity in a world of relentless transformation. This return to favour has been boosted by key events such as the queen's diamond jubilee celebrations, the opening ceremony of the Olympics and the wedding of Prince William to Kate Middleton.

The monarchy has successfully updated itself. As the queen's former press secretary, Ron Allison, points out:

If I'd suggested that someone plays their guitar on the roof of Buckingham Palace or that James Bond should walk into the palace to escort the queen by helicopter to the Olympics ... I would have got laughed out of Court ... amazing changes in attitude ... Wonderful.[46]

One person, however, failed to attend any of these gatherings – Baroness Thatcher. On the morning of Monday, 8 April 2013, sitting in an armchair in her suite looking at a picture book, she suffered another stroke. Within fifteen minutes of the attack, her heartbeat stopped. It was a quick and painless death. She was 87 years old.[47]

A Buckingham Palace spokesman issued a statement saying the queen was 'sad to hear of the news of the death of Baroness Thatcher', and that she would be sending a private message of sympathy to her family. Almost immediately the press speculated, 'Will the queen attend her funeral?' When it was announced that the queen would be attending, Sir Mark Thatcher appeared on the steps of Baroness Thatcher's Chester Square home. He stated, 'First of all, and most importantly, I would like to say how enormously proud and equally grateful we are that Her Majesty the Queen has agreed to attend the service next week at St Paul's. I know my mother would be greatly honoured as well as humbled by her presence.'[48]

In her final days, Margaret was surrounded by the people who cared for her most, and as one tabloid harshly pointed out, it had not been her family. Mark and Carol Thatcher were both abroad, Mark in Marbella and Carol in Switzerland. The *Daily Mirror* wrote, 'She died in a hotel room among the people who cared for her ... a devoted select group that did not include her own children.'[49] It seemed rather a lonely end; she was tended by two carers, Kate and Anne, with affection and gentle teasing. A small circle of long-standing friends, such as Conor Burns MP, who made weekly visits to see her, regularly visited her during her final days. Former defence secretary, Sir Gerald Howarth was another frequent visitor, as was Alison Wakeham, the wife of John Wakeham MP, who was so badly injured the night of the Brighton bomb. Others included Mark Worthington, who was her loyal private secretary for more than two decades, and Lord Powell, her foreign affairs advisor. Cynthia Crawford would stay for one or two weeks at a time and Sir Bernard Ingham, her indomitable press secretary, also visited.[50]

Julian Seymour, who became the head of Mrs Thatcher's private office in 1991, and who later handled all her legal, financial and administrative arrangements, was appointed the principal executor of her will. It was a simple document that divided her estate into three equal parts, one to Mark, one to Carol and one to her grandchildren.[51]

Margaret had meticulously planned her funeral. As early as 2002, during Tony Blair's premiership, discussion began with the Cabinet office, and before Gordon Brown left Downing Street in 2010 the detailed preparations for what was called 'a state funeral in all but name' had been approved.[52] A former royal courtier, Sir Malcolm Ross, who had overseen the funerals of the queen mother and Princess Diana, was a key figure in this process. The codename for the plans was 'True Blue', to give it a more Conservative feel.[53]

The press were divided about her death. Compared to the outpouring of grief for Princess Diana and the queen mother, there were split opinions. Several public figures, including the Bishop of Grantham, Lord Prescott and George Galloway MP, criticised the scale of the event, with estimates of the expense rising up to £10 million in total. In the event, it was reported by Downing Street that the cost to the government and taxpayer would be £3.6 million, of which £3.1 million was for police and security.[54] Following the bombing of the Boston Marathon on 17 April, two days before the funeral, 4,000 police officers were deployed.

The left wing *Daily Mirror* asked on its front page, 'Why is Britain's most divisive prime minister getting a ceremonial funeral fit for a queen?' Inside, another headline stated, 'No! No! No! Public don't want same send off as for royalty'.[55]

Amongst the bouquets that lay outside her home in Belgravia was a pint of milk, a reference to her early nickname as 'Thatcher the Milk Snatcher'. A petition was organised over the internet to demand that her funeral should be paid for entirely by her family, as a large proportion of the public hated her with a vengeance.

After anarchists had threatened a mass 'party' to celebrate her death, there were fears that there would be violent demonstrations, which would force the police to use the Public Order Act.[56] One of the more idiotic protests was a downloading campaign to ensure that the BBC were forced to play a 70-year-old number from

The Wizard of Oz ('Ding Dong! The Witch is Dead!') on their Top 40 chart show, The embarrassed BBC wasn't sure whether they should play it, and eventually, after tying themselves up in knots, gave it seven second's airtime on Radio 1. [57]

Many of her closest friends thought the funeral at St Paul's Cathedral was a little too much. 'I think it would have been much better to have had a great big do in Westminster Abbey ... all the pomp and ceremony, but no soldiers ... remarkable though she was, she wasn't Winston Churchill,' said Lord Carrington. [58]

'I was not in favour, and I think it went a little too far. That was my judgement beforehand,' said Michael Dobbs. 'My judgement afterwards was that actually they got away with it.' [59]

Sir Bernard Ingham disagrees:

Leave aside her being the first woman PM of the UK, she was the outstand-ing peacetime PM of the twentieth century, achieving more I think against a hostile environment than Attlee, who had vast public support. Mrs T came to office with the nation wondering whether Britain was governable anymore. She changed the nature of Britain and its standing in the world. I would have thought she was worth some ceremony on her death. [60]

The cost of the funeral threw the spotlight onto the ownership of Margaret Thatcher's £6 million home. The *Daily Mirror*'s chief reporter, Andy Lines, pointed out, in an article entitled 'Thatcher the Tax Snatcher?', that the property was, in fact, owned by what he called, 'a mysterious company with links to three notorious tax havens'. The paper's financial experts explained that it would have been a device to help her heirs avoid a potential £2.4 million bill for inheritance tax on the property.

The house was officially owned by Bakeland Property Company, based in the British Virgin Islands. The company's address was a post office box in a small town in Liechtenstein. John Christensen of the Tax Justice Network complained, 'This does not pass the smell test.' [61]

Other newspapers rushed to her defence, calling her 'The Woman Who Saved Britain', and demanded that the nation give her a state funeral. Simon Heffer, one of the leading *Daily Mail* columnists, said, 'it will be an insult to history to deny her this honour.' [62] The *Sun* called her a 'Humble grocer's girl who took on the world'.

On the day of the funeral itself, the national mood changed, and the student pro-tests and silly downloads evaporated. Amongst the crowds lining the streets, hostility was minimal, and not a single arrest was made. Thousands of Lady Thatcher's sup-porters cheered and applauded her cortège, drowning out the scattered protestors.

Inside St Paul's Cathedral, Queen Elizabeth and her husband Prince Philip led the 2,300 mourners. In a break with royal etiquette, they weren't the last to arrive. That honour was left to Margaret's coffin.

The funeral address was delivered by Margaret Thatcher's favourite bishop, Richard Chartres, Bishop of London, clad in a black cope designed for and last used at Churchill's funeral. Margaret, a devout Methodist in her youth who switched to the Church of England following her marriage, knew her *King James Bible*, Charles Wesley's hymns and Cardinal Newman's prayers. All were included, with the most powerful reading coming from her 19-year-old American-born granddaughter, Amanda Thatcher, who stole the show with her poise and confidence. The *Daily Mail* called her the 'Iron Granddaughter'.[63]

The queen's presence marked only the second time in her reign that she had attended the funeral of a former prime minister. The other time was the state funeral of Winston Churchill in 1965. Traditionally, the queen doesn't attend the funerals of 'commoners', normally sending representatives such as senior members of the household or members of the royal family. The perceived risk has always been that if she were to make herself available for one, she would need to for all, for every crowned head, foreign world leader and national dignitary. In 1881, this protocol prevented Queen Victoria from attending the funeral of Benjamin Disraeli, the prime minister that she had much loved. She compensated by sending a wreath of primroses, his favourite flowers.

The queen's attendance didn't stop the press speculating on their relationship in the days running up to the funeral. Articles appeared about their strained relationship: their clashes over the Commonwealth; Thatcher's refusal to impose sanctions on South Africa; and Elizabeth's 'dismay' about her 'uncaring' prime minister, who was dividing Britain. There were also anecdotal stories like the one concerning the depth of Margaret Thatcher's curtsies. Nevertheless, in the end Lady Thatcher would have been delighted that the king's daughter had paid such an enormous tribute to the grocer's daughter by attending her funeral.

Probably one of the more interesting and reflective tributes was made by actress Meryl Streep, who played Mrs Thatcher in *The Iron Lady* and won her third Oscar for the role:

> To me she was a figure of awe … To have come up, legitimately, through the ranks of the British political system, class bound and gender phobic as it was, in the time that she did and the way that she did, was a formidable achievement … To have given women and girls around the world reason to supplant fantasies of being princesses with a different dream: the real life option of leading their nation; this was groundbreaking and admirable.[64]

NOTES

Chapter 1

1   *The Path to Power*, Margaret Thatcher (HarperCollins, 1993).

2   *A Swim-on Part in the Goldfish Bowl*, Carol Thatcher (Headline, 2002).

3   *Margaret Thatcher*, Penny Junor (Sidgwick & Jackson, 1984).

4   *A Swim-on Part in the Goldfish Bowl*, Carol Thatcher (Headline, 2002).

5   Ibid.

6   *ITN News*, 4 May 1979.

7   Ibid.

8   'The Blooming of Margaret Thatcher', Gail Sheehy, *Vanity Fair*, June 1989.

9   Ibid.

10 *A Swim-on Part in the Goldfish Bowl*, Carol Thatcher (Headline, 2002).

11 *The Path to Power*, Margaret Thatcher (HarperCollins, 1993).

12 *The Constitution of the UK*, Peter Leyland (Oxford & Portland, 2012).

13 *The Audience*, Peter Morgan (Faber & Faber, 2013).

14 *Margaret Thatcher*, Penny Junor (Sidgwick & Jackson, 1984).

15 *Margaret Thatcher: Power and Personality*, Jonathan Aitken (Bloomsbury, 2013).

16 *Margaret Thatcher: The Authorised Biography (Volume One)*, Charles Moore (Allen Lane, 2013).

17 *Margaret Thatcher*, Penny Junor (Sidgwick & Jackson, 1984).

18 Interview, Ron Allison, 2013.

19 *Rejoice! Rejoice! Britain in the 1980s*, Alwyn W. Turner (Aurum Press, 2010).

20 *Elizabeth, the Queen*, Sally Bedell Smith (Penguin Books, 2012).

21 *The Queen: Elizabeth II and the Monarchy*, Ben Pimlott (HarperCollins, 1996).

22 *Elizabeth: Behind Palace Doors*, Nicholas Davies (Mainstream Publishing Projects, 2000).

23 Interview, Denis Healey, 2013.

24   *The Queen: Elizabeth II and the Monarchy*, Ben Pimlott (HarperCollins, 1996).

25   *Strange Rebels*, Christian Caryl (Basic Books, 2013).

26   *The Queen: Elizabeth II and the Monarchy*, Ben Pimlott (HarperCollins, 1996).

27   Joe Haines interview, *Daily Telegraph* article, 1979.

28   *Eminent Elizabethans*, Piers Brendon (Jonathan Cape, 2012).

29   *Margaret Thatcher*, Penny Junor (Sidgwick & Jackson, 1984).

30   'Mrs Thatcher and the Intellectuals', Brian Harrison, *Twentieth-Century British History*, 1994.

31   *The Diamond Queen*, Andrew Marr (Macmillan, 2011).

32   *Margaret Thatcher: From Childhood to Leadership*, George Gardiner MP (William Kimber & Co 1975).

33   *The Queen: Elizabeth II and the Monarchy*, Ben Pimlott (HarperCollins, 1996).

34   *Westmorland Gazette*, 13 April 2013.

35   *Elizabeth, the Queen*, Sally Bedell Smith (Penguin Books, 2012).

36   Ibid.

37   *Queen Elizabeth II: Her Life in Our Times*, Sarah Bradford (Viking, 2012).

38   *Inside Number 10*, Marcia Williams (Weidenfeld & Nicolson, 1972).

39   Ibid.

40   *Queen Elizabeth II: Her Life in Our Times*, Sarah Bradford (Viking, 2012).

41   *Elizabeth, the Queen*, Sally Bedell Smith (Penguin Books, 2012).

42   *The Queen: Elizabeth II and the Monarchy*, Ben Pimlott (HarperCollins, 1996).

43   Ibid.

44   *Harold Wilson*, Ben Pimlott (HarperCollins, 1992).

45   *Elizabeth, the Queen*, Sally Bedell Smith (Penguin Books, 2012).

46   Ibid.

47   *There is No Alternative*, Claire Berlinski (Basic Books, 2008).

48   NBC's *Meet the Press* interview with Prince Philip, 10 November 1969.

49   *Richard Crossland Diaries*, Richard Crossland (Book Clubs Associates, 1979).

50   *Inside View: Three Lectures on Prime Ministerial Government*, Richard Crossland (Cape, 1972).

51   *Times*, 28 May 1971.

52   *Queen Elizabeth II: Her Life in Our Times*, Sarah Bradford (Viking, 2012).

53   Ibid.

54   *The Queen: Elizabeth II and the Monarchy*, Ben Pimlott (HarperCollins, 1996).

55   *There is No Alternative*, Claire Berlinski (Basic Books, 2008).

56   *The Queen: Elizabeth II and the Monarchy*, Ben Pimlott (HarperCollins, 1996).

57   Ibid.

58   Interview, Ron Allison, 2013.

59   Interview, Edwina Currie, 2013.

60   Interview, Cecil Parkinson, 2013.

61   Interview, Edwina Currie, 2013.

62   *The Queen: Elizabeth II and the Monarchy*, Ben Pimlott (HarperCollins, 1996).

63   Ibid.

64   'The Blooming of Margaret Thatcher', Gail Sheehy, *Vanity Fair*, June 1989.

65   *A Swim-on Part in the Goldfish Bowl*, Carol Thatcher (Headline, 2002).

66   *Her Majesty, 60 Regal Years* (Diamond Jubilee Edition), Brian Hoey (Robson Press, 2012).

67   Ibid.

68   *Royal Secrets: The View from Downstairs*, Stephen P. Barry (Villard Books, 1985).

69   *Our Own Dear Queen*, Piers Brendon (Secker & Warburg, 1986).

70   *The Queen: Elizabeth II and the Monarchy*, Ben Pimlott (HarperCollins, 1996).

71   Ibid.

72   *The Journals of Woodrow Wyatt (Volume One)*, Sarah Curtis (Ed.) (Pan Books, 1998).

73   Interview, Ron Allison, 2013.

74   Interview, Lord Carrington, 2013.

75   BBC News Website, 22 November 2005.

76   'The Invincible Mrs Thatcher', Charles Moore, *Vanity Fair*, December 2011.

77   *There is No Alternative*, Claire Berlinski (Basic Books, 2008).

78   Interview, Tim Bell, 2013.

79   Interview, Jeffery Archer, 2013.

80   *Elizabeth: Behind Palace Doors*, Nicholas Davies (Mainstream Publishing Projects, 2000).

81   *The Queen: Elizabeth II and the Monarchy*, Ben Pimlott (HarperCollins, 1996).

82   *Thatcher & Sons*, Simon Jenkins (Penguin, 2007).

83   Interview, Lord Carrington, 2013.

84   Interview, Jeffrey Archer, 2013.

85   *Rejoice! Rejoice! Britain in the 1980s*, Alwyn W. Turner (Aurum Press, 2010).

Chapter 2

1   *Margaret Thatcher*, Penny Junor (Sidgwick & Jackson, 1984).

2   *The Iron Lady*, John Campbell (Penguin, 2009).

3   Author's correspondence with Sir Bernard Ingham, 2013.

4   *There is No Alternative*, Claire Berlinski (Basic Books, 2008).

5   'Did Blue Blood Run in Lady Thatcher's Veins?' *Daily Express*, 21 April 2013.

6   *There is No Alternative*, Claire Berlinski (Basic Books, 2008).

7   Interview, David Owen, 2013.

8   *Margaret Thatcher*, Penny Junor (Sidgwick & Jackson, 1984).

9   *Margaret Thatcher*, Tricia Murray (Star, 1978).

10   Simon Hoggart, *Tatler*, January 1984.

11   Robert Harris, *Observer*, 3 January 1988.

12   *Margaret, Daughter of Beatrice*, Leo Abse MP (Jonathan Cape, 1989).

13   Ibid.

14   'Reciprocal Rights and Responsibilities in Parent Child Relations', Diana Baumrind, *Journal of Social Issues*, 1978.

15   'The Blooming of Margaret Thatcher', Gail Sheehy, *Vanity Fair*, June 1989.

16   Ibid.

17   *Margaret Thatcher*, Penny Junor (Sidgwick & Jackson, 1984).

18   TV Interview for Yorkshire TV, *Woman to Woman* (transcript): Margaret Thatcher and Dr Miriam Stoppard interview, 2 October 1985. (Thatcher Archive.)

19   *The Thatcher Phenomenon*, Hugo Young and Ann Sloman (BBC Books, 1986).

20   *Margaret, Daughter of Beatrice*, Leo Abse MP (Jonathan Cape, 1989).

21   *Margaret Thatcher*, Tricia Murray (Star, 1978).

22   *The Iron Lady*, John Campbell (Penguin, 2009).

23   *Women in Power: The Personalities and Leadership Styles of Indira Gandhi, Golda Meir, and Margaret Thatcher*, Blema S. Steinberg (McGill–Queen's University Press, 2008).

24   *Margaret, Daughter of Beatrice*, Leo Abse MP (Jonathan Cape, 1989).

25   *Ronald Reagan and Margaret Thatcher: A Political Marriage*, Nicholas Wapshott (Penguin, 2007).

26   *Margaret Thatcher*, Penny Junor (Sidgwick & Jackson, 1984).

27   *Ronald Reagan and Margaret Thatcher: A Political Marriage*, Nicholas Wapshott (Penguin, 2007).

28   Ibid.

29   *The Path to Power*, Margaret Thatcher (HarperCollins, 1996).

30   *Margaret Thatcher*, Penny Junor (Sidgwick & Jackson, 1984).

31   *The Path to Power*, Margaret Thatcher (HarperCollins, 1996).

32   Ibid.

33   *Margaret Thatcher*, Penny Junor (Sidgwick & Jackson, 1984).

34   *Ronald Reagan and Margaret Thatcher: A Political Marriage*, Nicholas Wapshott (Penguin, 2007).

35   *The Path to Power*, Margaret Thatcher (HarperCollins, 1996).

36   *Margaret, Daughter of Beatrice*, Leo Abse MP (Jonathan Cape, 1989).

37   *Margaret Thatcher*, Penny Junor (Sidgwick & Jackson, 1984).

38   *There is No Alternative*, Claire Berlinski (Basic Books 2008).

39   *The Path to Power*, Margaret Thatcher (HarperCollins, 1996).

40   Ibid.

41   Ibid.

42   *Ronald Reagan and Margaret Thatcher: A Political Marriage*, Nicholas Wapshott (Penguin, 2007).

43   *The Path to Power*, Margaret Thatcher (HarperCollins, 1996).

44   'Thatcher and the Jews', Charles C. Johnson, *Tablet*, 28 December 2011.

45   *Margaret Thatcher*, Penny Junor (Sidgwick & Jackson, 1984).

46   *Margaret, Daughter of Beatrice*, Leo Abse MP (Jonathan Cape, 1989).

47   *Margaret Thatcher*, Penny Junor (Sidgwick & Jackson, 1984).

48   Ibid.

49   Ibid.

50   Ibid.

51   *Maggie*, Chris Ogden (Simon & Schuster, April 1990).

52   *Margaret Thatcher*, Penny Junor (Sidgwick & Jackson, 1984).

53   'The Blooming of Margaret Thatcher', Gail Sheehy, *Vanity Fair*, June 1989.

54   *Women in Power: The Personalities and Leadership Styles of Indira Gandhi, Golda Meir, and Margaret Thatcher*, Blema S. Steinberg (McGill-Queen's University Press, 2008).

55   *The Iron Lady*, Hugo Young (Noonday Press, November 1990).

56   *Margaret Thatcher*, Penny Junor (Sidgwick & Jackson, 1984).

57   Ibid.

58   Ibid.

59   'The Blooming of Margaret Thatcher', Gail Sheehy, *Vanity Fair*, June 1989.

60   Ibid.

61   *Margaret Thatcher*, Penny Junor (Sidgwick & Jackson, 1984).

62   *Ronald Reagan and Margaret Thatcher: A Political Marriage*, Nicholas Wapshott (Penguin, 2007).

63   Ibid.

64   *The Path to Power*, Margaret Thatcher (HarperCollins, 1996).

65   Ibid.

66   *Margaret Thatcher*, Penny Junor (Sidgwick & Jackson, 1984).

67   Ibid.

68   Ibid.

69   Ibid.

70 'The Blooming of Margaret Thatcher', Gail Sheehy, *Vanity Fair*, June 1989.

71 *Ronald Reagan and Margaret Thatcher: A Political Marriage*, Nicholas Wapshott (Penguin, 2007).

72 *Margaret Thatcher: Power and Personality*, Jonathan Aitken (Bloomsbury, 2013).

73 *Margaret Thatcher: The Authorised Biography (Volume One)*, Charles Moore (Allen Lane, 2013).

74 Ibid.

75 Ibid.

76 *Margaret Thatcher*, Penny Junor (Sidgwick & Jackson, 1984).

77 *Margaret Thatcher: Power and Personality*, Jonathan Aitken (Bloomsbury, 2013).

78 'The Blooming of Margaret Thatcher', Gail Sheehy, *Vanity Fair*, June 1989.

79 *Margaret, Daughter of Beatrice*, Leo Abse MP (Jonathan Cape, 1989).

80 *There is No Alternative*, Claire Berlinski (Basic Books, 2008).

81 *The Path to Power*, Margaret Thatcher (HarperCollins, 1996).

82 *There is No Alternative*, Claire Berlinski (Basic Books, 2008).

83 Interview, Cecil Parkinson, 2013.

84 Interview, Edwina Currie, 2013.

85 Interview, Cecil Parkinson, 2013.

86 Author's correspondence with Sir Bernard Ingham, 2013.

87 *Margaret Thatcher*, Tricia Murray (Star, 1978).

88 *Margaret Thatcher: Power and Personality*, Jonathan Aitken (Bloomsbury, 2013).

89 Sir Denis Thatcher Bt. Obituary, *Daily Telegraph*, 27 June 2003.

90 *Margaret Thatcher*, Penny Junor (Sidgwick & Jackson, 1984).

91 'The Blooming of Margaret Thatcher', Gail Sheehy, *Vanity Fair*, June 1989.

92 *There is No Alternative*, Claire Berlinski (Basic Books, 2008).

93 *Bang! A History of Britain in the 1980s*, Graham Stewart (Atlantic Books, 2013).

94 *Memories of Margaret Thatcher*, Iain Dale (Ed.) (Biteback Publishing, 2013).

95 *Eminent Elizabethans*, Piers Brendon (Jonathan Cape, 2012).

96 *The Path to Power*, Margaret Thatcher (HarperCollins, 1996).

97 *Eminent Elizabethans*, Piers Brendon (Jonathan Cape, 2012).

98 *Women in Power: The Personalities and Leadership Styles of Indira Gandhi, Golda Meir, and Margaret Thatcher*, Blema S. Steinberg (McGill–Queen's University Press, 2008).

99 Interview, Edwina Currie, 2013.

100 *Eminent Elizabethans*, Piers Brendon (Jonathan Cape, 2012).

101 Ibid.

102 *There is No Alternative*, Claire Berlinski (Basic Books, 2008).

103 Interview, Edwina Currie, 2013.

104 Interview, Tim Bell, 2013.

105 *Maggie*, Chris Ogden (Simon & Schuster, 1990).

106 *The Iron Lady*, John Campbell (Penguin, 2009).

107 *Margaret Thatcher: Power and Personality*, Jonathan Aitken (Bloomsbury, 2013).

108 Shirley Williams interview, *The Downing Street Years*, BBC.

109 *Margaret Thatcher*, Penny Junor (Sidgwick & Jackson, 1984).

110 *Women in Power: The Personalities and Leadership Styles of Indira Gandhi, Golda Meir, and Margaret Thatcher*, Blema S. Steinberg (McGill-Queen's University Press, 2008).

111 BBC Website: UK Confidential, 1 January 2001.

112 Interview, Lord Carrington, 2013.

113 *Margaret Thatcher*, Penny Junor (Sidgwick & Jackson, 1984).

114 Interview, Lord Carrington, 2013.

115 Ibid.

116 *Not for Turning*, Robin Harris (Bantam Press, 2013).

117 *Times* 'Diary', 11 September 1974.

118 Interview, Edwina Currie, 2013.

119 *Not for Turning*, Robin Harris (Bantam Press, 2013).

120 Interview, Edwina Currie, 2013.

121 'The Blooming of Margaret Thatcher', Gail Sheehy, *Vanity Fair*, June 1989.

122 'How Maggie Thatcher Was Remade', Patrick Sawer, *Daily Telegraph*, 8 January 2012.

123 *Not for Turning*, Robin Harris (Bantam Press, 2013).

124 *Eminent Elizabethans*, Piers Brendon (Jonathan Cape, 2012).

125 *Not for Turning*, Robin Harris (Bantam Press, 2013).

126 *Eminent Elizabethans*, Piers Brendon (Jonathan Cape, 2012).

127 *Not for Turning*, Robin Harris (Bantam Press, 2013).

128 'The Blooming of Margaret Thatcher', Gail Sheehy, *Vanity Fair*, June 1989.

129 *The Castle Diaries 1964–1976*, Barbara Castle (Macmillan, 1990).

130 Party Political Broadcast, 5 March 1975.

131 *Not for Turning*, Robin Harris (Bantam Press, 2013).

132 *The Path to Power*, Margaret Thatcher (HarperCollins, 1996).

133 *Women in Power: The Personalities and Leadership Styles of Indira Gandhi, Golda Meir, and Margaret Thatcher*, Blema S. Steinberg (McGill-Queen's University Press, 2008).

134 Interview, Tim Bell, 2013.

135 *Eminent Elizabethans*, Piers Brendon (Jonathan Cape, 2012).

136 *Thatcher's Britain*, Richard Vinen (Simon & Schuster, 2009).

137   *The Writing on the Wall: Britain in the Seventies*, Phillip Whitehead (Michael Joseph, 1985).

138   *Elizabeth, the Queen*, Sally Bedell Smith (Penguin Books, 2012).

139   *The Iron Lady*, Hugo Young (Noonday Press, November, 1990).

140   Interview, Tim Bell, 2013.

141   *Eminent Elizabethans*, Piers Brendon (Jonathan Cape, 2012).

142   Interview, Cecil Parkinson, 2013.

143   'Peasants' Uprising or Religious War? Re-Examining the 1975 Conservative Leadership Contest', Philip Cowley and Matthew Bailey, *British Journal of Political Science*, 2000.

144   *Eminent Elizabethans*, Piers Brendon (Jonathan Cape, 2012).

145   *Thatcher's Britain*, Richard Vinen (Simon & Schuster, 2009).

146   Interview, Edwina Currie, 2013.

147   Interview, Cecil Parkinson, 2013.

148   Interview, Lord Carrington, 2013.

149   Interview, Tim Bell, 2013.

150   *Eminent Elizabethans*, Piers Brendon (Jonathan Cape, 2012).

151   Ibid.

152   *Below the Parapet*, Carol Thatcher (HarperCollins, 1997).

153   *Margaret Thatcher*, Penny Junor (Sidgwick & Jackson, 1984).

154   *Not for Turning*, Robin Harris (Bantam Press, 2013).

155   *Elizabeth, the Queen*, Sally Bedell Smith (Penguin Books, 2012).

156   Article by Quentin Letts, *Daily Mail*, 9 April 2013.

157   *The Iron Lady*, John Campbell (Penguin, 2009).

158   Article by Quentin Letts, *Daily Mail*, 9 April 2013.

159   *Daily Mail*, 27 April 2004.

160   Article by Quentin Letts, *Daily Mail*, 9 April 2013.

Chapter 3

1   *Elizabeth, the Queen*, Sally Bedell Smith (Penguin Books, 2012).

2   *The Diamond Queen*, Andrew Marr (Macmillan, 2011).

3   *Elizabeth: Behind Palace Doors*, Nicholas Davies (Mainstream Publishing, 2000).

4   David Starkey's *Monarchy: The Windsors*, Documentary, Channel 4.

5   *The Untold Life of Queen Elizabeth, the Queen Mother*, Lady Colin Campbell (Dynasty Press, 2012).

6   Ibid.

7   *Elizabeth, the Queen*, Sally Bedell Smith (Penguin Books, 2012).

8   *George VI*, Sarah Bradford (Penguin, 1989).

9   David Starkey's *Monarchy: The Windsors*, Documentary, Channel 4.

10   *Elizabeth: Behind Palace Doors*, Nicholas Davies (Mainstream Publishing, 2000).

11   Ibid.

12   Speech, House of Commons, 11 February 1952.

13   *George VI*, Sarah Bradford (Penguin, 1989).

14   Nicholson, Balliol, 6 April 1955.

15   David Starkey's *Monarchy: The Windsors*, Documentary, Channel 4.

16   Ibid.

17   *George VI*, Sarah Bradford (Penguin, 1989).

18   *Our Own Dear Queen*, Piers Brendon (Secker & Warburg, 1986).

19   Ibid.

20   *This I Remember*, Eleanor Roosevelt (Greenwood Press, 1975).

21   *Our Own Dear Queen*, Piers Brendon (Secker & Warburg, 1986).

22   Ibid.

23   *The Little Princesses: The Story of the Queen's Childhood by her Nanny, Marion Crawford*, Marion Crawford (Orion, 2003).

24   *Our Own Dear Queen*, Piers Brendon (Secker & Warburg, 1986).

25   *George VI*, Sarah Bradford (Penguin, 1989).

26   Ibid.

27   *The Untold Life of Queen Elizabeth, the Queen Mother*, Lady Colin Campbell (Dynasty Press, 2012).

28   Ibid.

29   Ibid.

30   *Elizabeth, the Queen*, Sally Bedell Smith (Penguin Books, 2012).

31   *The Untold Life of Queen Elizabeth, the Queen Mother*, Lady Colin Campbell (Dynasty Press, 2012).

32   *George VI*, Sarah Bradford (Penguin, 1989).

33   Ibid.

34   *A Diary with Letters, 1931–1950*, Thomas Jones (Oxford, 1954).

35   *Elizabeth: Behind Palace Doors*, Nicholas Davies (Mainstream Publishing, 2000).

36   *The Untold Life of Queen Elizabeth, the Queen Mother*, Lady Colin Campbell (Dynasty Press, 2012).

37   *Elizabeth: Behind Palace Doors*, Nicholas Davies (Mainstream Publishing, 2000).

38   *The Diamond Queen,* Andrew Marr (Macmillan, 2011).

39   *Elizabeth: Behind Palace Doors,* Nicholas Davies (Mainstream Publishing, 2000).

40   *The Untold Life of Queen Elizabeth, the Queen Mother,* Lady Colin Campbell (Dynasty Press, 2012).

41   *The Queen: Elizabeth II and the Monarchy,* Ben Pimlott (HarperCollins, 1996).

42   Ibid.

43   *Elizabeth: Behind Palace Doors,* Nicholas Davies (Mainstream Publishing, 2000).

44   *George VI,* Sarah Bradford (Penguin, 1989).

45   *Elizabeth: Behind Palace Doors,* Nicholas Davies (Mainstream Publishing, 2000).

46   Ibid.

47   *Elizabeth: The Woman and Queen,* Graham Turner (Macmillan/*Daily Telegraph,* 24 May 2002).

48   Ibid.

49   Ibid.

50   *George VI,* Sarah Bradford (Penguin, 1989).

51   *The Queen: Elizabeth II and the Monarchy,* Ben Pimlott (HarperCollins, 1996).

52   *George VI,* Sarah Bradford (Penguin, 1989).

53   *Elizabeth: The Woman and Queen,* Graham Turner (Macmillan/*Daily Telegraph,* 24 May 2002).

54   Ibid.

55   Ibid.

56   Ibid.

57   Ibid.

58   *The Queen: Elizabeth II and the Monarchy,* Ben Pimlott (HarperCollins, 1996).

59   Ibid.

60   *Elizabeth: Behind Palace Doors,* Nicholas Davies (Mainstream Publishing, 2000).

61   *The Queen: Elizabeth II and the Monarchy,* Ben Pimlott (HarperCollins, 1996).

62   *George VI,* Sarah Bradford (Penguin, 1989).

63   *Elizabeth: Behind Palace Doors,* Nicholas Davies (Mainstream Publishing, 2000).

64   Ibid.

65   *Elizabeth: The Woman and Queen,* Graham Turner (Macmillan/*Daily Telegraph,* 24 May 2002).

66   Ibid.

67   *George VI,* Sarah Bradford (Penguin, 1989).

68   Ibid.
69   *The Rise and Fall of the House of Windsor*, A.N. Wilson (W.W. Norton, 1993).
70   *Elizabeth: The Woman and Queen*, Graham Turner (Macmillan/*Daily Telegraph*, 24 May 2002).
71   Interview, David Owen, 2013.
72   *The Baltimore Sun*, 8 February 1957.
73   *Our Own Dear Queen*, Piers Brendon (Secker & Warburg, 1986).
74   Ibid.
75   *The Queen: Elizabeth II and the Monarchy*, Ben Pimlott (HarperCollins, 1996).
76   *Our Own Dear Queen*, Piers Brendon (Secker & Warburg, 1986).
77   *The Iron Lady*, John Campbell (Penguin, 2009).
78   Article by Gordon Rayer, *Daily Mail*, 2 December 2011.

Chapter 4

1   *The Iron Lady*, John Campbell (Penguin, 2009).
2   *Queen Elizabeth II: Her Life in Our Times*, Sarah Bradford (Viking, 2012).
3   *Daily Mail*, 15 December 2013.
4   Internal Downing Street memo, sent by Caroline Stephens to Clive Whitmore, 24 July 1980. (Obtained by the *Daily Mail* under the Freedom of Information Act.)
5   *Daily Mail*, 15 December 2013.
6   Ibid.
7   *The Queen: Elizabeth II and the Monarchy*, Ben Pimlott (HarperCollins, 1996).
8   *Always Right*, Niall Ferguson (Kindle Single, Odyssey Editions, 2013).
9   'Why I Wanted to Make *The Audience* Public', Peter Morgan, *Guardian*, 13 January 2013.
10   *The Royals*, Kitty Kelly (H.B. Productions Inc., 1997).
11   *Independent*, 13 April 2003.
12   *A View from the Wings*, Ronald Millar (Weidenfeld & Nicolson, 1993).
13   Interview, Lord Carrington, 2013.
14   Interview, Edwina Currie, 2013.
15   *The Shah's Last Ride*, William Shawcross (Chatto & Windus, 1989).
16   Ibid.
17   Ibid.
18   Interview, Lord Carrington, 2013.
19   *The Shah's Last Ride*, William Shawcross (Chatto & Windus, 1989).

20   Interview, Lord Carrington, 2013.

21   *Margaret Thatcher: Power and Personality*, Jonathan Aitken (Bloomsbury, 2013).

22   *Elizabeth, the Queen*, Sally Bedell Smith (Penguin Books, 2012).

23   'Last Secrets of the Queen Mother's Favourite Traitor', Geoffrey Levy, *Daily Mail*, 27 June, 2009.

24   *The Climate of Treason*, Andrew Boyle (Hutchinson, 1979).

25   *Margaret Thatcher: Power and Personality*, Jonathan Aitken (Bloomsbury, 2013).

26   *The Windsors*, Piers Brendon and Phillip Whitehead (Pimlico, 2000).

27   Ibid.

28   Interview, David Owen, 2013

29   *Margaret Thatcher: Power and Personality*, Jonathan Aitken (Bloomsbury, 2013).

30   Ibid.

31   *Anthony Blunt: His Lives*, Miranda Carter (Pan, 2002).

32   *Diaries*, Alan Clark (Weidenfeld & Nicolson, 1993).

33   *Hidden Agenda*, Martin Allen (M. Evans & Co, 2002).

34   Ibid.

35   Ibid.

36   *Anthony Blunt: His Lives*, Miranda Carter (Pan, 2002).

37   Ibid.

38   Ibid.

39   *Elizabeth: The Woman and Queen*, Graham Turner (Macmillan/*Daily Telegraph*, 24 May 2002).

40   Blunt letter, Margaret Thatcher to Ted Leadbitter, 1 July 1980. (Margaret Thatcher Foundation.)

41   Author's correspondence with Sir Bernard Ingham, 2013.

42   *Diaries*, Alan Clark (Weidenfeld & Nicolson, 1993).

43   *Conspiracy of Silence*, Barrie Penrose and Simon Freeman (HarperCollins, 1987).

44   *Anthony Blunt: His Lives*, Miranda Carter (Pan, 2002).

45   *Conspiracy of Silence*, Barrie Penrose and Simon Freeman (HarperCollins, 1987).

46   *The Windsors*, Piers Brendon and Phillip Whitehead (Pimlico, 2000).

47   'Last Secrets of the Queen Mother's Favourite Traitor', Geoffrey Levy, *Daily Mail*, 27 June, 2009.

48   *The Windsors*, Piers Brendon and Phillip Whitehead (Pimlico, 2000).

49   *Spycatcher*, Peter Wright (Viking, 1987).

50   Ibid.

51   *The Iron Lady*, John Campbell (Penguin, 2009).

52   *The Queen: Elizabeth II and the Monarchy*, Ben Pimlott (HarperCollins, 1996).

53 *On Royalty*, Jeremy Paxman (Penguin, 2006).

54 Interview, David Owen, 2013

55 *On Royalty*, Jeremy Paxman (Penguin, 2006).

56 *Ornamentalism: How the British Saw Their Empire*, David Cannadine (Allen Lane, 2001).

57 *Queen Elizabeth II: Her Life in Our Times*, Sarah Bradford (Viking, 2012).

58 *Elizabeth, the Queen*, Sally Bedell Smith (Penguin Books, 2012).

59 *Margaret, Daughter of Beatrice*, Leo Abse MP (Jonathan Cape, 1989).

60 Ibid.

61 *Elizabeth, the Queen*, Sally Bedell Smith (Penguin Books, 2012).

62 Interview, David Owen, 2013

63 *Our Queen*, Robert Hardman (Hutchinson, 2011).

64 *Elizabeth, the Queen*, Sally Bedell Smith (Penguin Books, 2012).

65 *Eminent Elizabethans*, Piers Brendon (Jonathan Cape, 2012).

66 *The Windsors*, Piers Brendon and Phillip Whitehead (Pimlico, 2000).

67 Ibid.

68 *The History of Modern Britain*, Andrew Marr (Macmillan, 2007).

69 'Africans Blast British at Lusaka Commonwealth Meeting', *Executive Intelligence Review*, 7–13 August 1979.

70 *Queen Elizabeth II: Her Life in Our Times*, Sarah Bradford (Viking, 2012).

71 *The Windsors*, Piers Brendon and Phillip Whitehead (Pimlico, 2000).

72 *George VI*, Sarah Bradford (Penguin, 1989).

73 *Financial Times*, 19 July 1986.

74 *The Queen: Elizabeth II and the Monarchy*, Ben Pimlott (HarperCollins, 1996).

75 Ibid.

76 *Queen Elizabeth II: Her Life in Our Times*, Sarah Bradford (Viking, 2012).

77 *Elizabeth, the Queen*, Sally Bedell Smith (Penguin Books, 2012).

78 *A Journey with Margaret Thatcher: Foreign Policy under the Iron Lady*, Robin Renwick (Biteback Publishing, 2013).

79 *The Windsors*, Piers Brendon and Phillip Whitehead (Pimlico, 2000).

80 Ibid.

81 *A Journey with Margaret Thatcher: Foreign Policy under the Iron Lady*, Robin Renwick (Biteback Publishing, 2013).

82 *Elizabeth, the Queen*, Sally Bedell Smith (Penguin Books, 2012).

83 Interview, David Owen, 2013.

Chapter 5

1   *Our Queen*, Robert Hardman (Hutchinson, 2011).
2   *Thatcher's Britain*, Richard Vinen (Simon & Schuster, 2009).
3   *The Royals*, Kitty Kelly (H.B. Productions Inc., 1997).
4   *Elizabeth, the Queen*, Sally Bedell Smith (Penguin Books, 2012).
5   *Economist*, 13–19 April 2013.
6   *Time of My Life*, Denis Healey (Michael Joseph, 1989).
7   *Eminent Elizabethans*, Piers Brendon (Jonathan Cape, 2012).
8   *A Journey with Margaret Thatcher: Foreign Policy under the Iron Lady*, Robin Renwick (Biteback Publishing, 2013).
9   *Ronald Reagan and Margaret Thatcher: A Political Marriage*, Nicholas Wapshott (Penguin, 2007).
10   *Margaret Thatcher: The Authorised Biography*, Charles Moore (Penguin, 2013).
11   *Ronald Reagan and Margaret Thatcher: A Political Marriage*, Nicholas Wapshott (Penguin, 2007).
12   *Eminent Elizabethans*, Piers Brendon (Jonathan Cape, 2012).
13   *Below the Parapet*, Carol Thatcher (HarperCollins, 1996).
14   Falklands – Ridley minute to Carrington, 20 May 1980. (Margaret Thatcher Foundation.)
15   Falklands – Carrington minute to Margaret Thatcher, 20 September 1979. (Margaret Thatcher Foundation.)
16   *Eminent Elizabethans*, Piers Brendon (Jonathan Cape, 2012).
17   'How Britain Averted a Falklands Invasion in 1977', *Guardian*, 1 June 2005.
18   Interview, David Owen, 2013.
19   *Margaret Thatcher: The Authorised Biography*, Charles Moore (Penguin, 2013).
20   *There is No Alternative*, Claire Berlinski (Basic Books, 2008).
21   'The Blooming of Margaret Thatcher', Gail Sheehy, *Vanity Fair*, June 1989.
22   Interview, Lord Carrington, 2013.
23   *There is No Alternative*, Claire Berlinski (Basic Books, 2008).
24   'The Blooming of Margaret Thatcher', Gail Sheehy, *Vanity Fair*, June 1989.
25   *The Downing Street Years*, Margaret Thatcher (HarperCollins, 2011).
26   Reagan's letter to Margaret Thatcher, 5 May 1982. (Margaret Thatcher Foundation.)
27   Interview, Lord Carrington, 2013.
28   Interview, David Owen, 2013.
29   *The Downing Street Years*, Margaret Thatcher (HarperCollins, 2011).
30   Ibid.

31 *Ronald Reagan and Margaret Thatcher: A Political Marriage*, Nicholas Wapshott (Penguin, 2007).

32 *There is No Alternative*, Claire Berlinski (Basic Books, 2008).

33 Interview, Cecil Parkinson, 2013.

34 *The Windsors*, Piers Brendon and Phillip Whitehead (Pimlico, 2000).

35 *Elizabeth, the Queen*, Sally Bedell Smith (Penguin Books, 2012).

36 *The Windsors*, Piers Brendon and Phillip Whitehead (Pimlico, 2000).

37 Ibid.

38 Interview, David Owen, 2013.

39 Interview, Ron Allison, 2013.

40 *One of Us*, Hugo Young (Pan, 2013).

41 *Royal Secrets: The View from Downstairs*, Stephen P. Barry (Villard Books, 1988).

42 *Royal Fortune*, Phillip Hall (Bloomsbury, 1992).

43 *Ronald Reagan and Margaret Thatcher: A Political Marriage*, Nicholas Wapshott (Penguin, 2007).

44 Ibid.

45 *Nancy Reagan*, Kitty Kelly (Bantam, 1992).

46 *The Queen: Elizabeth II and the Monarchy*, Ben Pimlott (HarperCollins, 1996).

47 *Ronald Reagan and Margaret Thatcher: A Political Marriage*, Nicholas Wapshott (Penguin, 2007).

48 Programme for the Windsor Castle banquet, 8 June 1982. (Margaret Thatcher Foundation.)

49 Ibid.

50 *Ronald Reagan and Margaret Thatcher: A Political Marriage*, Nicholas Wapshott (Penguin, 2007).

51 *Queen Elizabeth II*, Sarah Bradford (Viking, 2012).

52 *Thatcher & Sons*, Simon Jenkins (Penguin, 2007).

53 'The Blooming of Margaret Thatcher', Gail Sheehy, *Vanity Fair*, June 1989.

54 Interview, Cecil Parkinson, 2013.

55 Interview, David Owen, 2013.

56 'The Blooming of Margaret Thatcher', Gail Sheehy, *Vanity Fair*, June 1989.

57 *Eminent Elizabethans*, Piers Brendon (Jonathan Cape, 2012).

58 *Elizabeth, the Queen*, Sally Bedell Smith (Penguin Books, 2012).

59 Interview, David Owen, 2013.

60 Ibid.

61 *Eminent Elizabethans*, Piers Brendon (Jonathan Cape, 2012).

62 Interview, Edwina Currie, 2013.

63 *Elizabeth, the Queen*, Sally Bedell Smith (Penguin Books, 2012).

64 *The Windsors*, Piers Brendon and Phillip Whitehead (Pimlico, 2000).
65 'The Blooming of Margaret Thatcher', Gail Sheehy, *Vanity Fair*, June 1989.
66 *Eminent Elizabethans*, Piers Brendon (Jonathan Cape, 2012).
67 *Diary of an Election*, Carol Thatcher (Sidgwick & Jackson, 1983).
68 *Thatcher & Sons*, Simon Jenkins (Penguin, 2007).
69 *Thatcher's Britain*, Richard Vinen (Simon & Schuster, 2009).
70 *The Iron Lady*, John Campbell (Penguin, 2009).
71 *Eminent Elizabethans*, Piers Brendon (Jonathan Cape, 2012).
72 *The Iron Lady*, John Campbell (Penguin, 2009).
73 *Women in Power: The Personalities and Leadership Styles of Indira Gandhi, Golda Meir, and Margaret Thatcher*, Blema S. Steinberg (McGill-Queen's University Press, 2008).
74 Interview, Lord Carrington, 2013.
75 *Margaret Thatcher: Power and Personality*, Jonathan Aitken (Bloomsbury, 2013).
76 Ibid.
77 *Eminent Elizabethans*, Piers Brendon (Jonathan Cape, 2012).
78 *Observer*, 5 June 1983.
79 *The Queen: Elizabeth II and the Monarchy*, Ben Pimlott (HarperCollins, 1996).
80 *Ronald Reagan and Margaret Thatcher: A Political Marriage*, Nicholas Wapshott (Penguin, 2007).
81 *Elizabeth, the Queen*, Sally Bedell Smith (Penguin Books, 2012).
82 *Grenada: Revolution and Invasion*, A. Payne, P. Sutton and T. Thorndike (Crown Helm, 1984).
83 *Ronald Reagan and Margaret Thatcher: A Political Marriage*, Nicholas Wapshott (Penguin, 2007).
84 Ibid.
85 *The Queen: Elizabeth II and the Monarchy*, Ben Pimlott (HarperCollins, 1996).
86 *Ronald Reagan and Margaret Thatcher: A Political Marriage*, Nicholas Wapshott (Penguin, 2007).
87 *An American Life*, Ronald Reagan (Simon & Schuster, 1990).
88 Ibid.
89 *The Downing Street Years*, Margaret Thatcher (HarperCollins, 2011).
90 *Ronald Reagan and Margaret Thatcher: A Political Marriage*, Nicholas Wapshott (Penguin, 2007).
91 Interview Edwina Currie, 2013.
92 *Ronald Reagan and Margaret Thatcher: A Political Marriage*, Nicholas Wapshott (Penguin, 2007).
93 *The Royals*, Kitty Kelly (H.B. Productions Inc., 1997).

94   Interview, David Owen, 2013.

95   Interview, Lord Carrington, 2013.

96   Interview, Cecil Parkinson, 2013.

97   *Observer*, 30 October 1983.

98   Interview, Cecil Parkinson, 2013.

99   *A Journey with Margaret Thatcher: Foreign Policy under the Iron Lady*, Robin Renwick (Biteback Publishing, 2013).

100   *Ronald Reagan and Margaret Thatcher: A Political Marriage*, Nicholas Wapshott (Penguin, 2007).

Chapter 6

1   *The Iron Lady*, John Campbell (Penguin, 2009).

2   *Stick it Up Your Punter*, Peter Chippindale and Chris Horrie (William Heinemann, 1990).

3   Interview, Cecil Parkinson, 2013.

4   Author's correspondence with Sir Bernard Ingham, 2013.

5   Interview, Tim Bell, 2013.

6   Interview, Edwina Currie, 2013.

7   *Elizabeth, the Queen*, Sally Bedell Smith (Penguin Books, 2012).

8   *The Man Who Owns the News*, Michael Wolff (Bodley Head, 2008).

9   Ibid.

10   *Dial M for Murdoch*, by Tom Watson and Martin Hickman (Allen Lane, 2012).

11   *The Rise and Fall of the Murdoch Empire*, John Lisners (John Blake, 2012).

12   *Eminent Elizabethans*, Piers Brendon (Jonathan Cape, 2012).

13   'The *News of the World* History: All Human Life Was There', Roy Stockdill, *Guardian*, 10 July 2011.

14   *Eminent Elizabethans*, Piers Brendon (Jonathan Cape, 2012).

15   Ibid.

16   *Stick it Up Your Punter*, Peter Chippindale and Chris Horrie (William Heinemann, 1990).

17   *Eminent Elizabethans*, Piers Brendon (Jonathan Cape, 2012).

18   *Stick it Up Your Punter*, Peter Chippindale and Chris Horrie (William Heinemann, 1990).

19   Ibid.

20   Interview, Tim Bell, 2013.

21   *The Diamond Queen*, Andrew Marr (Macmillan, 2011).

22   *Eminent Elizabethans*, Piers Brendon (Jonathan Cape, 2012).

23   *Stick it Up Your Punter*, Peter Chippindale and Chris Horrie (William Heinemann, 1990).

24   *Queen Elizabeth II: Her Life in Our Times*, Sarah Bradford (Viking, 2012).

25   *Stick it Up Your Punter*, Peter Chippindale and Chris Horrie (William Heinemann, 1990).

26   *Our Own Dear Queen*, Piers Brendon (Secker & Warburg, 1986).

27   *Eminent Elizabethans*, Piers Brendon (Jonathan Cape, 2012).

28   *Elizabeth: The Woman and Queen*, Graham Turner (Macmillan/ *Daily Telegraph*, 24 May 2002).

29   *The Queen: Elizabeth II and the Monarchy*, Ben Pimlott (HarperCollins, 1996).

30   Ibid.

31   *Elizabeth: Behind Palace Doors*, Nicholas Davies (Mainstream Publishing, 2000).

32   *The Queen: Elizabeth II and the Monarchy*, Ben Pimlott (HarperCollins, 1996).

33   'Queen Obtains Ban on Gossip Articles', R.W. Apple Jr, *New York Times*, 24 February 1983.

34   *The Royals*, Kitty Kelly (H.B. Productions Inc., 1997).

35   *Stick it Up Your Punter*, Peter Chippindale and Chris Horrie (William Heinemann, 1990).

36   *The Path to Power*, Margaret Thatcher (HarperCollins, 2012).

37   *Stick it Up Your Punter*, Peter Chippindale and Chris Horrie (William Heinemann, 1990).

38   *Popular Newspapers, the Labour Party and British Politics*, James Thomas (Routledge, 2005).

39   *Margaret Thatcher: Power and Personality*, Jonathan Aitken (Bloomsbury, 2013).

40   *Stick it Up Your Punter*, Peter Chippindale and Chris Horrie (William Heinemann, 1990).

41   *Rejoice! Rejoice! Britain in the 1980s*, Alwyn W. Turner (Aurum Press, 2010).

42   *Stick it Up Your Punter*, Peter Chippindale and Chris Horrie (William Heinemann, 1990).

43   Ibid.

44   *The Man Who Owns the News*, Michael Wolff (Bodley Head, 2008).

45   *Murdoch's Politics*, David McKnight (Pluto Press, 2013).

46   *Eminent Elizabethans*, Piers Brendon (Jonathan Cape, 2012).

47   *The Man Who Owns the News*, Michael Wolff (Bodley Head, 2008).

48   Ibid.

49   Ibid.

50   *The Iron Lady*, John Campbell (Penguin, 2009).

51   *The Man Who Owns the News*, Michael Wolff (Bodley Head, 2008).

52   *Stick it Up Your Punter*, Peter Chippindale and Chris Horrie (William Heinemann, 1990).

53   Obituary, Lord Thomas of Fleet, 12 June 2006.

54   *Margaret Thatcher: Power and Personality*, Jonathan Aitken (Bloomsbury, 2013).

55   Interview, Tim Bell, 2013.

56   Author's correspondence with Sir Bernard Ingham, 2013.

57   *The Journals of Woodrow Wyatt*, Sarah Curtis (Ed.) (Macmillan, 1999).

58   Ibid.

59   *The Iron Lady*, John Campbell (Penguin, 2009).

60   *Hugh Trevor-Roper: The Biography*, Adam Sisman (Weidenfeld & Nicolson, 2010).

61   *The Man Who Owns the News*, Michael Wolff (Bodley Head, 2008).

62   *Eminent Elizabethans*, Piers Brendon (Jonathan Cape, 2012).

63   Ibid.

64   Ibid.

65   *Stick it Up Your Punter*, Peter Chippindale and Chris Horrie (William Heinemann, 1990).

66   Ibid.

67   *The Royals*, Kitty Kelly (H.B. Productions Inc., 1997).

68   Ibid.

69   *Stick it Up Your Punter*, Peter Chippindale and Chris Horrie (William Heinemann, 1990).

70   *The Royals*, Kitty Kelly (H.B. Productions Inc., 1997).

71   Ibid.

72   Ibid.

73   *Stick it Up Your Punter*, Peter Chippindale and Chris Horrie (William Heinemann, 1990).

74   Ibid.

75   *The Queen: Elizabeth II and the Monarchy*, Ben Pimlott (HarperCollins, 1996).

76   *The Diamond Queen*, Andrew Marr (Macmillan, 2011).

77   *Stick it Up Your Punter*, Peter Chippindale and Chris Horrie (William Heinemann, 1990).

78   *The Windsors*, Piers Brendon and Phillip Whitehead (Pimlico, 2000).

79   *The Wapping Dispute*, S.M. Littleton (Avebury, 1992).

80   Ibid.

81   *Eminent Elizabethans*, Piers Brendon (Jonathan Cape, 2012).

82   *Murdoch's Politics*, David McKnight (Pluto Press, 2013).

83   *Eminent Elizabethans*, Piers Brendon (Jonathan Cape, 2012).

84   *The End of the Street*, L. Melvern (Methuen, 1986).

85   *The Iron Lady*, John Campbell (Penguin, 2009).

86   *Full Disclosure*, Andrew Neil (Macmillan, 1996).

87   *The Iron Lady*, John Campbell (Penguin, 2009).

88   *The Wapping Dispute*, S.M. Littleton (Avebury, 1992).

89   *The Journals of Woodrow Wyatt*, Sarah Curtis (Ed.) (Macmillan, 1999).

90   Ibid.

91   *Citizen Murdoch*, Thomas Kiernan (Dodd, Mead & Co., 1986).

92   *Murdoch's Politics*, David McKnight (Pluto Press, 2013).

93   *The Journals of Woodrow Wyatt*, Sarah Curtis (Ed.) (Macmillan, 1999).

94   Ibid.

95   Ibid.

96   'Rupert Murdoch and the *Sunday Times*: A Lamp Goes Out', Hugo Young, *Political Quarterly*, October–December 1984.

97   *Dial M for Murdoch*, by Tom Watson and Martin Hickman (Allen Lane, 2012).

98   *Murdoch's Politics*, David McKnight (Pluto Press, 2013).

99   'Maxwell Tried to get Thatcher to Bail Him Out', Maurice Chittenden, *Sunday Times*, 29 January 2006.

Chapter 7

1   *Diaries*, Alan Clark (Weidenfeld & Nicolson, 1993).

2   *Elizabeth, the Queen*, Sally Bedell Smith (Penguin Books, 2012).

3   *The Rise and Fall of the House of Windsor*, A.N. Wilson (W.W. Norton & Co., 1993).

4   *Elizabeth, the Queen*, Sally Bedell Smith (Penguin Books, 2012).

5   'Portrait of a Marriage', *Daily Telegraph*, 5 September 2004.

6   *Elizabeth, the Queen*, Sally Bedell Smith (Penguin Books, 2012).

7   *The Queen: Elizabeth II and the Monarchy*, Ben Pimlott (HarperCollins, 1996).

8   Ibid.

9   *The Windsors*, Piers Brendon and Phillip Whitehead (Pimlico, 2000).

10   'The Blooming of Margaret Thatcher', Gail Sheehy, *Vanity Fair*, June 1989.

11   Ibid.

12   *Elizabeth, the Queen*, Sally Bedell Smith (Penguin Books, 2012).

13   Ibid.

14 *Thatcher & Sons*, Simon Jenkins (Penguin, 2007).

15 Interview, David Owen, 2013.

16 Ibid.

17 *The Audience*, Peter Morgan (Faber & Faber, 2013).

18 *One of Us*, Hugo Young (Macmillan, 1989).

19 *Charles: A Biography*, Anthony Holden (Corgi, 1999).

20 *Manchester Evening News*, 23 October 1985.

21 *Glasgow Herald*, 11 April 1988.

22 *Charles: A Biography*, Anthony Holden (Corgi, 1999).

23 Ibid.

24 *The Royals*, Kitty Kelly (H.B. Productions Inc., 1997).

25 *Having It So Good*, Peter Hennessy (Allen Lane, 2006).

26 *There is No Alternative*, Claire Berlinski (Basic Books, 2008).

27 Ibid.

28 National Archives – papers released in 2014.

29 *There is No Alternative*, Claire Berlinski (Basic Books, 2008).

30 'The Blooming of Margaret Thatcher', Gail Sheehy, *Vanity Fair*, June 1989.

31 *Strange Rebels*, Christian Caryl (Basic Books, 2013).

32 *There is No Alternative*, Claire Berlinski (Basic Books, 2008).

33 *Iron Lady*, Stephen Blake and Andrew John (Michael O'Mara Books, 2003).

34 *There is No Alternative*, Claire Berlinski (Basic Books, 2008).

35 'The Blooming of Margaret Thatcher', Gail Sheehy, *Vanity Fair*, June 1989.

36 *Upwardly Mobile*, Norman Tebbit (Weidenfeld and Nicolson, 1988).

37 *Iron Lady*, Stephen Blake and Andrew John (Michael O'Mara Books, 2003).

38 *Courier*, 12 August 1984.

39 *Montreal Gazette*, 13 August 1984.

40 *Elizabeth: Behind Palace Doors*, Nicholas Davies (Mainstream Publishing, 2000).

41 'True Spies', *BBC News*, 2002.

42 *The Queen: Elizabeth II and the Monarchy*, Ben Pimlott (HarperCollins, 1996).

43 *Full Disclosure*, Andrew Neil (Macmillan, 1996).

44 Interview, Edwina Currie, 2013

45 *The Windsors*, Piers Brendon and Phillip Whitehead (Pimlico, 2000).

46 Ibid.

47 Author's correspondence with Sir Bernard Ingham, 2013.

48 *Full Disclosure*, Andrew Neil (Macmillan, 1996).

49 Ibid.

50 Ibid.

51 'The African Queen', Michael Jones and Simon Freeman, *Sunday Times*, 20 July 1986.
52 Ibid.
53 *One of Us*, Hugo Young (Macmillan, 1989).
54 Ibid.
55 *Elizabeth, the Queen*, Sally Bedell Smith (Penguin Books, 2012).
56 'The African Queen', Michael Jones and Simon Freeman, *Sunday Times*, 20 July 1986.
57 *The Queen: Elizabeth II and the Monarchy*, Ben Pimlott (HarperCollins, 1996).
58 'The African Queen', Michael Jones and Simon Freeman, *Sunday Times*, 20 July 1986.
59 *The Queen: Elizabeth II and the Monarchy*, Ben Pimlott (HarperCollins, 1996).
60 Ibid.
61 *Full Disclosure*, Andrew Neil (Macmillan, 1996).
62 Author's correspondence with Bernard Ingham, 2013.
63 Ibid.
64 *Full Disclosure*, Andrew Neil (Macmillan, 1996).
65 Ibid.
66 Ibid.
67 *The Journals of Woodrow Wyatt*, Sarah Curtis (Ed.) (Macmillan, 1999).
68 *Full Disclosure*, Andrew Neil (Macmillan, 1996).
69 *The Windsors*, Piers Brendon and Phillip Whitehead (Pimlico, 2000).
70 Ibid.
71 *Full Disclosure*, Andrew Neil (Macmillan, 1996).
72 Ibid.
73 Ibid.
74 *The Queen: Elizabeth II and the Monarchy*, Ben Pimlott (HarperCollins, 1996).
75 *Observer*, 27 July 1987.
76 *Full Disclosure*, Andrew Neil (Macmillan, 1996).
77 Interview, Ronald Allison, 2013.
78 *Full Disclosure*, Andrew Neil (Macmillan, 1996).
79 Interview, Ronald Allison, 2013.
80 *The Queen: Elizabeth II and the Monarchy*, Ben Pimlott (HarperCollins, 1996).
81 Interview, Lord Carrington, 2013.
82 Interview, David Owen, 2013.
83 Ibid.
84 *Guardian*, 21 July 1986.
85 *Elizabeth: Behind Palace Doors*, Nicholas Davies (Mainstream Publishing, 2000).

86   *The Queen: Elizabeth II and the Monarchy*, Ben Pimlott (HarperCollins, 1996).

87   *The Journals of Woodrow Wyatt*, Sarah Curtis (Ed.) (Macmillan, 1999).

88   *Sunday Telegraph*, 27 July 1986.

89   *The Downing Street Years*, Margaret Thatcher (HarperCollins, 1993).

90   *Full Disclosure*, Andrew Neil (Macmillan, 1996).

91   *The Journals of Woodrow Wyatt*, Sarah Curtis (Ed.) (Macmillan, 1999).

92   *Full Disclosure*, Andrew Neil (Macmillan, 1996).

93   *The Queen: Elizabeth II and the Monarchy*, Ben Pimlott (HarperCollins, 1996).

94   *Conflict of Loyalty*, Geoffrey Howe (Pan, 1995).

95   Author's correspondence with Sir Bernard Ingham, 2013.

96   *The Journals of Woodrow Wyatt*, Sarah Curtis (Ed.) (Macmillan, 1999).

97   Author's correspondence with David Steel, 2013.

98   Interview, Michael Dobbs, 2013.

99   *The Journals of Woodrow Wyatt*, Sarah Curtis (Ed.) (Macmillan, 1999).

100   Interview, Tim Bell, 2013.

101   Interview, David Owen, 2013.

102   *Full Disclosure*, Andrew Neil (Macmillan, 1996).

103   *Elizabeth: The Woman and Queen*, Graham Turner (Macmillan/*Daily Telegraph*, 24 May 2002).

Chapter 8

1   *The Rise and Fall of the House of Windsor*, A.N. Wilson (W.W. Norton & Co., 1993).

2   *The Windsors*, Piers Brendon and Phillip Whitehead (Pimlico, 2000).

3   Ibid.

4   Ibid.

5   Interview, David Owen, 2013.

6   Interview, Ron Allison, 2013.

7   *Guardian*, 26 November 1982.

8   *The Windsors*, Piers Brendon and Phillip Whitehead (Pimlico, 2000).

9   *The Rise and Fall of the House of Windsor*, A.N. Wilson (W.W. Norton & Co., 1993).

10   *The Iron Lady*, John Campbell (Penguin, 2009).

11   *Just in Time: Inside the Thatcher Revolution*, J. Hoskyns (Aurum, 2000).

12   *One of Us*, Hugo Young (Pan, 2013).

13   Lord Hailsham, *Richard Dimbleby Lecture*, BBC, 1976.

14   Lord Hailsham, *Richard Dimbleby Lecture*, BBC, 1976.

15   'The Blooming of Margaret Thatcher', Gail Sheehy, *Vanity Fair*, June 1989.

16   *The Iron Lady*, John Campbell (Penguin, 2009).

17   *The Windsors*, Piers Brendon and Phillip Whitehead (Pimlico, 2000).

18   *One of Us*, Hugo Young (Pan, 2013).

19   *The Windsors*, Piers Brendon and Phillip Whitehead (Pimlico, 2000).

20   *Elizabeth: Behind Palace Doors*, Nicholas Davies (Mainstream Publishing, 2000).

21   *Sun*, 4 January 1989.

22   *Hour*, 5 January 1989.

23   *Elizabeth: The Woman and Queen*, Graham Turner (Macmillan/ *Daily Telegraph*, 24 May 2002).

24   'Charles's Visit Calms Anger in Lockerbie', Press Association, 25 January 1989.

25   Ibid.

26   'The Blooming of Margaret Thatcher', Gail Sheehy, *Vanity Fair*, June 1989.

27   Ibid.

28   *Rejoice! Rejoice! Britain in the 1980s*, Alwyn W. Turner (Aurum Press, 2010).

29   'The Blooming of Margaret Thatcher', Gail Sheehy, *Vanity Fair*, June 1989.

30   National Archives, 2014.

31   Interview, Dr Daniel Conway, 2013.

32   *Eminent Elizabethans*, Piers Brendon (Jonathan Cape, 2012).

33   *One of Us*, Hugo Young (Pan, 2013).

34   Interview, Ron Allison, 2013.

35   Interview, Edwina Currie, 2013.

36   *The Windsors*, Piers Brendon and Phillip Whitehead (Pimlico, 2000).

37   Ibid.

38   'Battle Royal Erupts Over Queen Rumour', Dan Fisher. *LA Times*, 23 November 1988.

39   Interview, Dr Daniel Conway, 2013.

40   *The Queen: Elizabeth II and the Monarchy*, Ben Pimlott (HarperCollins, 1996).

41   *The Enchanted Glass: Britain and its Monarchy*, Tom Nairn (Verso, 2011).

42   *Times*, 30 January 1992.

43   'The Blooming of Margaret Thatcher', Gail Sheehy, *Vanity Fair*, June 1989.

44   *The Windsors*, Piers Brendon and Phillip Whitehead (Pimlico, 2000).

45   Author's correspondence with Sir Bernard Ingham, 2013.

46   *The Royals*, Kitty Kelly (H.B. Productions Inc., 1997).

47   Interview, David Owen, 2013.

48   Interview, Michael Dobbs, 2013.

49 *Eminent Elizabethans*, Piers Brendon (Jonathan Cape, 2012).

50 *Guardian*, 21 January 1990.

51 *The Iron Lady*, John Campbell (Penguin, 2009).

52 Ibid.

53 *The Queen: Elizabeth II and the Monarchy*, Ben Pimlott (HarperCollins, 1996).

54 Margaret Thatcher letter to Lady Moore, 13 September 1982. (Margaret Thatcher Foundation.)

55 *A Journey*, Tony Blair (Arrow, 2011).

56 Interview, Ron Alison, 2013.

57 *Elizabeth, the Queen*, Sally Bedell Smith (Penguin Books, 2012).

58 *Royal Secrets: The View from Downstairs*, Stephen P. Barry (Villard Books, 1985).

59 *The Prince of Wales*, Jonathan Dimbleby (Little Brown, 1994).

60 *Royal Secrets: The View from Downstairs*, Stephen P. Barry (Villard Books, 1985).

61 Interview, David Owen, 2013.

62 *Elizabeth: The Woman and Queen*, Graham Turner (Macmillan/*Daily Telegraph*, 24 May 2002).

63 *The Diamond Queen*, Andrew Marr (Macmillan, 2011).

64 Ibid.

65 *Our Queen*, Robert Hardman (Hutchinson, 2011).

66 *The Diamond Queen*, Andrew Marr (Macmillan, 2011).

67 Interview, Edwina Currie, 2013.

68 *The Prince of Wales*, Jonathan Dimbleby (Little Brown, 1994).

69 *Elizabeth, the Queen*, Sally Bedell Smith (Penguin Books, 2012).

70 *Eminent Elizabethans*, Piers Brendon (Jonathan Cape, 2012).

71 *Elizabeth: The Woman and Queen*, Graham Turner (Macmillan/*Daily Telegraph*, 24 May 2002).

72 *One of Us*, Hugo Young (Pan, 2013).

73 *Elizabeth: The Woman and Queen*, Graham Turner (Macmillan/*Daily Telegraph*, 24 May 2002).

74 *The Journals of Woodrow Wyatt*, Sarah Curtis (Ed.) (Macmillan, 1999).

75 Ibid.

76 'The Queen Mother on Margaret Thatcher', Andrew Pierce, *Daily Telegraph*, 17 September 2009.

77 Ibid.

78 Interview, Jeffery Archer, 2013.

79 *The Queen: Elizabeth II and the Monarchy*, Ben Pimlott (HarperCollins, 1996).

80 Ibid.

81 *Sunday Times*, 18 March 2012.

Chapter 9

1   *The Queen: Elizabeth II and the Monarchy*, Ben Pimlott (HarperCollins, 1996).

2   *Eminent Elizabethans*, Piers Brendon (Jonathan Cape, 2012).

3   *Charles: A Biography*, Anthony Holden (Corgi, 1999).

4   *The Royals*, Kitty Kelly (H.B. Productions Inc., 1997).

5   *Sydney Morning Herald*, 5 May 1958.

6   *The Royals*, Kitty Kelly (H.B. Productions Inc., 1997).

7   Ibid.

8   *The Royals*, Kitty Kelly (H.B. Productions Inc., 1997).

9   *Elizabeth: The Woman and Queen*, Graham Turner (Macmillan/ *Daily Telegraph*, 24 May 2002).

10   *Charles: A Biography*, Anthony Holden (Corgi, 1999).

11   *Daily Telegraph*, 22 February 1954.

12   *Elizabeth, the Queen*, Sally Bedell Smith (Penguin Books, 2012).

13   Ibid.

14   *The Prince of Wales*, Jonathan Dimbleby (Little Brown, 1994).

15   *The Royals*, Kitty Kelly (H.B. Productions Inc., 1997).

16   *Charles: A Biography*, Anthony Holden (Corgi, 1999).

17   *The Prince of Wales*, Jonathan Dimbleby (Little Brown, 1994).

18   *The Royals*, Kitty Kelly (H.B. Productions Inc., 1997).

19   *The Prince of Wales*, Jonathan Dimbleby (Little Brown, 1994).

20   *Charles: A Biography*, Anthony Holden (Corgi, 1999).

21   *Eminent Elizabethans*, Piers Brendon (Jonathan Cape, 2012).

22   *The Diamond Queen*, Andrew Marr (Macmillan, 2011).

23   *Eminent Elizabethans*, Piers Brendon (Jonathan Cape, 2012).

24   *The Rise and Fall of the House of Windsor*, A.N. Wilson (W.W. Norton & Co., 1993).

25   *Queen Elizabeth II: Her Life in Our Times*, Sarah Bradford (Viking, 2012).

26   *Royal Secrets: The View from Downstairs*, Stephen P. Barry (Villard Books, 1985).

27   *The Diamond Queen*, Andrew Marr (Macmillan, 2011).

28   *The Rise and Fall of the House of Windsor*, A.N. Wilson (W.W. Norton & Co., 1993).

29   *Elizabeth: The Woman and Queen*, Graham Turner (Macmillan/ *Daily Telegraph*, 24 May 2002).

30   Quoted in the *Scotsman*, May 7 2003.

31   *Elizabeth: The Woman and Queen*, Graham Turner (Macmillan/ *Daily Telegraph*, 24 May 2002).

32   Ibid.
33   *Callaghan: A Life*, by Kenneth O. Morgan (Oxford University Press, 1997).
34   *The Monarchy: The Oral Biography of Elizabeth II*, Deborah Strober (Broadway, 2002).
35   *Queen Elizabeth II: Her Life in Our Times*, Sarah Bradford (Viking, 2012).
36   *Anne*, Brian Hoey (Sidgwick & Jackson, 1997).
37   *Elizabeth: The Woman and Queen*, Graham Turner (Macmillan/*Daily Telegraph*, 24 May 2002).
38   Ibid.
39   *Queen Elizabeth II: Her Life in Our Times*, Sarah Bradford (Viking, 2012).
40   *A Journey*, Tony Blair (Arrow, 2011).
41   'Oh Carol, Why Are We So in Love with You?', Gillian Bowditch, *The Scotsman*, 27 December 2005.
42   *Not for Turning*, Robin Harris (Bantam Press, 2013).
43   *Thatcher's Gold*, Paul Halloran and Mark Hollingsworth (Simon & Schuster, 1995).
44   *Margaret Thatcher*, George Gardiner (HarperCollins, 1975).
45   Interview, Edwina Currie, 2013.
46   Interview, Lord Carrington, 2013.
47   'The Mummy's Boy and a Daughter who Always felt Second Best', by Geoffrey Levy, *Daily Mail*, 9 April 2013.
48   *Not for Turning*, Robin Harris (Bantam Press, 2013).
49   *The Iron Lady*, John Campbell (Penguin, 2009).
50   *In the Limelight*, BBC TV, 11 August 1980.
51   *Thatcher*, Nicholas Wapshott and George Brock (Macdonald, 1983).
52   *The Iron Lady*, John Campbell (Penguin, 2009).
53   *The Path to Power*, Margaret Thatcher (HarperCollins 1993).
54   *Margaret Thatcher: Power and Personality*, Jonathan Aitken (Bloomsbury, 2013).
55   *Below the Parapet*, Carol Thatcher (HarperCollins, 1996).
56   *Margaret Thatcher*, Penny Junor (Sidgwick & Jackson, 1984).
57   *Today*, 26 November 1993.
58   *Margaret Thatcher: Power and Personality*, Jonathan Aitken (Bloomsbury, 2013).
59   Ibid.
60   Ibid.
61   Ibid.
62   *Independent*, 10 October 1994.
63   *Margaret Thatcher: Power and Personality*, Jonathan Aitken (Bloomsbury, 2013).
64   *Independent*, 10 October 1994.

65   Mark Thatcher's letters to his mother. (Margaret Thatcher Foundation.)

66   *Independent*, 10 October 1994.

67   Ibid.

68   *Thatcher's Gold*, Paul Halloran and Mark Hollingsworth (Simon & Schuster, 1995).

69   *Independent*, 10 October 1994.

70   *Thatcher's Gold*, Paul Halloran and Mark Hollingsworth (Simon & Schuster, 1995).

71   *Independent*, 10 October 1994.

72   *Daily Telegraph*, 24 November 1994.

73   *Thatcher's Gold*, Paul Halloran and Mark Hollingsworth (Simon & Schuster, 1995).

74   *Independent*, 10 October 1994.

75   *Thatcher's Gold*, Paul Halloran and Mark Hollingsworth (Simon & Schuster, 1995).

76   *Thatcher's Gold*, Paul Halloran and Mark Hollingsworth (Simon & Schuster, 1995).

77   *One of Us*, Hugo Young (Pan, 2013).

78   *Daily Telegraph*, 16 January 1982.

79   Confidential interview, 2013.

80   *Thatcher's Gold*, Paul Halloran and Mark Hollingsworth (Simon & Schuster, 1995).

81   *Observer*, 15 January 1984.

82   The text of the draft statement in the Cabinet Office. It is undated, but is likely to have been drafted in February, 1984.

83   Hansard, Column 218, 29 February 1984.

84   Letter to Peter Shore MP, 12 April 1984. (Margaret Thatcher Foundation.)

85   *Thatcher's Gold*, Paul Halloran and Mark Hollingsworth (Simon & Schuster, 1995).

86   *The Iron Lady*, John Campbell (Penguin, 2009).

87   *Thatcher's Gold*, Paul Halloran and Mark Hollingsworth (Simon & Schuster, 1995).

88   *Independent*, 10 October 1994.

89   *Thatcher's Gold*, Paul Halloran and Mark Hollingsworth (Simon & Schuster, 1995).

90   Ibid.

91   Ibid.

92   *Mail on Sunday*, 16 April 1995.

93   *Independent*, 10 October 1994.

94   *Thatcher's Gold*, Paul Halloran and Mark Hollingsworth (Simon & Schuster, 1995).

95   *Times*, 7 February 1995.

96   *Sunday Times*, 8 December 1996.

97   *Independent*, 12 August 1996.

98   Author's correspondence with Sir Bernard Ingham, 2013.

99   Confidential interview, 2013

100   'The Trouble with Andrew', Edward Klein, *Vanity Fair*, August 2011.

101   *Elizabeth, the Queen*, Sally Bedell Smith (Penguin Books, 2012).

102   'The Trouble with Andrew', Edward Klein, *Vanity Fair*, August 2011.

103   Ibid.

104   *The Royals*, Kitty Kelly (H.B. Productions Inc., 1997).

105   'The Trouble with Andrew', Edward Klein, *Vanity Fair*, August 2011.

106   *Daily Mail*, 7 March 2011.

107   'The Trouble with Andrew', Edward Klein, *Vanity Fair*, August 2011.

108   Ibid.

109   *Daily Telegraph*, 26 May 2012.

110   *Daily Mail*, 7 March 2011.

111   Ibid.

112   'The Trouble with Andrew', Edward Klein, *Vanity Fair*, August 2011.

113   *Daily Mail*, 7 March 2011.

114   'The Trouble with Andrew', Edward Klein, *Vanity Fair*, August 2011.

115   *Daily Mail*, 5 March 2011.

116   'The Trouble with Andrew', Edward Klein, *Vanity Fair*, August 2011.

117   *Observer*, 13 March 2011.

118   Ibid.

119   'The Trouble with Andrew', Edward Klein, *Vanity Fair*, August 2011.

120   *Royal Secrets: The View from Downstairs*, Stephen P. Barry (Villard Books, 1985).

Chapter 10

1   'Margaret Thatcher and the Queen: The Two Most Powerful Women in the World', *Independent*, 16 April 2013.

2   Interview, Edwina Currie, 2013.

3   Interview, Tim Bell, 2013.

4   'The Poll Tax Battle of Trafalgar Square', *Daily Telegraph*, 1 April 1990.

5   *The Downing Street Years*, Margaret Thatcher (HarperCollins, 2012).

6   *Hamlet*, William Shakespeare.

7   Interview, Nigel Lawson, *The Downing Street Years*, BBC Documentary.

8   Interview, Lord Carrington, 2013.

9   *Margaret Thatcher: Power and Personality*, Jonathan Aitken (Bloomsbury, 2013).

10   Ibid.

11   Interview, Edwina Currie, 2013.

12   *Margaret Thatcher: Power and Personality*, Jonathan Aitken (Bloomsbury, 2013).

13   Ibid.

14   *The Queen: Elizabeth II and the Monarchy*, Ben Pimlott (HarperCollins, 1996).

15   Interview, Nigel Lawson, *The Downing Street Years*, BBC Documentary.

16   *Margaret Thatcher: Power and Personality*, Jonathan Aitken (Bloomsbury, 2013).

17   Interview, Geoffrey Howe, *The Downing Street Years*, BBC Documentary.

18   Ibid.

19   *Conflict of Loyalty*, Geoffrey Howe (Pan, 1995).

20   Hansard, HL, Official Report, 10 April 2013. 'Death of a Member: Baroness Thatcher, Tributes'.

21   Interview, Margaret Thatcher, *The Downing Street Years*, BBC Documentary.

22   Howe attack paves the way for Heseltine. 14 November 1990.

23   *Margaret Thatcher: Power and Personality*, Jonathan Aitken (Bloomsbury, 2013).

24   Interview, Margaret Thatcher, *The Downing Street Years*, BBC Documentary.

25   *Below the Parapet*, Carol Thatcher (HarperCollins, 1996).

26   *Margaret Thatcher: Power and Personality*, Jonathan Aitken (Bloomsbury, 2013).

27   Interview, Cynthia Crawford, *Maggie – the First Lady* (documentary), Brook Lapping, 2003.

28   *Below the Parapet*, Carol Thatcher (HarperCollins, 1996).

29   Interview, Cecil Parkinson, 2013.

30   Ibid.

31   Interview, Edwina Currie, 2013.

32   *The Turbulent Years*, Kenneth Baker (Faber & Faber, 1993).

33   Speaking to her Cabinet, 22 November 1990. (Margaret Thatcher Foundation.)

34   'Cabinet Revolt Ends Thatcher's Eleven Year Reign', *Daily Telegraph*, 23 November 1990.

35   *Elizabeth, the Queen*, Sally Bedell Smith (Penguin Books, 2012).

36   *The Journals of Woodrow Wyatt*, Sarah Curtis (Ed.) (Macmillan, 1999).

37   Hansard, HC, 22 November 1990.

38   Ibid.

39 *Margaret Thatcher: Power and Personality*, Jonathan Aitken (Bloomsbury, 2013).

40 Hansard, HC, 22 November 1990.

41 Ibid.

42 *Margaret Thatcher: Power and Personality*, Jonathan Aitken (Bloomsbury, 2013).

43 *Daily Mail*, 23 November 1990.

44 *Margaret Thatcher: Power and Personality*, Jonathan Aitken (Bloomsbury, 2013).

45 Interview, Edwina Currie, 2013.

46 *Below the Parapet*, Carol Thatcher (HarperCollins, 1996).

47 *A View from the Wings*, Ronald Millar (Weidenfeld & Nicolson, 1993).

48 Interview, Denis Oliver, BBC Radio 4, 11 April 2013.

49 *Woman's Own*, 23 September 1987.

50 *Sultan in Arabia*, John Beasant and Christopher Long (Mainstream, 2004).

51 Ibid.

52 *Reading Eagle*, 3 October 1991.

53 *Edwina Currie: Diaries*, Edwina Currie (Biteback, 2012).

54 *John Major: The Autobiography*, (HarperCollins, 2010).

55 Interview, Edwina Currie, 2013.

56 *The Journals of Woodrow Wyatt*, Sarah Curtis (Ed.) (Macmillan, 1999).

57 *Margaret Thatcher: Power and Personality*, Jonathan Aitken (Bloomsbury, 2013).

58 Ibid.

59 Interview, Tim Bell, 2013.

60 *Margaret Thatcher: Power and Personality*, Jonathan Aitken (Bloomsbury, 2013).

61 Interview, Edwina Currie, 2013.

62 *Not for Turning*, Robin Harris (Bantam Press, 2013).

63 'Diary of Judith Chaplin', *Daily Telegraph*, 19 September 1990.

64 *Thatcher's Fortunes: The Life and Times of Mark Thatcher*, Mark Hollingsworth and Paul Halloran (Mainstream, 2005).

65 *Sultan in Arabia*, John Beasant and Christopher Long (Mainstream, 2004).

66 *Margaret Thatcher: Power and Personality*, Jonathan Aitken (Bloomsbury, 2013).

67 Author's correspondence with Sir Bernard Ingham, 2013.

68 *The Iron Lady*, John Campbell (Penguin, 2009).

69 Ibid.

70 *Sunday Times*, 21 March 2004.

71 *Elizabeth, the Queen*, Sally Bedell Smith (Penguin Books, 2012).

72 *The Enchanted Glass: Britain and its Monarchy*, Tom Nairn (Verso, 2011).

73 *Sunday Times*, 14 October 1984.

74 *The Rise and Fall of the House of Windsor*, A.N. Wilson (W.W. Norton, 1993).

75 *Queen Elizabeth II: Her Life in Our Times*, Sarah Bradford (Viking, 2012).

76   *The Journals of Woodrow Wyatt*, Sarah Curtis (Ed.) (Macmillan, 1999).

77   *Spectator*, 19 August 1989.

78   *The Journals of Woodrow Wyatt*, Sarah Curtis (Ed.) (Macmillan, 1999).

79   Letter sent to the Prince and Princess of Wales by HM the Queen, 20 December 1995.

80   *Elizabeth, the Queen*, Sally Bedell Smith (Penguin Books, 2012).

81   *Queen Elizabeth II: Her Life in Our Times*, Sarah Bradford (Viking, 2012).

82   Ibid.

83   *A Journey*, Tony Blair (Arrow, 2011).

84   *Queen Elizabeth II: Her Life in Our Times*, Sarah Bradford (Viking, 2012).

85   *Elizabeth: The Woman and Queen*, Graham Turner (Macmillan/*Daily Telegraph*, 24 May 2002).

86   *A Journey*, Tony Blair (Arrow, 2011).

87   Ibid.

88   Ibid.

89   *Elizabeth: The Woman and Queen*, Graham Turner (Macmillan/*Daily Telegraph*, 24 May 2002).

90   *The Audience*, Peter Morgan (Faber & Faber, 2013).

91   *Daily Mail*, 21 September 2013.

92   *Power Trip*, Damian McBride (Biteback Publishing, 2013).

Chapter 11

1   'The Lighter and Softer Side of the Iron Lady', Andrew Roberts, *Sunday Telegraph*, 14 April 2013.

2   *Muddling Through: Power Politics and the Quality of Government in Post-War Britain*, Peter Hennessy (Victor Gollancz, 1996).

3   *Elizabeth: The Woman and Queen*, Graham Turner (Macmillan/*Daily Telegraph*, 24 May 2002).

4   Ibid.

5   Ibid.

6   Interview, Tim Bell, 2013.

7   *Memories of Margaret Thatcher: A Portrait*, Iain Dale (Biteback Publishing, 2013).

8   'Far from the Madding Crowd', *Sunday Times*, 21 March 2004.

9   *Edwina Currie: Diaries*, Edwina Currie (Biteback Publishing, 2012).

10   *Not for Turning*, Robin Harris (Bantam Press, 2013).

11   Interview, Tim Bell, 2013.

12 *Diaries*, Alan Clark (Weidenfeld & Nicolson, 1993).

13 *Thatcher's Gold*, Paul Halloran and Mark Hollingsworth (Simon & Schuster, 1995).

14 'Maggie's Big Problem', Maureen Orth, *Vanity Fair*, June 1991.

15 *Thatcher's Gold*, Paul Halloran and Mark Hollingsworth (Simon & Schuster, 1995).

16 'Maggie's Big Problem', Maureen Orth, *Vanity Fair*, June 1991.

17 *Margaret Thatcher: Power and Personality*, Jonathan Aitken (Bloomsbury, 2013).

18 Interview, Lord Carrington, 2013.

19 *Sunday Times*, 21 April 1991.

20 *Observer*, 25 June 1991.

21 'Far from the Madding Crowd', *Sunday Times*, 21 March 2004.

22 *Not for Turning*, Robin Harris (Bantam Press, 2013).

23 *Thatcher's Fortunes: The Life and Times of Mark Thatcher*, Mark Hollingsworth and Paul Halloran (Mainstream, 2005).

24 *Not for Turning*, Robin Harris (Bantam Press, 2013).

25 *Margaret Thatcher: Power and Personality*, Jonathan Aitken (Bloomsbury, 2013).

26 *The Iron Lady*, John Campbell (Penguin, 2009).

27 Interview, Tim Bell, 2013.

28 Interview, Michael Dobbs, 2013.

29 'The Woman Who Saved Britain', *Daily Mail*, 9 April 2013.

30 *Below the Parapet*, Carol Thatcher (HarperCollins, 1996).

31 *Margaret Thatcher: Power and Personality*, Jonathan Aitken (Bloomsbury, 2013).

32 *A Swim-on Part in the Goldfish Bowl*, Carol Thatcher (Headline, 2002).

33 *Not for Turning*, Robin Harris (Bantam Press, 2013).

34 *Daily Mirror*, 10 April 2013.

35 *Times*, 14 October 2005.

36 Ibid.

37 Interview, Cecil Parkinson, 2013.

38 'Frail Final Years', Andrew Pierce, *Daily Mail*, 9 April 2013.

39 Ibid.

40 *The Queen: Elizabeth II and the Monarchy*, Ben Pimlott (HarperCollins, 1996).

41 Ibid.

42 Ibid.

43 *Elizabeth: The Woman and Queen*, Graham Turner (Macmillan/ *Daily Telegraph*, 24 May 2002).

44 Ibid.

45 'The Forgotten Prince', *Time Magazine*, 4 September 2013.

46   Interview, Ron Allison, 2013.
47   *Daily Telegraph*, 10 April 2013.
48   *Daily Mail*, 9 April 2013.
49   *Daily Mirror*, 10 April 2013.
50   'Frail Final Years', Andrew Pierce, *Daily Mail*, 9 April 2013.
51   *Daily Mirror*, 10 April 2013.
52   *Margaret Thatcher: Power and Personality*, Jonathan Aitken (Bloomsbury, 2013).
53   *Daily Telegraph*, 9 April 2013.
54   'Margaret Thatcher's Funeral', Oliver Wright, *Independent*, 9 April 2013.
55   *Daily Mirror*, 9 April 2013.
56   BBC News, 25 April 2013.
57   *Daily Mirror*, 10 April 2013.
58   Interview, Lord Carrington, 2013.
59   Interview, Michael Dobbs, 2013.
60   Author's correspondence with Sir Bernard Ingham, 2013.
61   *Daily Mirror*, 10 April 2013.
62   *Daily Mail*, 9 April 2013.
63   *Daily Mail*, 18 April 2013.
64   *Hollywood Reporter*, April 2013.

BIBLIOGRAPHY

Abse, Leo, *Margaret, Daughter of Beatrice* (Jonathan Cape, 1989).

Aitken, Jonathan, *Margaret Thatcher: Power and Personality* (Bloomsbury, 2013).

Allen, Martin, *Hidden Agenda* (M. Evans & Co., 2002).

Baker, Kenneth, *The Turbulent Years* (Faber & Faber, 1993).

Barry, Stephen P., *Royal Secrets: The View from Downstairs* (Villard Books, 1985).

Beasant, John and Christopher Long, *Sultan in Arabia* (Mainstream, 2004).

Berlinski, Claire, *There is No Alternative* (Basic Books, 2008).

Blair, Tony, *A Journey* (Arrow, 2011).

Blake, Stephen and Andrew John, *Iron Lady* (Michael O'Mara Books, 2003).

Boyle, Andrew, *The Climate of Treason* (Hutchinson, 1979).

Bradford, Sarah, *George VI* (Penguin, 1989).

Bradford, Sarah, *Queen Elizabeth II: Her Life in Our Times*, (Viking, 2012).

Brendon, Piers, *Eminent Elizabethans* (Jonathan Cape, 2012).

Brendon, Piers, *Our Own Dear Queen* (Secker & Warburg, 1986).

Brendon, Piers and Phillip Whitehead, *The Windsors* (Pimlico, 2000).

Campbell, Lady Colin, *The Untold Life of Queen Elizabeth, the Queen Mother* (Dynasty Press, 2012).

Campbell, John, *The Iron Lady* (Penguin, 2009).

Cannadine, David, *Ornamentalism: How the British Saw Their Empire* (Allen Lane, 2001).

Carter, Miranda, *Anthony Blunt: His Lives* (Pan, 2002).

Caryl, Christian, *Strange Rebels* (Basic Books, 2013).

Chippindale, Peter and Chris Horrie, *Stick it Up Your Punter* (William Heinemann, 1990).

Clark, Alan, *Diaries* (Weidenfeld & Nicolson, 1993).

Crawford, Marion, *The Little Princesses: The Story of the Queen's Childhood by her Nanny Marion Crawford* (Orion, 2003).

Crossland, Richard, *Richard Crossland Diaries* (Book Clubs Associates, 1979).

Curtis, Sarah (Ed.) *The Journals of Woodrow Wyatt* (Macmillan, 1999).

Dale, Iain, *Memories of Margaret Thatcher: A Portrait* (Biteback Publishing, 2013).

Davies, Nicholas, *Elizabeth: Behind Palace Doors* (Mainstream Publishing, 2000).

Dimbleby, Jonathan, *The Prince of Wales* (Little, Brown, 1994).

Ferguson, Niall, *Always Right* (Kindle Edition, 2013).

Gardiner, George, *Margaret Thatcher: From Childhood to Leadership* (William Kimber & Co., 1975).

Hall, Phillip, *Royal Fortune* (Bloomsbury, 1992).

Halloran, Paul and Mark Hollingsworth, *Thatcher's Gold* (Simon & Schuster, 1995).

Hardman, Robert, *Our Queen* (Hutchinson, 2011).

Harris, Robin, *Not for Turning* (Bantam Press, 2013).

Hennessy, Peter, *Having It So Good* (Allen Lane, 2006).

Hennessy, Peter, *Muddling Through: Power Politics and the Quality of Government in Post War Britain* (Victor Gollancz, 1996).

Hoey, Brian, *Anne* (Sidgwick & Jackson, 1997).

Hoey, Brian, *Her Majesty, 60 Regal Years* (Diamond Jubilee Edition) (Robson Press, 2012).

Holden, Anthony, *Charles: A Biography* (Corgi, 1999).

Hoskyns, J., *Just in Time: Inside the Thatcher Revolution* (Aurum, 2000).

Jenkins, Simon, *Thatcher & Sons* (Penguin, 2007).

Judd, Denis, *George VI* (I.B. Tauris & Co., 2012).

Junor, Penny, *Margaret Thatcher* (Sidgwick & Jackson, 1984).

Kelly, Kitty, *The Royals* (H.B. Productions Inc., 1997).

Kiernan, Thomas, *Citizen Murdoch* (New York: Dodd, Mead & Co., 1986).

Leyland, Peter, *The Constitution of the UK* (Oxford & Portland, 2012).

Lisners, John, *The Rise and Fall of the Murdoch Empire* (John Blake, 2012).

Littleton, S.M., *The Wapping Dispute* (Avebury, 1992).

McKnight, David, *Murdoch's Politics* (Pluto Press, 2013).

Marr, Andrew, *The Diamond Queen* (Macmillan, 2011).

Marr, Andrew, *The History of Modern Britain* (Macmillan, 2007).

Millar, Ronald, *A View from the Wings* (Weidenfeld & Nicolson, 1993).

Montefiore, Simon Sebag, *Titans of History* (Quercus, 2012).

Moore, Charles, *Margaret Thatcher: The Authorised Biography* (Volume One) (Allen Lane, 2013).

Morgan, Kenneth O., *Callaghan: A Life* (Oxford University Press, 1997).

Morgan, Peter, *The Audience* (Faber & Faber, 2013).

Murray, Tricia, *Margaret Thatcher* (Star, 1978).

Neil, Andrew, *Full Disclosure* (Macmillan, 1996).

Ogden, Chris, *Maggie* (Simon & Schuster, 1990).

Paxman, Jeremy, *On Royalty* (Penguin, 2006).

Payne, A., Paul Sutton and Tony Thorndike, *Grenada: Revolution and Invasion* (Crown Helm, 1984).

Penrose, Barrie and Simon Freeman, *Conspiracy of Silence* (HarperCollins, 1987).

Pimlott, Ben, *Harold Wilson* (HarperCollins, 1992).

Pimlott, Ben, *The Queen: Elizabeth II and the Monarchy* (HarperCollins, 1996).

Reagan, Ronald, *An American Life* (Simon & Schuster, 1990).

Renwick, Robin, *A Journey with Margaret Thatcher: Foreign Policy Under the Iron Lady* (Biteback Publishing, 2013).

Ring, Anne, *The Story of Princess Elizabeth* (Murray, 1930).

Roosevelt, Eleanor, *This I Remember* (Greenwood Press, 1975).

Shawcross, William, *The Shah's Last Ride* (Chatto & Windus, 1989).

Shea, Michael, *A Cold Conspiracy*, (Severn House, 2000).

Shea, Michael, *Influence: How to Make the System Work for You* (Ebury, 1988).

Shea, Michael, *Spin Doctor* (HarperCollins, 1996).

Shea, Michael, *To Lie Abroad: Diplomacy Reviews* (Sinclair-Stevenson, 1996).

Shea, Michael, *A View from the Sidelines* (Sutton, 2003).

Sisman, Adam, *Hugh Trevor-Roper* (Weidenfeld & Nicolson, 2010).

Smith, Sally Bedell, *Elizabeth, the Queen* (Penguin Books 2012).

Starkey, Dr David, *Crown and Country* (HarperCollins, 2010).

Steinberg, Blema S., *Women in Power: The Personalities and Leadership Styles of Indira Gandhi, Golda Meir, and Margaret Thatcher* (McGill-Queen's University Press, 2008).

Stewart, Graham, *Bang! A History of Britain in the 1980s* (Atlantic Books, 2013).

Tebbit, Norman, *Upwardly Mobile* (Weidenfeld and Nicolson, 1988).

Thatcher, Carol, *Below the Parapet* (HarperCollins, 1997).

Thatcher, Carol, *Diary of an Election* (Sidgwick & Jackson, 1983).

Thatcher, Carol, *A Swim-on Part in the Goldfish Bowl* (Headline, 2002).

Thatcher, Margaret, *The Downing Street Years* (HarperCollins, 2011).

Thatcher, Margaret, *The Path to Power* (HarperCollins, 1993).

Thatcher, Margaret, *Statecraft* (HarperCollins, 2002).

Thomas, James, *Popular Newspapers, the Labour Party and British Politics* (Routledge, 2005).

Turner, Alwyn W., *Rejoice! Rejoice! Britain in the 1980s* (Aurum Press, 2010).

Turner, Graham, *Elizabeth: The Woman and Queen* (Macmillan/ *Daily Telegraph*, 24 May 2002).

Vinen, Richard, *Thatcher's Britain* (Simon & Schuster, 2009).

Wapshott, Nicholas, *Ronald Reagan and Margaret Thatcher: A Political Marriage* (Penguin, 2007).

Watson, Tom and Martin Hickman, *Dial M for Murdoch* (Allen Lane, 2012).

Whitehead, Phillip, *The Writing on the Wall: Britain in the Seventies* (Michael Joseph, 1985).

Wilson. A.N., *The Rise and Fall of the House of Windsor* (W.W. Norton, 1993).

Wolff, Michael, *The Man Who Owns the News* (Bodley Head, 2008).

Young, Hugo, *The Iron Lady* (Noonday Press, 1990).

Young, Hugo, *One of Us* (Pan, 2013).

Young, Hugo and Ann Sloman, *The Thatcher Phenomenon* (BBC Books, 1986).

Articles

'The Blooming of Margaret Thatcher', Gail Sheehy, *Vanity Fair*, June 1989.

'The Invincible Mrs Thatcher', Charles Moore, *Vanity Fair*, December 2011.

'The Trouble with Andrew', Edward Klein, *Vanity Fair*, August, 2011.

INDEX